OXFORD WORLD'S CLASSICS

ON MURDER

THOMAS DE QUINCEY (1785–1859) was born in Manchester to a prosperous linen merchant. As a young boy he read widely and acquired a reputation as a brilliant classicist. At 17 he ran away from Manchester Grammar School and spent five harrowing months penniless and hungry on the streets of London. Reconciled with his family, he entered Oxford University in 1803, but left five years later without taking his degree and moved to the English Lake District to be near his two literary idols, William Wordsworth and Samuel Taylor Coleridge. In 1813 he became dependent on opium, a drug he began experimenting with during his days at Oxford, and over the next few years he slid deeper into debt and addiction. His most famous work, *Confessions of an English Opium-Eater*, appeared in the *London Magazine* in 1821, and launched his career as a contributor to the leading magazines of the day, where he wrote on a wide variety of subjects, including politics, literature, history, philosophy, and economics. In 1823 he published his most famous piece of literary criticism, 'On the Knocking at the Gate in Macbeth', in which he explored the representation and psychology of violence. Four years later in *Blackwood's Magazine* he published his brilliant exercise in black humour, 'On Murder Considered as One of the Fine Arts', which he followed with a 'Second Paper On Murder' in 1839 and a 'Postscript' in 1854. De Quincey also wrote terror fiction, and in 1838 produced 'The Avenger', his most disturbing treatment of retribution and racial violence. De Quincey spent much of his life battling poverty, debt, and addiction, but his work was widely admired, and British and American editions of his writings began to appear in the 1850s. He died in Edinburgh on 8 December 1859.

ROBERT MORRISON is Professor of English literature at Queen's University, Kingston, Ontario. He has edited writings by Leigh Hunt, Richard Woodhouse, and Jane Austen. With Chris Baldick, he produced editions of *The Vampyre and Other Tales of the Macabre* and *Tales of Terror from Blackwood's Magazine* for Oxford World's Classics.

OXFORD WORLD'S CLASSICS

*For over 100 years Oxford World's Classics have brought
readers closer to the world's great literature. Now with over 700
titles—from the 4,000-year-old myths of Mesopotamia to the
twentieth century's greatest novels—the series makes available
lesser-known as well as celebrated writing.*

*The pocket-sized hardbacks of the early years contained
introductions by Virginia Woolf, T. S. Eliot, Graham Greene,
and other literary figures which enriched the experience of reading.
Today the series is recognized for its fine scholarship and
reliability in texts that span world literature, drama and poetry,
religion, philosophy and politics. Each edition includes perceptive
commentary and essential background information to meet the
changing needs of readers.*

OXFORD WORLD'S CLASSICS

THOMAS DE QUINCEY

On Murder

Edited with an Introduction and Notes by
ROBERT MORRISON

OXFORD
UNIVERSITY PRESS

OXFORD

UNIVERSITY PRESS

Great Clarendon Street, Oxford OX2 6DP

Oxford University Press is a department of the University of Oxford.
It furthers the University's objective of excellence in research, scholarship,
and education by publishing worldwide in

Oxford New York

Auckland Cape Town Dar es Salaam Hong Kong Karachi
Kuala Lumpur Madrid Melbourne Mexico City Nairobi
New Delhi Shanghai Taipei Toronto

With offices in

Argentina Austria Brazil Chile Czech Republic France Greece
Guatemala Hungary Italy Japan Poland Portugal Singapore
South Korea Switzerland Thailand Turkey Ukraine Vietnam

Oxford is a registered trade mark of Oxford University Press
in the UK and in certain other countries

Published in the United States
by Oxford University Press Inc., New York

Editorial matter © Robert Morrison 2006

The moral rights of the author have been asserted

Database right Oxford University Press (maker)

First published as an Oxford World's Classics paperback 2006
Reissued 2009

British Library Cataloguing in Publication Data

Data available

Library of Congress Cataloging in Publication Data

Data available

ISBN 978-0-19-953904-8

15

Typeset in Ehrhardt
by RefineCatch Limited, Bungay, Suffolk
Printed in Great Britain by
Clays Ltd, Elcograf S.p.A.

CONTENTS

ACKNOWLEDGEMENTS

LIKE all critics of De Quincey, I am deeply indebted to Grevel Lindop, who developed the idea for this volume, and who has repeatedly challenged and broadened my understanding of De Quincey. I would also like to thank Judith Luna for her enthusiasm and support. For expertise and advice of all kinds, I am grateful to Chris Baldick, Bonnie Brooks, Iain Brown, Jeff Cowton, Michael Cummings, Jeff Eckert, Robert Freeman, Louis Godbout, Clifford Jackman, Heather Jackson, Robin Jackson, Adam Johnstone, Mark Jones, Frank Jordan, Bernard Kavanagh, Larry Krupp, Justin Jaron Lewis, Charles Mahoney, Julian North, Seamus Perry, William Reeve, Christopher Ricks, David Smith, Paul Stanwood, Barry Symonds, Beert Verstraete, Paul Wiens, and Romira Worvill. Special thanks to Brandon Alakas for his hard work, insightful questions, and meticulous scholarship. I am indebted to the staffs of several libraries: the National Library of Scotland; the Dove Cottage Library, Grasmere; and the Countway Library of Medicine, Houghton Library, and Widener Library, Harvard University. I would especially like to thank the staffs of the Joseph S. Stauffer Library and the W. D. Jordan Special Collections, Douglas Library, Queen's University. My research on this edition was greatly facilitated by generous grants from the Social Sciences and Humanities Research Council of Canada and the Advisory Research Committee of Queen's University.

My greatest debt, comme toujours, is to Carole, Zachary, and Alastair.

INTRODUCTION

'MAY I quote Thomas De Quincey?' asks the murderer politely in Peter Ackroyd's *Dan Leno and the Limehouse Golem*. 'In the pages of his essay "On Murder Considered as One of the Fine Arts" I first learned of the Ratcliffe Highway deaths, and ever since that time his work has been a source of perpetual delight and astonishment to me.'[1] De Quincey burst onto the literary scene in 1821 with his best-known publication, *Confessions of an English Opium-Eater*, and in the decades that followed he produced works of fiction, biography, and various modes of autobiography, as well as essays on a remarkably diverse range of topics, from literary theory, science, and political economics to philology, geography, philosophy, and history. Perhaps De Quincey's most thoroughgoing preoccupation, however, was violence. He wrote often of murderers, exploiting sources from Roman biographies to contemporary newspapers, but at the centre of his fascination stands John Williams, the presumed killer in 1811 of seven people in two different incidents separated by only twelve days and a few city streets in London's East End. De Quincey's response to Williams's attacks were written over the course of more than thirty years, and ranged from penetrating literary and aesthetic criticism to disturbing fictive transpositions, brilliantly funny satiric high jinks, and gruesomely vivid reportage. The works collected in this volume brought De Quincey great contemporary notoriety, and inspired a long line of writers on crime, detection, aesthetics, and violence. They also hold a peculiar appeal to the modern reader, for they presage academic and popular assaults on conventional morality, the highly diverse commodification of violence, and the world-weariness that regards the spectacle of murder with both cynicism and fascination.

De Quincey's keen interest in violence and crime is part of a broad and longstanding tradition in Britain and well beyond. 'If all novels and dramas turning upon startling crimes were to be expunged from our literature, we should have to make a surprisingly clean sweep,' remarked Leslie Stephen in 'The Decay of Murder' (1869). '*Hamlet*

---

[1] Peter Ackroyd, *Dan Leno and the Limehouse Golem* (London, 1994), 30.

and *Othello* and *King Lear* would have to go at once.'[2] In the seventeenth century highly popular broadsheets, pamphlets, and squibs describing gruesome murders and execution scenes were typically framed by a piously insistent morality which made clear that bad guys finish last. Providential fictions such as John Reynolds's *Triumph of God's Revenge* (1621–35) featured a wrathful God who smote sinners, and combined 'impassioned Moralizing' with a 'heart & soul . . . swallowed up in the notion of "Murder" ', as Samuel Taylor Coleridge observed.[3] By the eighteenth century notorious thieves such as John Sheppard and Dick Turpin had become favourite figures in ballads, plays, romances, and burlesques, while the first *Newgate Calendar* (1773), running to five volumes and dealing with the violent excesses of dozens of major criminals, fed a voracious public appetite and spawned many imitations. John Villette's *Annals of Newgate* (1776) extended the pattern of blending violence and morality 'to expose . . . the infamy and punishments naturally attending those who deviate from the paths of virtue'.[4] At the same time, the novel was evolving in close connection with criminality and transgression. Daniel Defoe's *Roxana* (1724) is a tale of thievery which ends in murder and remorse, while Henry Fielding's *Jonathan Wild* (1743) is a fictionalized version of the life of the infamous criminal executed in 1725. The maudlin extremes of the novel of sentiment culminated in Johann Wolfgang von Goethe's *Sorrows of Young Werther* (1774), where the eponymous hero, ravaged by hopeless passion and half in love with death, put a bullet through his head and touched off a suicide epidemic across Europe. The gothicism of Horace Walpole's *Castle of Otranto* (1764), Matthew Lewis's *The Monk* (1796), Ann Radcliffe's *The Italian* (1797), and Charlotte Dacre's *Zofloya* (1805) employed the paraphernalia of dungeons, castles, subterranean passageways, virtuous maidens, and tormented villains, but had at their heart a preoccupation with emotional extremity, brutal usurpation, and murderous vengeance. The noble criminal at war with society dominated works from Friedrich Schiller's *Robbers* (1781) to Victor Hugo's *Hernani* (1830), while

---

[2] Leslie Stephen, 'The Decay of Murder', *Cornhill Magazine*, 20 (December 1869), 722.

[3] *The Collected Works of Samuel Taylor Coleridge: Marginalia IV*, ed. H. J. Jackson and George Whalley (Princeton, 1998), 237–8.

[4] Laurence Senelick, *The Prestige of Evil: The Murderer as Romantic Hero from Sade to Lacenaire* (New York, 1987), p. xviii.

English writers such as William Blake, Lord Byron, Mary Shelley, and Percy Shelley produced re-evaluations of mythic rebels like Prometheus and Cain. In the early 1830s Newgate novels by Edward Bulwer Lytton and William Harrison Ainsworth featured compassionate or glamorized portraits of actual eighteenth-century thieves and murderers, and provoked responses such as Charles Dickens's *Oliver Twist* (1837–8) and William Thackeray's *Catherine* (1839–40), both of which presented a harshly realistic view of criminal life.

De Quincey's interest in violence, and especially murder, played a key role in the evolution of crime literature, and was persistent, various, and wide-ranging. He surveyed the distant past for striking examples of murder, and highlighted in particular the Roman Emperors Caligula and Nero, the Judaean King Herod the Great, and the Thugs of India, a confederacy of professional assassins that 'gave rise to endless speculation' in De Quincey, as his publisher James Hogg put it. 'The far-reaching power of this mysterious brotherhood, the swiftness and certainty of its operations, the strange gradations of official rank, and the curious disguises adopted—all these exercised an influence on his mind which seemed never to wane.'[5] De Quincey had an extensive knowledge of seventeenth- and eighteenth-century gallows writing, including cases such as 'the old Parisian jeweller Cardillac, in Louis XIV.'s time, who was stung with a perpetual lust for murdering the possessors of fine diamonds'.[6] As a young man, De Quincey was an enthusiastic reader of the *Newgate Calendar*, and a great admirer of the gothic fantasies of Schiller, Lewis, and especially Radcliffe, whom he described as 'the great enchantress' of a generation.[7] As a writer, he frequently examined literary texts through the lens of crime, as when he observed that 'the archangel Satan' in Milton's *Paradise Lost* must contend with an 'angelic . . . constable or an inspector of police'[8] stationed at the gates of Paradise. During his editorship of the *Westmorland Gazette* (1818–19) De Quincey filled the columns of the newspaper with assize reports and lurid murder stories, and over the next forty years

[5] James Hogg, *De Quincey and his Friends* (London, 1895), 174.
[6] *The Works of Thomas De Quincey: Volume Nine*, ed. Grevel Lindop, Robert Morrison, and Barry Symonds (London, 2001), 46.
[7] *The Works of Thomas De Quincey: Volume Two*, ed. Grevel Lindop (London, 2000), 146.
[8] *The Works of Thomas De Quincey: Volume Eighteen*, ed. Edmund Baxter (London, 2001), 35–6.

paid close attention to the trials and circumstances of several notorious murderers, including William Burke and William Hare, William
Palmer, Madeleine Smith, and Thomas Griffiths Wainewright, who
dined with De Quincey in London in 1821 and later revealed himself
as 'a murderer of a freezing class; cool, calculating, wholesale in his
operations, and moving all along under the advantages of unsuspecting domestic confidence and domestic opportunities'.[9]

No killer, however, captured De Quincey's imagination like John
Williams, the man thought responsible for two horrendous acts of
carnage in late 1811. Near midnight on Saturday, 7 December,
Williams entered Timothy Marr's lace and pelisse warehouse at 29
Ratcliffe Highway. Once inside he locked the door, and within a
matter of minutes ruthlessly dispatched all four inhabitants. The
servant girl, Margaret Jewell (called 'Mary' by De Quincey), had
been sent out to fetch dinner, and when she returned to find the door
locked she raised the alarm. A neighbour gained entry at the back of
the house and the front door was quickly opened. Eyewitnesses saw
Marr's wife Celia sprawled lifelessly headlong. Marr himself was
dead behind the store counter. The apprentice James Gowen was
stretched out in the back near a door that led to a staircase. Most
sinisterly, downstairs in the kitchen, three-month-old Timothy
Marr, junior, was found dead. 'Sooner murder an infant in its cradle
than nurse unacted desires,' wrote William Blake in *The Marriage of
Heaven and Hell*.[10] Williams took Blake at his word. He crushed
the skulls and cut the throats of all four victims. Twelve days later—
again around midnight, again in the same East London area—
Williams struck again, this time at the household of a publican named
John Williamson. 'A man named Williams does quite accidentally
murder a man named Williamson,' observed G. K. Chesterton; 'it
sounds like a sort of infanticide.'[11] Williams's attack on this second
occasion was not as successful, but his savagery was equally chilling.
Williamson himself was found dead in the cellar. He had apparently
been thrown down the stairs. His throat was cut. His wife Elizabeth
and the maid Anna Bridget Harrington were discovered on the main

---

[9] *The Works of Thomas De Quincey: Volume Sixteen*, ed. Robert Morrison (London, 2003), 388.
[10] *The Complete Poetry and Prose of William Blake*, ed. David V. Erdman, commentary by Harold Bloom (New York, 1982), 38.
[11] G. K. Chesterton, *Father Brown: A Selection*, ed. W. W. Robson (Oxford, 1995), 6.

floor, their skulls battered and their throats slit. A lodger named John Turner, however, managed to escape by climbing out of a third-floor window and calling for help. An angry crowd gathered, but by the time they entered the house Williams had fled. Kitty Stillwell, the 14-year-old granddaughter of the Williamsons, had been asleep upstairs the entire time. She was unharmed. Several suspects were arrested in connection with the atrocities, including Williams, who was detained on 22 December and who was found hanged in his prison cell four days later, an apparent suicide. The court chose to hear the evidence against him, but the circumstances of his death were widely interpreted as a confession of guilt. On New Year's Eve Williams's body was publicly exhibited in a procession through the Ratcliffe Highway and then driven to the nearest crossroads, where it was forced into a narrow hole and a stake driven through the heart. In response to these horrors, Leigh Hunt wrote of 'Watchmen' and the dangers of 'such ferocious fellows as *Williams*', while Robert Southey told a friend that 'no circumstances which did not concern myself ever disturbed me so much. I . . . never had so mingled a feeling of horror, and indignation, and astonishment, with a sense of insecurity too'.[12] Not everyone, however, adopted this solemn tone. When Charles Lamb asked his friend George Dyer 'what he thought of the terrible Williams, the Ratcliffe Highway murderer', there was a 'pause for consideration' and then 'the answer came: "I should think, Mr Lamb, he must have been rather an eccentric character" '.[13]

De Quincey's reaction to Williams and the Ratcliffe murders ranged from impassioned solemnity to black humour, and the essays and fictions of the present volume are all haunted by his presence, sometimes directly, sometimes only in outline. De Quincey published 'On the Knocking at the Gate in Macbeth' in the *London Magazine* in 1823, just two years after he had launched himself to notoriety in the same magazine with the publication of his *Confessions of an English Opium-Eater*. 'On the Knocking' is his most celebrated piece of literary criticism, and brings the murderer and the writer into the same orbit, for both are interested in pleasure and power, and both seek freedom by outstripping or subverting the social institutions they feel thwart or confine them. Shakespeare and

[12] Leigh Hunt, 'Watchmen', *The Examiner*, 212 (19 January 1812), 33; *Selections from the Letters of Robert Southey*, ed. J. W. Warter, 4 vols. (London, 1856), ii. 248.

[13] E. V. Lucas, *The Life of Charles Lamb*, 2 vols. (London, 1905), i. 163.

Williams are both creators of bloody dramas, great artists who perform upon the stage of London, and awe their audiences with supreme moments of self-assertion and violence. 'Murder is negative creation', writes W. H. Auden, 'and every murderer is therefore the rebel who claims the right to be omnipotent.'[14] In 'On the Knocking', De Quincey characteristically approaches Williams from at least two different angles. On the one hand, he introduces the satiric aesthetic that enables him to see Williams's performance 'on the stage of Ratcliffe Highway' as 'making the connoisseur in murder very fastidious in his taste, and dissatisfied with any thing that has been since done in that line. All other murders look pale by the deep crimson of his' (p. 4). The essays 'On Murder' that follow spring from the seedbed of this aesthetic. Yet on the other hand, the circumstances surrounding Williams's extreme brutality reveal to De Quincey the emotional impact of a particular moment in *Macbeth*, and lead also to reflections on the psychology of murder and the representation of violence. 'Murder in ordinary cases . . . is an incident of coarse and vulgar horror,' he asserts; 'and for this reason—that it flings the interest exclusively upon the natural but ignoble instinct by which we cleave to life.' Such an attitude is ill-suited to 'the purposes of the poet', and so Shakespeare throws 'the interest on the murderer', where 'there must be raging some great storm of passion,—jealousy, ambition, vengeance, hatred,—which will create a hell within him; and into this hell we are to look' (pp. 4–5). In an 1818 essay, William Hazlitt remarked that 'at present we are less exposed to the vicissitudes of good or evil. . . . The police spoils all; and we now hardly so much as dream of a midnight murder. Macbeth is only tolerated in this country for the sake of the music.'[15] De Quincey, however, dreamt often of midnight murder, and in his response to Hazlitt he reveals *Macbeth* as a play where the world of violence is 'cut off by an immeasurable gulph from the ordinary tide and succession of human affairs' (p. 6), and where the mind of murder is acutely and unnervingly revealed.

Within two years of publishing 'On the Knocking' De Quincey had left the *London Magazine*, and by 1826 he had returned to

---

[14] W. H. Auden, 'The Guilty Vicarage', in *The Complete Works of W. H. Auden*, 4 vols. (1988—continuing), iv. 265.

[15] *The Complete Works of William Hazlitt*, ed. P. P. Howe, 21 vols. (London, 1930–4), v. 10.

Blackwood's Edinburgh Magazine, where he had begun his career as a magazinist in 1819. *Blackwood's*, with its owner William Blackwood as editor and De Quincey's closest friend John Wilson as lead writer, was the most exuberant, popular, and unpredictable magazine of the age. It prized erudition, outrage, irony, and extremity, combining urbanity and elitism with what De Quincey described as a 'spirit of jovial and headlong gaiety' that meant 'an occasional use of street slang was not out of harmony'.[16] The magazine is most frequently cited for its truculent Toryism and vitriolic assaults on the so-called 'Cockney School of Poetry', which included Leigh Hunt and John Keats, but it also published some remarkably insightful literary criticism, especially on William Wordsworth and Percy Shelley, and it was famous for the concentrated dread and precisely calculated alarm which shaped its tales of terror and guilt, many of which were written by distinguished authors, including Walter Scott, John Galt, James Hogg, and of course De Quincey himself.[17] De Quincey reviewed Robert Gillies's edition of *German Stories* in *Blackwood's* for December 1826, and offered readers a characteristic blend of mirth, scholarship, wit, and colloquiality. Several of the tales in Gillies's collection turned upon the 'appalling interest of secret and mysterious murder', but in other instances De Quincey could not avoid a more humorous tack: 'Pleasant it is, no doubt, to drink tea with your sweetheart, but most disagreeable to find her bubbling in the tea-urn.'[18] In 1828 Blackwood complained that he 'always' had 'a superabundance of what may be called good articles', but what he wanted were 'articles which have some distinctive or superior cast about them'.[19] In early 1827 he published De Quincey's engaging assessments of Gotthold Ephraim Lessing and Immanuel Kant, but De Quincey's next essay—'On Murder Considered as One of the Fine Arts'—revealed how fully he could exploit the *Blackwood's* context of irony, subversion, and extravagance. In the words of

---

[16] *The Works of Thomas De Quincey: Volume Seven*, ed. Robert Morrison (London, 2000), 80.

[17] See *Tales of Terror from Blackwood's Magazine*, ed. Robert Morrison and Chris Baldick (Oxford, 1995).

[18] *The Works of Thomas De Quincey: Volume Six*, ed. David Groves and Grevel Lindop (London, 2000), 19, 15–16.

[19] Irene Mannion, 'Criticism "Con Amore": A Study of *Blackwood's Magazine* 1817–1834', Ph.D. diss., University of California at Los Angeles, 1984, 102.

Edgar Allan Poe, De Quincey knew 'How to Write a Blackwood Article'.[20]

'On Murder' seizes on the satiric and artistic approach to murder that De Quincey introduced in 'On the Knocking', pushing the logic of such a rationale in ways that are both disturbing and seductive, and submerging the ethical to the aesthetic. 'Everything in this world has two handles,' he argues with the deadpan aplomb that gives the essay such energy. 'Murder, for instance, may be laid hold of by its moral handle . . . and *that*, I confess, is its weak side; or it may also be treated *aesthetically* . . . that is, in relation to good taste' (pp. 10–11). De Quincey was not the first to employ such a breezy and ironized attitude toward violence and crime. In John Gay's *The Beggar's Opera* (1728), Peachum notes that 'Murder is as fashionable a Crime as a Man can be guilty of. How many fine Gentlemen have we in *Newgate* every Year, purely upon that Article!'[21] Denis Diderot's narrator in *Rameau's Nephew* (written 1761–74) begins 'to find irksome the presence of a man who discussed a horrible act, an execrable crime, like a connoisseur of painting or poetry'.[22] The Marquis de Sade's *Juliette* (1797) features 'the Sodality of the Friends of Crime', while in Thomas Love Peacock's *Nightmare Abbey* (1818), Mr Flosky asserts that 'if a man knocks me down, and takes my purse and watch by main force, I turn him to account, and set him forth in a tragedy as a dashing young fellow'.[23] De Quincey's views on murder are also buttressed by a variety of philosophical sources, including Aristotle's notion of catharsis: 'the final purpose of murder, considered as a fine art, is precisely the same as that of Tragedy, in Aristotle's account of it, viz. "to cleanse the heart by means of pity and terror" ' (p. 32). De Quincey also reworked and extended key eighteenth-century notions of the sublime. In *A Philosophical Enquiry into the Origin of our Ideas of the Sublime and Beautiful* (1757), Edmund Burke describes a theatre audience anxiously awaiting the performance of 'the most sublime and affecting tragedy'

[20] 'How to Write a Blackwood Article', in *Collected Works of Edgar Allan Poe*, ed. Thomas Ollive Mabbott, 3 vols. (Cambridge, Mass., 1969–78), ii. 334–62.

[21] John Gay, *Dramatic Works*, ed. John Fuller, 2 vols. (Oxford, 1983), ii. 7–8.

[22] Denis Diderot, *Rameau's Nephew*, trans. Leonard Tancock (Harmondsworth, 1966), 97.

[23] Marquis de Sade, *Juliette*, trans. Austryn Wainhouse (New York, 1968), 417; 'Nightmare Abbey' in *The Works of Thomas Love Peacock*, ed. H. F. B. Brett-Smith and C. E. Jones (London, 1924–34), iii. 52.

when it is 'reported that a state criminal of high rank is on the point of being executed in the adjoining square'. The theatre of course empties in a moment, demonstrating 'the comparative weakness of the imitative arts' and proclaiming 'the triumph of real sympathy'.[24] Art and violence are again conjoined: Shakespeare is good, but the spectacle of public execution is better. In *The Critique of Judgement* (1790), Kant defines the sublime as that which does 'violence to our imagination', and acknowledges that dreadful natural calamities—'volcanoes with their all-destroying violence, hurricanes with the devastation they leave behind'—may evoke the sublime 'as long as we find ourselves in safety'.[25] De Quincey saw clearly the openings and opportunities that such positions allowed, and he moved quickly down a very slippery slope. For 'once natural violence was considered as a possible source of aesthetic experience,' Joel Black observes, 'what was to prevent human violence, which inspired perhaps even greater terror, from making aesthetic claims as well?'[26] De Quincey's reply in 'On Murder' is 'nothing', and in the essay he launches himself and his readers into an exhilarating and disorientating world of irony and aesthetics. In 1829, two years after De Quincey's first essay 'On Murder' appeared, Walter Scott was approached by 'one David Paterson', who had worked for the Edinburgh anatomist Dr Robert Knox, and who had been involved in buying bodies from the serial killers William Burke and William Hare. Paterson asked Scott if he was interested in writing about 'the awfull tragedy of burke and hare', and offered 'sketches of one or two persons who I dair say will be promenent characters'. Scott declined with immediate and heartfelt disgust: 'The scoundrel has been the companion and patron of such atrocious murderers and kidnappers and he has the impudence to write to any decent man.'[27] De Quincey felt no such inhibitions. When faced with similar opportunities to explore and exploit contemporary murders, he embraced notoriety and gleefully ignored the 'decent man' in favour of the aesthete.

[24] Edmund Burke, *Philosophical Enquiry into the Origin of our Ideas of the Sublime and Beautiful*, ed. Adam Phillips (Oxford, 1990), 43.

[25] Immanuel Kant, *Critique of the Power of Judgment*, ed. Paul Guyer (Cambridge, 2000), 129, 144.

[26] Joel Black, *The Aesthetics of Murder: A Study in Romantic Literature and Contemporary Culture* (Baltimore, 1991), 14.

[27] *The Journal of Sir Walter Scott*, ed. W. E. K. Anderson (Oxford, 1972), 542–3.

Yet De Quincey's subversion of morality is perhaps not as clean or complete as he would have us believe. In *Confessions of an English Opium-Eater* he grappled with similar issues, dismissing morality and attempting to slip into the freedom of aesthetics. 'Let no man expect to frighten me, by a few hard words, into embarking . . . upon desperate adventures of morality,' he declares. Earlier, he confesses it, 'as a besetting infirmity of mine, that . . . I hanker too much after a state of happiness. . . . I cannot face misery'.[28] But De Quincey cannot escape misery either, and is repeatedly staggered by his own suffocating sense of humiliation and paralysis. 'I had the power, if I could raise myself, to will it', he writes; 'and yet again had not the power, for the weight of twenty Atlantics was upon me, or the oppression of inexpiable guilt.'[29] As hedonism collides with shame, De Quincey often half admits the very sin he is bent on denying: 'Guilt . . . I do not acknowledge: and, if I did, it is possible that I might still resolve on the present act of confession.'[30] A similar dynamic is at work within 'On Murder'. De Quincey wants the liberation and fun that comes from a temporary release from social values, and he achieves this through a blandly outrageous misappropriation of language, and a prolonged series of ironic deflations, substitutions, and inversions that enable him to keep morbidity at bay and graze the brink between comedy and horror. His remark that 'every philosopher of eminence for the two last centuries has either been murdered, or, at the least, been very near it' initiates a hilarious survey, often tinged with fact, in which he observes that René Descartes was almost murdered by 'professional men', Thomas Hobbes 'was not murdered' but 'was three times very near being murdered', Nicolas Malebranche was in fact murdered by George Berkeley, and Immanuel Kant 'had a narrower escape from a murderer than any man we read of, except Des Cartes' (pp. 16, 20, 23). In a discussion of artistic preconception, De Quincey bemoans the fact that 'people will not submit to have their throats cut quietly; they will run, they will kick, they will bite; and, whilst the portrait painter often has to complain of too much torpor in his subject, the artist, in our line, is generally embarrassed by too much animation' (p. 26). Such outrageously poker-faced lamentations run riot throughout the essay but, as in *Confessions*, De Quincey in 'On Murder' only stays or

---

[28] *The Works of Thomas De Quincey: Volume Two*, 232, 54.
[29] Ibid. 73–4.   [30] Ibid. 10.

upends ethical judgement: he does not escape it. As editor of the
Westmorland Gazette, he justifies including dozens of assize reports
of murders and rapes because they teach 'the more uneducated
classes' their 'social duties', and 'present the best indications of the
moral condition of society'.[31] In 'On Murder', De Quincey insists
that the victim 'ought to be a good man', and 'severe good taste'
demands that 'the subject chosen ought also to have a family of
young children wholly dependent on his exertions'. The better the
person, the more aesthetically satisfying the murder: 'how can there
be any pity for one tiger destroyed by another tiger?' (pp. 31–3).
The murderous narrator in Philip Kerr's thriller *A Philosophical
Investigation* (1992) writes that in 'On Murder' the 'moral issue is
neatly disposed of by De Quincey'.[32] But 'you can never draw
the line between aesthetic criticism and moral and social criticism,'
T. S. Eliot observed; 'however rigorous an aesthete you may be, you
are over the frontier into something else sooner or later.' In 'On
Murder' the relationship between the aesthetic and the moral is 'one
of ironic connection rather than of mutual exclusion', as Angela
Leighton puts it. 'Text and context, style and reference, are dialogi-
cally related, so that the one frets against the other. . . . Aesthetic
pleasure is challenged by ideological guilt.'[33]

De Quincey extended his 1827 thoughts 'On Murder' a year
later in a manuscript essay that was apparently designed to introduce another manuscript fragment that he seems to have written
around 1825, and that concerned the German murderer Peter
Anthony Fonk. De Quincey's source for his account of Fonk is the
Conversations-Lexicon, published in Leipzig in 1824, and the relatively straightforward and reportorial tone of the essay suggests that
it was written before he developed the extravagant conceit of the
1827 *Blackwood's* essay. The 1828 manuscript, however, is directed
'To the Editor of Blackwood's Magazine' and builds on the ironies
and inversions of the published essay, as when the narrator who is
'most decidedly for goodness and morality' warns a servant of a
dreadful downward slide from 'Murder . . . to highway robbery; and

---

[31] *The Works of Thomas De Quincey: Volume One*, ed. Barry Symonds (London, 2000), 147.

[32] Philip Kerr, *A Philosophical Investigation* (London, 1992), 241.

[33] T. S. Eliot, 'A Dialogue on Dramatic Poetry', in *Selected Essays* (New York, 1960), 42; Angela Leighton, 'De Quincey and Women', in *Beyond Romanticism*, ed. Stephen Copley and John Whale (London, 1992), 165.

from highway robbery . . . to petty larceny. And when once you are got to *that*, there comes in sad progression sabbath-breaking, drunkenness, and late hours; until the awful climax terminates in neglect of dress, non-punctuality, and general waspishness' (p. 157). Both papers are of considerable interest but William Blackwood was apparently unimpressed and declined to publish either of them, perhaps fearing too much of a good thing. De Quincey, however, remained keenly interested in the satiric treatment of murder, and in 1839 he offered Robert and Alexander Blackwood (managers of the magazine since the death of their father in 1834) a 'Second Paper on Murder Considered as One of the Fine Arts', which exploited the same satiric topsy-turviness of the 1827 essay, and which duly appeared in *Blackwood's* in the November issue. The essay centres on a dinner for murder connoisseurs who celebrate the achievements of practitioners from the Jewish Sicarii and the Old Man of the Mountain to more recent adepts such as the Edinburgh killers William Burke and William Hare. It features the curmudgeonly Toad-in-the-hole, who is given new life when he learns of John Williams's sensationally murderous career in the Ratcliffe Highway, for ' "this is the real thing—this is genuine—this is what you can approve, can recommend to a friend" ' (p. 86). De Quincey's 1844 manuscript, 'A New Paper on Murder', is yet another spirited turn on this familiar pattern. William Burke, De Quincey reliably informs us, was 'a man of fine sensibility', but his partner William Hare was 'a man of principle, a man that you could depend upon—order a corpse for Friday, and on Friday you had it' (p. 164).

De Quincey's obsession with murder and mystery, however, did not always involve extravagance, deflation, and satire. In 1838, a year before the appearance of his 'Second Paper on Murder', he took a very different approach to crime and violence in his tale 'The Avenger', which he published in *Blackwood's*, and which drew on and extended the magazine's well-established preoccupation with terror fiction. 'The Avenger' is a story of suspense and retribution in which De Quincey offers a 'moral lesson' that 'deserves the deep attention of coming generations', though the corrupt and bloody world of the tale makes it difficult to determine what exactly that moral lesson is (p. 35). Maximilian Wyndham is an idealized hero who returns from the Napoleonic Wars to settle in a quiet town in north-eastern Germany. Before long a series of brutal murders takes place in which the killer plants himself within a house and then exterminates all occupants. The townsfolk are gripped by panic and an acute sense of vulnerability, 'like that which sometimes takes possession of the mind in dreams—when one feels oneself sleeping alone, utterly divided from all call or hearing of friends' (p. 36). The murderer is eventually revealed to be Maximilian himself, who is Jewish, and whose mother was publicly flogged to death in the town when Maximilian was a boy. He swears vengeance for her death, and then returns to the town as an adult to embark on his ruthlessly ingenious career of vindictive assassination. Yet while 'The Avenger' features a brilliant military hero who murders as a fine art, De Quincey often deviates from his own aesthetic injunctions for heightened effect as articulated in his first essay 'On Murder'. Many of Maximilian's victims are not young but old, and De Quincey goes so far as to note that in one of the recent murders 'there had not been much to call forth sympathy. The family consisted of two old bachelors, two sisters, and one grand-niece. The niece was absent on a visit, and the two old men were cynical misers, to whom little personal interest attached' (p. 52). Similarly, while the 1827 essay 'On Murder' emphasizes that the emotional impact is far greater when 'good' people die innocently, De Quincey debunks such effects in 'The Avenger' by revealing the seemingly peaceful and innocent inhabitants of the town as bigots and fanatics who killed others for the crime of their race (p. 31). Murder for murder's sake is the disinterested aesthetic ideal, but in 'The Avenger' Maximilian wages a personal vendetta with clearly established interests and objectives. What is more, as Maximilian's secret career is gradually unfolded, he comes to occupy a highly ambivalent position within the tale as outcast and god, protector and destroyer, saviour and suicide. He is Kurt Hiller's 'intelligent terrorist' whose argument is, 'if I do not kill I shall never establish the world dominion of justice'.[34] As a vigilante Maximilian soon comes to seem at least as cruel as his victims, though he continues to insist that their wrongs create his rights. When his vengeance careens so far out of control that he accidentally takes the life of his wife Margaret, he regards her death not as a confirmation of the dead-end futility of violence, but as a final sacrifice that affirms the divinity of his mission.

[34] Walter Benjamin, 'Critique of Violence', in *Reflections: Essays, Aphorisms, Auto-biographical Writings*, ed. Peter Demetz, trans. Edmund Jephcott (New York, 1978), 298.

De Quincey is similarly sombre in his brilliant 1854 'Postscript' to 'On Murder', where he returns again to the scene of the crime that had preoccupied him over the course of more than forty years, for the essay offers his most detailed and searching exploration of the Williams murders. The 'Postscript' is rooted in contemporary accounts of the crime in newspapers and pamphlets (as the endnotes to this volume demonstrate), yet De Quincey also omits and distorts events in order to intensify the sense of panic, terror, and defencelessness. He draws plainly on his previous work on the Williams case. In 'On the Knocking', he was prompted by his recollection of the moment in the Marr murders when the servant girl Mary returned from an errand, rang the outside bell 'and at the same time very gently knocked. . . . Yet how is this? To her astonishment, but with the astonishment came creeping over her an icy horror, no stir nor murmur was heard ascending from the kitchen' (p. 109). The black humour of the first two published essays 'On Murder' returns fitfully, as when De Quincey observes that 'it is really wonderful and most interesting to pursue the successive steps of this monster', or that 'our present murderer is fastidiously finical in his exactions—a sort of martinet in the scenical grouping and draping of the circumstances in his murders' (pp. 107, 129). Like Maximilian in 'The Avenger', De Quincey's attitude toward Williams is highly ambivalent: he is a 'solitary artist' who 'walked in darkness', yet he is also 'one born of hell' and an 'accursed hound' (pp. 98, 104, 114). Both the 'Postscript' and 'The Avenger' plumb the particular horror of unknown assailants descending on an urban household which is surrounded by unsuspecting neighbours. Both also insist on the strange and aesthetic allure of a clean and catastrophic fell swoop. It is one of Maximilian's trademarks, for he is behind 'ten cases of total extermination, applied to separate households', while Williams seeks Mary because, 'if caught and murdered', she 'perfected and rounded the desolation of the house. . . . The whole covey of victims was thus netted; the household ruin was thus full and orbicular' (pp. 36, 111). The 'Postscript' concludes with De Quincey's account of the M'Kean brothers' botched attempt to rob an isolated inn just outside Manchester, and includes the gruesome description of a servant who is stabbed but not killed: 'Solemnly, and in ghostly silence, uprose in her dying delirium the murdered girl; she stood upright, she walked steadily for a moment or two, she bent her steps towards the door' (p. 139). In its coherence, intensity, and detail, the 'Post-script' is De Quincey's most lurid exploration of violence.

Yet for all his fixation with murder, De Quincey approached the subject from a remarkably varied series of perspectives and sym-pathies. De Quincey undoubtedly identified with the destructive power of the murderer. Wilson observed tellingly that De Quincey's was 'a nature of dreadful passions subdued by reason', and De Quincey himself often gave vent to feelings of profound hostility, as when he acknowledged himself 'to have been long alienated from Wordsworth; sometimes even I feel a rising emotion of hostility— nay, something, I fear, too nearly akin to vindictive hatred'.[35] De Quincey worried often that he might be responsible for someone's death, such as the mysterious Malay in *Confessions*, or the young woman in the gig in 'The English Mail-Coach'. He joked uneasily that if he had 'a *doppelganger*, who went about personating me . . . philosopher as I am, I might . . . be so far carried away by jealousy as to attempt the crime of murder upon his carcass'.[36] De Quincey projected a work entitled *Confessions of a Murderer*, and he exulted in the thought of retaliation: 'revenge', he wrote, 'is a luxury . . . so inebriating that possibly a man would be equally liable to madness, from the perfect gratification of his vindictive hatred or its perfect defeat'.[37] John Williams was a brutal psychopath who left large clues at the scenes of his murders, and who was not able to escape detec-tion for more than two weeks. But De Quincey often entertained sublime and strange fantasies of vengeance, and in his mind Williams came to symbolize an agency and energy that he himself found absent in his own meek will. Maximilian is a brutal and unrepentant mass murderer, but he accesses that 'tremendous power which is laid open in a moment to any man who can reconcile himself to the abjuration of all conscientious restraints' (p. 99). De Quincey, so often powerless and paralysed by addiction and guilt, glories in the transgressions of the criminal, and embodies what Michel Foucault calls 'the desire to know and narrate how men have been able to rise

---

[35] Mary Gordon, *'Christopher North': A Memoir of John Wilson* (New York, 1863), 326; *The Works of Thomas De Quincey: Volume Eleven*, ed. Julian North (London, 2003), 62.

[36] *The Works of Thomas De Quincey: Volume Sixteen*, 52.

[37] *The Works of Thomas De Quincey: Volume Ten*, ed. Alina Clej (London, 2003), 261.

against power, traverse the law, and expose themselves to death through death'.[38]

Yet De Quincey also sympathized with the victim, and while in 'On the Knocking' he instructed the poet not to look into the hearts of those cowering for fear of their own lives, in his first paper 'On Murder' he contradicts this directive by declaring that the 'tendency in murder' is 'to excite and irritate the subject' (p. 26). In 'interesting illustration of this fact', De Quincey offers the case of the 'pursy, unwieldy, half cataleptic' Mannheim baker who mustered the strength to go twenty-six rounds with an English boxer and assassin, demonstrating 'what an astonishing stimulus to latent talent is contained in any reasonable prospect of being murdered' (pp. 26, 29). Less risible examples occur in 'The Avenger'. As terror descends upon the town, 'some, alas for the dignity of Man! drooped into helpless imbecility', but 'some started up into heroes under the excitement' (p. 51). One hero is Louisa, a 13-year-old student who hears footsteps on the stairs and later spies the murderer's leg in the closet, but manages to save both herself and her sister through a display not of hysteria or abjection but 'blind inspiration' and a 'matchless . . . presence of mind' (pp. 57, 56). Similarly, in the 'Postscript' the young boy finds himself trapped between the two M'Kean brothers. 'On the landing at the head of the stairs was one murderer, at the foot of the stairs was the other: who could believe that the boy had the shadow of a chance for escaping?' And yet he does escape, for in his 'horror, he laid his left hand on the balustrade, and took a flying leap over it, which landed him at the bottom of the stairs, without having touched a single stair'. It was a jump from 'a height, such as he will never clear again to his dying day' (pp. 139, 26). De Quincey often highlighted the clarity and courage of those who found themselves face to face with murderous violence.

De Quincey, however, did not stop at the murderer and the victim, for he was also fascinated by the position and anxieties of the witness. Given the insights of 'On the Knocking', the clear expectation in the 'Postscript' is that the focus will be on the psychology of the murderer Williams. But it is not. Once Williams is inside the Marr household, De Quincey makes a striking decision: 'Let us leave the murderer alone with his victims' and 'in vision, attach ourselves' to

---

[38] *I, Pierre Rivière*, ed. Michel Foucault, trans. Frank Jellinek (New York, 1975), 206.

Mary, who has been sent to fetch oysters for dinner (p. 108). Williams inflicts his atrocities while we accompany an anxious innocent. And when Mary returns to the Marr front door and begins her slide into panic, De Quincey remains with her, positioning her just beyond Williams's reach, not directly exposed to his savagery, but hovering on the periphery, a witness to the events rather than a victim of them. 'The unknown murderer and she have both their lips upon the door, listening, breathing hard', whispers De Quincey; 'but luckily they are on different sides of the door; and upon the least indication of unlocking or unlatching, she would have recoiled into the asylum of general darkness' (p. 111). What is more, in his account of the Williamson murders, De Quincey follows the same pattern. He is with neither Williams nor Williamson, but accompanies the journey-man John Turner, 'the secret witness, from his secret stand' who waits breathlessly on the staircase while Williams hangs over the dead body of Mrs Williamson and then searches for keys (p. 124). The murderer's coat is lined with silk and his shoes creak, for 'the young artisan, paralysed as he had been by fear, and evidently fascin-ated for a time so as to walk right towards the lion's mouth, yet found himself able to notice everything important'. Eventually the mur-derer walks off 'to the hidden section of the parlour' and Turner, seeing 'at last . . . the sudden opening for an escape', makes his way upstairs and then out of his bedroom window and down into the street, 'the solitary spectator' who watched spellbound in horror but evaded Williams's brutality (pp. 123, 125, 102). In *Macbeth*, we as audience witness the two murderers shortly after their killing of Duncan. In his representation of both the Marr and Williamson atro-cities, De Quincey places us in the same position. Bound to the viewpoint of the witness, we listen to or watch Williams just moments after his carnage is complete. In the 'Postscript', De Quincey builds his aesthetic of violence from this perspective, for we look on—rather than within—Williams. The terrified bystander is endangered but ultimately released, and reader, witness, and mur-derer fixed together in a closed and rapt space that descends towards the brink of terror before allowing an escape for help and the reasser-tion of the ethical world of human action. The three scenes are closely related in terms of structure and emotion, but in *Macbeth* we are with the murderer while in the 'Postscript' we are with the witness.

De Quincey's sympathies, however, were divided even beyond

murderer, victim, and witness, for he also paved the way for the appearance of the detective, not with the introduction of the actual figure, but by putting in place key features that helped to initiate the enormous and enduring popularity of murder mysteries and detective fiction. De Quincey aestheticized violence, transforming it into liberating and intellectual entertainment and then marketing it in a variety of fictive, impassioned, and satiric guises, where it was rapidly consumed by a reading public insatiably interested in palatable versions of murder that disturbed in order to excite and seduce. 'From the adventure story to de Quincey, or from the *Castle of Otranto* to Baudelaire', asserts Foucault, 'there is a whole aesthetic rewriting of crime, which is also the appropriation of criminality in acceptable forms.'[39] De Quincey stressed the intellectualism and design of brilliant crime. He was not interested in the murder of 'some huge farmer returning drunk from a fair', for while 'there would be plenty of blood', that can hardly be taken 'in lieu of taste, finish, scenical grouping' (p. 83). He delighted to piece together clues: 'It is really wonderful and most interesting to pursue the successive steps of this monster [Williams], and to notice the absolute certainty with which the silent hieroglyphics of the case betray to us the whole process and movements of the bloody drama' (p. 107). His mind demanded mystery. William Godwin's *Caleb Williams* (1794) is often taken as one of the first novels of detection, but De Quincey roundly condemned it because the plot was not 'managed with art, and covered with mystery'.[40] Most strikingly, in 'The Avenger' De Quincey adopts the whole rhetoric of detective fiction. Footsteps in the chapel promise to 'furnish a clue to the discovery of one at least amongst the murderous band', while the terrified townsfolk grapple with 'the mystery of the *how*, and the profounder mystery of the *why*' (pp. 47, 52). Maximilian's confessional letter explains the inspired ways in which he committed his acts of murderous vengeance and marks 'the solution of that mystery which caused such perplexity' (pp. 77–8). In his aestheticization and commodification of crime, as well as in the rhetoric, suspense, violence, reversals, and ingenuity of 'The Avenger', De Quincey maps in key features of detective fiction.

  De Quincey's writings on murder were received with a great deal

---

[39] Michel Foucault, *Discipline and Punish*, trans. Alan Sheridan (New York, 1979), 68.
[40] *The Works of Thomas De Quincey: Volume Fifteen*, ed. Frederick Burwick (London, 2003), 266.

of contemporary enthusiasm. 'He has written a thing about Macbeth better than anything I could write,' remarked Charles Lamb of 'On the Knocking'; '—no—not better than anything I could write, but I could not write anything better'.[41] The *Gentleman's Magazine* thought the first essay 'On Murder' ran over 'with a ripe and laughter-moving humour from the first page to the last', while the *Eclectic Review* considered it 'as perfect a piece of pure cynicism as any in our language; not savage, like some of Swift's or Carlyle's pieces, but playful and full of humour'.[42] In 'The Avenger', notes L. W. Spring, 'the plot darkens; the crisis gathers; loud and more tumultuous waxes the fiendish tumult, until all lesser passions are swallowed up, and the empire of a blank, rayless revenge is triumphant; we are spellbound amid the successive stages of the demoniac tragedy; we start up convulsively, as from the horrors of nightmare at its ghastly catastrophe'.[43] The 'Postscript' drew equal praise. 'I know of no writer but De Quincey who invests mysteries of this tragic order with their appropriate drapery', wrote H. M. Alden, 'so that they shall, to our imaginations, unfold the full measure of their capacities for striking awe into our hearts.'[44] The *Eclectic Review* observed that 'anything more horribly interesting cannot be imagined, than his description of Williams, and the murder of the Marrs; it has a magnetic force of attraction, a fascination which the reader vainly endeavours to dispel'.[45] The *British Quarterly Review* declared that 'it is long since we read' the 'Postscript', but 'its bloody horrors are still fresh, and are, even to this day, sometimes tyrannous. It is simply terrible in its power; and for long after we read it, every night brought a renewal of the most real shuddering, the palsying dread, and the nightmare impotence with which its first perusal cursed us'.[46] In 1874 Leslie Stephen asserted that De Quincey's essays 'On Murder' were 'probably the most popular of his writings'.[47]

The essays, satires, and fictions collected in this volume have had

---

[41] E. V. Lucas, *The Life of Charles Lamb*, 2 vols. (London, 1905), ii. 69.

[42] Anonymous, 'Thomas De Quincey', *Gentleman's Magazine*, 203 (August 1857), 111; Anonymous, 'Thomas De Quincey', *Eclectic Review*, 8th ser., 15 (August 1868), 115.

[43] L. W. Spring, 'Thomas De Quincey and his Writings', *Continental Monthly*, 5 (June 1864), 662.

[44] H. M. Alden, 'Thomas De Quincey', *Atlantic Monthly*, 12 (September 1863), 362.

[45] Anonymous, 'Thomas De Quincey', *Eclectic Review*, 8th ser., 15 (August 1868), 115.

[46] Anonymous, '*The Works of Thomas De Quincey*', *British Quarterly Review*, 38 (July 1863), 22.

[47] 'Leslie Stephen on De Quincey', in *De Quincey*, ed. M. R. Ridley (Oxford, 1927), 16.

an enormous impact that can be felt across a wide-ranging series of works. Edgar Allan Poe seized on De Quinceyan precedents to fashion the first fictional detective, Auguste Dupin, and to produce a powerful series of tales that explore murder as a fine art.[48] In 'Proem at the Paris Station' (1849), Dante Gabriel Rossetti sees a stabbed body pulled from the Seine and conjectures that

> he who did the job
> Was standing among those who stood with us,
> To look upon the corpse. You fancy him—
> Smoking an early pipe, and watching, as
> An artist, the effect of his last work.[49]

Charles Dickens encapsulates the humour and mobility of De Quincey's aesthetic in *Great Expectations* (1860–1). 'A highly popular murder had been committed, and Mr Wopsle was imbrued in blood to the eyebrows', writes Dickens. 'He gloated over every abhorrent adjective in the description, and identified himself with every witness at the Inquest. He faintly moaned, "I am done for", as the victim, and he barbarously bellowed, "I'll serve you out", as the murderer. . . . He enjoyed himself thoroughly, and we all enjoyed ourselves, and were delightfully comfortable.'[50] G. K. Chesterton declares that De Quincey is 'the first and most powerful of the decadents', and that 'any one still smarting from the pinpricks' of Oscar Wilde or James Whistler 'will find most of what they said said better in *Murder as One of the Fine Arts*'.[51] Similarly, Wyndham Lewis remarks that De Quincey's 'exaltation of the murderer' puts him in a group of 'distinguished diabolists' that includes 'Lord Byron, Huysmans, Baudelaire, Wilde, De Lautréamont. . . . It is a history of a century of diabolics'.[52] In the twentieth century George Orwell's 'Decline of the English Murder' (1946) is among the most famous tributes. 'Before returning to this pitiful and sordid case', writes Orwell, '. . . let me try to define what it is that the readers of

---

[48] Robert Morrison, 'Poe's De Quincey, Poe's Dupin', *Essays in Criticism*, 51/4 (2001), 424–41.

[49] Dante Gabriel Rossetti, *Collected Poetry and Prose*, ed. Jerome McGann (New Haven, 2003), 354.

[50] Charles Dickens, *Great Expectations*, ed. Margaret Cardwell (Oxford, 1993), 132.

[51] G. K. Chesterton, *The Victorian Age in Literature* (New York, 1913), 24–5.

[52] Wyndham Lewis, *Men Without Art*, ed. Seamus Cooney (Santa Rosa, Calif., 1987), 143.

Sunday papers mean when they say fretfully that "you never seem to get a good murder nowadays".[53] Malcolm Lowry's *Under the Volcano* (1947) features the mescal-sodden Consul's recollections of 'Old De Quincey; the knocking on the gate in Macbeth. Knock, knock, knock: who's there? Cat. Cat who? Catastrophe'.[54] In Vladimir Nabokov's *Despair* (1966), the murderer states flatly, 'any remorse on my part is absolutely out of the question: an artist feels no remorse, even when his work is not understood, not accepted'.[55] Iain Sinclair opens his *Lud Heat* (1975) with a quotation from the 'Postscript' to 'On Murder', and observes that in the essay itself 'De Quincey, at his speed and exhaustion of operation, fending off the monkey, digressing obsessively towards overlapping versions of the truth, couldn't help getting in among the authentic substrata'.[56] Peter Ackroyd is as fixated with the Ratcliffe murders as De Quincey, and in *Hawksmoor* (1985) he recalls how Williams 'was transformed . . . according to De Quincey, into a "mighty murderer" ', and then buried at a crossroads, where 'as far as Hawksmoor knew', he lay buried still: 'it was the spot where he had this morning seen the crowd pressing against the cordon set up by the police'.[57] De Quincey's work altered the ways in which murder was represented and recreated, taking us from Radcliffe novels to Ratcliffe highway, from *Caleb Williams* to John Williams, and from Edmund Burke to William Burke. His interpretations of murder frequently confound the reader between sympathy and voyeurism, but reveal the ways in which what would horrify us in life will entertain us in art. In his hands, violent crime became a subject which could be detached from social circumstances and then ironized, tamed, analysed, exploited, and avidly enjoyed by his burgeoning magazine audiences, and by generations of murder mystery connoisseurs and armchair detectives who enjoy the intellectual challenge, rapt exploration, and satiric safety of murder as a fine art.

[53] George Orwell, *Smothered under Journalism, 1946*, ed. Peter Davison (London, 1998), 108–9.
[54] Malcolm Lowry, *Under the Volcano*, intro. Michael Schmidt (London, 2000), 140.
[55] Vladimir Nabokov, *Despair* (New York, 1966), 187.
[56] Iain Sinclair, *Lud Heat and Suicide Bridge* (London, 1998), 13, 23.
[57] Peter Ackroyd, *Hawksmoor* (London, 1985), 116.

NOTE ON THE TEXT

THE copy text for the four essays and one tale of terror reprinted in
the main section of this volume is the first published version. Details
of dates and the place of publication appear in the Explanatory
Notes. All five texts have been standardized in a number of ways:
double quotation marks have been changed to single, quotation
marks have been removed from around indented quotations, full
stops have been removed from terms of address ('Mrs', 'Mr', 'Dr',
'St'), a standard format has been adopted for the headings, and
square brackets have been changed to round. Obvious typographical
errors have been silently corrected. Inconsistencies in punctuation,
capitalization, and spelling have been retained.

The three appendices in this volume contain manuscript fragments intended by De Quincey to form part of the 'On Murder
Considered as One of the Fine Arts' series, though in each instance
the fragment remained unpublished until well after his death. Head-
notes to each appendix give details on manuscript location, date
or probable date of composition, and any distinctive or anomalous
features.

Throughout the volume, De Quincey's footnotes are cued by
superior figures and editorial endnotes are cued by asterisks.

SELECT BIBLIOGRAPHY

Bibliographies

Dendurent, H. O., *Thomas De Quincey: A Reference Guide* (Boston, 1978).

Morrison, Robert, 'Essayists of the Romantic Period: De Quincey, Hazlitt, Hunt, and Lamb', in *Literature of the Romantic Period: A Bibliographical Guide*, ed. Michael O'Neill (Oxford, 1998), 341–63.

Biographies

Eaton, H. A., *Thomas De Quincey* (New York, 1936).

Lindop, Grevel, *The Opium-Eater: A Life of Thomas De Quincey* (London, 1981).

Sackville-West, Edward, *A Flame in Sunlight: The Life and Works of Thomas De Quincey* (London, 1936; reprinted, ed. John Jordan, London, 1974).

Editions

The Works of Thomas De Quincey, gen. ed. Grevel Lindop, 21 vols. (London, 2000–3).

Letters

De Quincey at Work, ed. W. H. Bonner (Buffalo, 1936).

De Quincey to Wordsworth, ed. John E. Jordan (Berkeley, 1963).

'De Quincey and his Publishers', ed. Barry Symonds, Ph.D. thesis, University of Edinburgh, 1994.

Criticism

Appleman, Philip, 'D. H. Lawrence and the Intrusive Knock', *Modern Fiction Studies*, 3 (1958), 328–32.

Barrell, John, *The Infection of Thomas De Quincey* (New Haven, 1991).

Baxter, Edmund, *De Quincey's Art of Autobiography* (Edinburgh, 1990).

Benjamin, Walter, 'Critique of Violence', in *Reflections: Essays, Aphorisms, Autobiographical Writings*, ed. Peter Demetz, trans. Edmund Jephcott (New York, 1978), 277–300.

Black, Joel, *The Aesthetics of Murder: A Study in Romantic Literature and Contemporary Culture* (Baltimore, 1991).

Breton, André, 'Thomas De Quincey', in *Anthology of Black Humour*, trans. Mark Polizzotti (San Francisco, 1997), 53–8.

Burke, Thomas, 'The Obsequies of Mr Williams: New Light on De Quincey's Famous Tale of Murder', *The Bookman*, 68 (1928), 257–63.

Burwick, Frederick, 'De Quincey and the Aesthetics of Violence', *Words-worth Circle*, 27 (1996), 78–86.

Byerly, Alison, 'Accident or Murder? Intentionality, the Picturesque, and the Body of Thomas De Quincey', *Nineteenth-Century Prose*, 29/2 (2002), 48–68.

Carnall, Geoffrey, 'De Quincey on the Knocking at the Gate', *Review of English Literature*, 2 (1961), 49–57.

Chandler, Raymond, 'The Simple Art of Murder: An Essay', in *The Simple Art of Murder* (New York, 1988), 1–18.

Cohen, Michael, *Murder Most Fair* (Madison, 2000).

Critchley, T. A., and James, P. D., *The Maul and the Pear Tree: The Ratcliffe Highway Murders, 1811* (London, 1971).

De Luca, V. A., *Thomas De Quincey: The Prose of Vision* (Toronto, 1980).

Goldman, Albert, *The Mine and the Mint: Sources for the Writings of Thomas De Quincey* (Carbondale, Ill., 1965).

Gossman, Ann, 'On the Knocking at the Gate in "Markheim" ', *Nineteenth-Century Fiction*, 17 (1962), 73–6.

Katz, Jack, *Seductions of Crime: Moral and Sensual Attractions in Doing Evil* (New York, 1988).

Leask, Nigel, 'Toward a Universal Aesthetic: De Quincey on Murder as Carnival and Tragedy', in *Questioning Romanticism*, ed. John Beer (Baltimore, 1995), 92–120.

Lehman, David, *The Perfect Murder: A Study in Detection* (Ann Arbor, 2000).

Leighton, Angela, 'De Quincey and Women', in *Beyond Romanticism*, ed. Stephen Copley and John Whale (London, 1992), 160–77.

Lindop, Grevel, 'Innocence and Revenge: The Problem of De Quincey's Fiction', in *Thomas De Quincey: Bicentenary Studies*, ed. Robert Lance Snyder (Norman, Okla., 1985), 213–37.

Long, John C., 'Thomas De Quincey, Clinician', *Wordsworth Circle*, 24 (1993), 170–7.

McDonagh, Josephine, 'Do or Die: Problems of Agency and Gender in the Aesthetics of Murder', *Genders*, 5 (1989), 120–34.

Malkan, Jeffrey, 'Aggressive Text: Murder and the Fine Arts Revisited', *Mosaic*, 23 (1990), 101–14.

Mandel, Ernest, *Delightful Murder: A Social History of the Crime Story* (Minneapolis, 1984).

Mayoux, Jean-Jacques, 'De Quincey: Humour and the Drugs', in *Veins of Humour*, ed. Harry Levin (Cambridge, Mass., 1972), 109–29.

Moldenhauer, Joseph, 'Murder as a Fine Art: Basic Connections between Poe's Aesthetics, Psychology, and Moral Vision', *PMLA*, 83 (1968), 284–97.

Morrison, Robert, 'Poe's De Quincey, Poe's Dupin', *Essays in Criticism*, 51/4 (2001), 424–41.

Most, Glenn W., and Stowe, William W. (eds.), *The Poetics of Murder: Detective Fiction and Literary Theory* (New York, 1983).

O'Quinn, Daniel, 'Murder, Hospitality, Philosophy: De Quincey and the Complicitous Grounds of National Identity', *Studies in Romanticism*, 38 (1999), 135–70.

Orwell, George, 'Decline of the English Murder', in *Smothered under Journalism, 1946*, ed. Peter Davison (London, 1998), 108–10.

Playfair, G. M. H., 'De Quincey: The Murderer Williams', *Notes and Queries*, 11th ser., 5 (January 1912), 6.

Plotz, Judith, 'On Guilt Considered as One of the Fine Arts: De Quincey's Criminal Imagination', *Wordsworth Circle*, 19 (1988), 83–8.

Plumtree, A. S., 'The Artist as Murderer: De Quincey's Essay "On Murder Considered as One of the Fine Arts" ', in *Thomas De Quincey: Bicentenary Studies*, ed. Robert Lance Snyder (Norman, Okla., 1985), 140–63.

Rzepka, Charles, *Sacramental Commodities: Gift, Text, and the Sublime in De Quincey* (Amherst, 1995).

Sartre, Jean-Paul, 'On the Fine Arts Considered as Murder', in *Saint Genet: Actor and Martyr*, trans. Bernard Frechtman (New York, 1963), 483–543.

Sedgwick, Eve Kosofsky, 'Language as Live Burial: Thomas De Quincey', in *The Coherence of Gothic Conventions* (New York, 1980), 37–96.

Senelick, Laurence, *The Prestige of Evil: The Murderer as Romantic Hero from Sade to Lacenaire* (New York, 1987).

Snyder, Robert Lance, 'De Quincey's Liminal Interspaces: On Murder Considered as One of the Fine Arts" ', *Nineteenth-Century Prose*, 28/2 (2001), 102–18.

Stephen, Leslie, 'The Decay of Murder', *Cornhill Magazine*, 20 (December 1869), 722–33.

Sullivan, Margo Ann, *Murder and Art: Thomas De Quincey and the Ratcliffe Highway Murders* (New York, 1987).

Super, Robert H., 'De Quincey and a Murderer's Conscience', *Times Literary Supplement* (5 December 1936), 1016.

Whale, John, ' "In a Stranger's Ear": De Quincey's Polite Magazine Context', in *Thomas De Quincey: Bicentenary Studies*, ed. Robert Lance Snyder (Norman, Okla., 1985), 35–53.

Ziolkowski, Theodore, 'A Portrait of the Artist as a Criminal', in *Dimensions of the Modern Novel: German Texts and European Contexts* (Princeton, 1969), 289–331.

Fiction and Poetry

Ackroyd, Peter, *Dan Leno and the Limehouse Golem* (London, 1994).
—— *Hawksmoor* (London, 1985).
Kerr, Philip, *A Philosophical Investigation* (London, 1992).
Long, Gabrielle Margaret Vere [as Joseph Shearing], 'Blood and Thunder',
    in *Orange Blossoms* (London, 1938).
Nabokov, Vladimir, *Despair* (New York, 1966).
Sinclair, Iain, *Lud Heat* (London, 1975; repr. in *Lud Heat and Suicide
    Bridge*, London, 1998).

Further Reading in Oxford World's Classics

De Quincey, Thomas, *Confessions of an English Opium-Eater and Other
    Writings*, ed. Grevel Lindop.
Doyle, Arthur Conan, *The Adventures of Sherlock Holmes*, ed. Richard
    Lancelyn Green.
—— *The Memoirs of Sherlock Holmes*, ed. Christopher Roden.
Hogg, James, *The Private Memoirs and Confessions of a Justified Sinner*, ed.
    John Carey.
Le Fanu, Joseph Sheridan, *In a Glass Darkly*, ed. Robert Tracy.
Poe, Edgar Allan, *Selected Tales*, ed. David Van Leer.
The Vampyre and Other Tales of the Macabre, ed. Robert Morrison and
    Chris Baldick.
Wilde, Oscar, *The Picture of Dorian Gray*, ed. Isobel Murray.

A CHRONOLOGY OF
THOMAS DE QUINCEY

1785 Born (15 August) in Manchester, son of Thomas Quincey, textile importer, and Elizabeth Penson.

1790 Death of his sister Jane, aged 3.

1792 Death of his sister Elizabeth, aged 9.

1793 Death of his father.

1796 Moves to Bath and enters Bath Grammar School. His mother takes the name 'De Quincey'.

1799 Enters Winkfield School, Wiltshire. Reads Wordsworth and Coleridge's *Lyrical Ballads*, which he later describes as 'the greatest event in the unfolding of my own mind'.

1800 Translation from Horace's Twenty-Second Ode wins third prize in a contest, and is published in the *Monthly Preceptor*. Accidentally meets George III at Frogmore. Summer holiday in Ireland. Enters Manchester Grammar School.

1801 Spends summer in Everton, near Liverpool, where he meets William Roscoe, James Currie, and other Whig intellectuals.

1802 Flees from Manchester Grammar School. Wanders in North Wales and then spends five months penniless and hungry on the streets of London.

1803 Reconciled with his mother and guardians. Spends another summer in Everton. Reads gothic fiction voraciously. Deepening admiration for Coleridge, whom he begins to think 'the greatest man that has ever appeared'. Writes fan letter to Wordsworth, and the two begin a correspondence. Enters Worcester College, Oxford.

1804 Begins occasional use of opium. Meets Charles Lamb.

1805 Travels to the Lake District at the invitation of Wordsworth, but loses his nerve and turns back without meeting the poet.

1806 Travels again to the Lake District to meet Wordsworth, and again loses his nerve.

1807 Meets Coleridge. Gives him £300 under the polite pretence of a 'loan'. Escorts Coleridge's family to the Lake District and meets Wordsworth at Grasmere.

1808 Sees Coleridge daily and assists him with his lectures for the Royal

Institution, on Poetry and Principles of Taste. Bolts from Oxford midway through his final examinations and does not receive his degree. Introduced to John Wilson, the future 'Christopher North' of *Blackwood's Magazine*. The two become close friends.

1809 Supervises the printing of Wordsworth's pamphlet on *The Convention of Cintra*, and contributes a lengthy 'Postscript on Sir John Moore's Letters'. Moves to Grasmere, where he rents Dove Cottage, the former home of the Wordsworths.

1810 Enters period of greatest intimacy with Wordsworth and Coleridge. Reads manuscript of Wordsworth's *Prelude*. With Wilson and Alexander Blair, contributes the 'Letter of Mathetes' to Coleridge's metaphysical newspaper, *The Friend*.

1812 Enters the Middle Temple briefly to read for the Bar. Grief-stricken by the death of Wordsworth's 3-year-old daughter Catherine.

1813 Becomes addicted to opium. Strained relations with the Wordsworths. Courts Margaret Simpson, the daughter of a Lake District farmer.

1814 Visits Edinburgh with Wilson, where he meets leading members of the Scottish literary scene, including J. G. Lockhart, the future biographer of Walter Scott, and James Hogg, the 'Ettrick Shepherd'.

1816 Birth of son, William Penson, by Margaret Simpson. Estranged from the Wordsworths.

1817 Marries Margaret Simpson. William Blackwood founds and edits *Blackwood's Magazine*, with Wilson, Lockhart, and Hogg as major contributors.

1818 With Wordsworth, publishes the Tory jeremiad *Close Comments upon a Straggling Speech*, a denunciation of Henry Brougham, Independent Whig candidate in the parliamentary election campaign in Westmorland. Appointed editor of the local Tory newspaper, the *Westmorland Gazette*. Slides deeper into debt and addiction. Lucid opium nightmares.

1819 Dismissed from editorship of the *Westmorland Gazette*. With Wilson and Lockhart, writes review of Percy Bysshe Shelley's *The Revolt of Islam* for *Blackwood's Magazine*.

1821 'The Sport of Fortune', translated from Friedrich Schiller's 'Spiel des Schicksals', published in *Blackwood's Magazine*. Quarrels with William Blackwood. Publishes *Confessions of an English Opium-Eater* in the *London Magazine*. Conversations with John Keats's friend Richard Woodhouse. Meets William Hazlitt.

1822 First publication of the *Confessions* in book form. Projects a work entitled *Confessions of a Murderer* but it does not appear.

1823 'Notes from the Pocket Book of a Late Opium-Eater', including 'On the Knocking at the Gate in Macbeth', in the *London Magazine*. Appears as 'The Opium-Eater' in the *Noctes Ambrosianae*, a series of raucous and wide-ranging dialogues published in *Blackwood's Magazine* (completed 1835).

1824 Reviews Goethe's *Wilhelm Meister's Apprenticeship*, a translation by Thomas Carlyle, in the *London Magazine*.

1825 Translates and abridges the German pseudo-Waverley novel *Walladmor*. Probably composes manuscript on Peter Anthony Fonk, which he later attempts to incorporate into a sequel to 'On Murder Considered as One of the Fine Arts'. Leaves the *London Magazine*.

1826 Rejoins *Blackwood's Magazine*, where he publishes his review of Robert Gillies's *German Stories*.

1827 'On Murder Considered as One of the Fine Arts' in *Blackwood's Magazine*. Begins to write for the *Edinburgh Saturday Post*. Meets Carlyle and an intimacy develops.

1828 'Toilette of the Hebrew Lady' and 'Elements of Rhetoric' in *Blackwood's Magazine*. Writes the manuscript fragment 'To the Editor of Blackwood's Magazine', which he attempts to incorporate into a sequel to 'On Murder Considered as One of the Fine Arts'.

1829 'Sketch of Professor Wilson' in the *Edinburgh Literary Gazette*.

1830 'Kant in his Miscellaneous Essays', 'Richard Bentley', and a series of heated Tory diatribes, including 'French Revolution' and 'Political Anticipations', in *Blackwood's Magazine*. Moves permanently to Edinburgh.

1831 'Dr Parr and his Contemporaries' in *Blackwood's Magazine*. Prosecuted and briefly imprisoned for debt.

1832 *Klosterheim: or, the Masque*, a one-volume gothic romance, published by Blackwood.

1833 Contributes 'The Age of the Earth', translated from Kant's 'Die Frage, ob die Erde veralte, physicalisch erwogen', and an assessment, 'Mrs Hannah More', to *Tait's Magazine*, the leading Scottish rival of *Blackwood's Magazine*. Twice prosecuted for debt. Takes refuge in the debtor's sanctuary at Holyrood. Death of son Julius, aged 3.

1834 'Samuel Taylor Coleridge' and 'Sketches of Life and Manners from the Autobiography of a Late Opium-Eater' (sporadically until 1841) in *Tait's Magazine*. Three times prosecuted for debt. Death of Samuel Taylor Coleridge, Charles Lamb, and William Blackwood. Blackwood's sons Robert and Alexander take over the management of the magazine.

1835 'Oxford' and 'A Tory's Account of Toryism, Whiggism, and Radicalism' in *Tait's Magazine*.

1837 'The Revolt of the Tartars' in *Blackwood's Magazine*. Twice prosecuted for debt. Death of his wife Margaret.

1838 Two tales of terror, 'The Household Wreck' and 'The Avenger', in *Blackwood's Magazine*. 'Recollections of Charles Lamb' in *Tait's Magazine*.

1839 'Second Paper on Murder Considered as One of the Fine Arts' in *Blackwood's Magazine*. 'William Wordsworth' in *Tait's Magazine*.

1840 'The Opium and the China Question' in *Blackwood's Magazine*. Prosecuted for debt.

1843 Moves to Mavis Bush Cottage, Lasswade, outside Edinburgh.

1844 Publishes one-volume treatise, *The Logic of Political Economy*, with Blackwood. Manuscript fragment of 'a new paper on Murder as a Fine Art'.

1845 'Coleridge and Opium-Eating' and 'Suspiria de Profundis' in *Blackwood's Magazine*. 'On Wordsworth's Poetry' and 'Notes on Gilfillan's "Gallery of Literary Portraits": Godwin, Foster, Hazlitt, Shelley, Keats' (completed 1846) in *Tait's Magazine*.

1846 'System of the Heavens as Revealed by Lord Rosse's Telescope' in *Tait's Magazine*.

1847 'Joan of Arc' and 'The Nautico–Military Nun of Spain' in *Tait's Magazine*.

1848 'Final Memorials of Charles Lamb' in *North British Review*. Meets Ralph Waldo Emerson.

1849 'The English Mail-Coach', his last essay for *Blackwood's Magazine*.

1850 Contributes several essays to the Edinburgh publisher James Hogg's weekly magazine, *The Instructor*. Ticknor, Reed, and Fields of Boston begin publication of *De Quincey's Writings* (twenty-two volumes, completed 1856). Death of Wordsworth.

1851 'Lord Carlisle on Pope', his last essay for *Tait's Magazine*.

1853 Begins sometimes extensive revision of his work for *Selections Grave and Gay*, an edition issued by Hogg (fourteen volumes, completed 1860). *Autobiographic Sketches* (completed 1854) appear as volumes i and ii of *Selections Grave and Gay*.

1854 Takes lodgings at 42 Lothian Street, Edinburgh. Publishes his 'Postscript' to 'On Murder Considered as One of the Fine Arts' in volume iv of *Selections Grave and Gay*. Death of Wilson.

1856 *Confessions of an English Opium-Eater*, revised and expanded, appears as volume v of *Selections Grave and Gay*. Begins to contribute to Hogg's monthly magazine, *The Titan*.

1857 Publishes pamphlet on *China* with Hogg. Articles on the Indian Mutiny for *The Titan* (completed 1858).

1859 Dies (8 December) in Edinburgh. Buried beside Margaret in St Cuthbert's churchyard.

ON MURDER

ON THE KNOCKING AT THE GATE
IN MACBETH

FROM my boyish days I had always felt a great perplexity on one point in Macbeth: it was this: the knocking at the gate, which succeeds to the murder of Duncan,* produced to my feelings an effect for which I never could account: the effect was—that it reflected back upon the murder a peculiar awfulness and a depth of solemnity: yet, however obstinately I endeavoured with my understanding to comprehend this, for many years I never could see *why* it should produce such an effect.—

Here I pause for one moment to exhort the reader never to pay any attention to his understanding when it stands in opposition to any other faculty of his mind. The mere understanding, however useful and indispensable, is the meanest faculty in the human mind and the most to be distrusted: and yet the great majority of people trust to nothing else; which may do for ordinary life, but not for philosophic purposes. Of this, out of ten thousand instances that I might produce, I will cite one. Ask of any person whatsoever, who is not previously prepared for the demand by a knowledge of perspective, to draw in the rudest way the commonest appearance which depends upon the laws of that science—as for instance, to represent the effect of two walls standing at right angles to each other, or the appearance of the houses on each side of a street, as seen by a person looking down the street from one extremity. Now in all cases, unless the person has happened to observe in pictures how it is that artists produce these effects, he will be utterly unable to make the smallest approximation to it. Yet why?—For he has actually seen the effect every day of his life. The reason is—that he allows his understanding to overrule his eyes. His understanding, which includes no intuitive knowledge of the laws of vision, can furnish him with no reason why a line which is known and can be proved to be a horizontal line, should not *appear* a horizontal line: a line, that made any angle with the perpendicular less than a right angle, would seem to him to indicate that his houses were all tumbling down together. Accordingly he makes the line of his houses a horizontal line, and fails of course to produce the effect demanded. Here then is one instance out of many, in which not only the understanding is allowed to overrule the eyes, but where the understanding is positively allowed to obliterate the eyes as it were: for not only does the man believe the evidence of his understanding in opposition to that of his eyes, but (which is monstrous!) the idiot is not aware that his eyes ever gave such evidence. He does not know that he has seen (and therefore *quoad** his consciousness has *not* seen) that which he *has* seen every day of his life. But, to return from this digression,—my understanding could furnish no reason why the knocking at the gate in Macbeth should produce any effect direct or reflected: in fact, my understanding said positively that it could *not* produce any effect. But I knew better: I felt that it did: and I waited and clung to the problem until further knowledge should enable me to solve it.—At length, in 1812, Mr Williams* made his *début* on the stage of Ratcliffe Highway, and executed those unparalleled murders which have procured for him such a brilliant and undying reputation. On which murders, by the way, I must observe, that in one respect they have had an ill effect, by making the connoisseur in murder very fastidious in his taste, and dissatisfied with any thing that has been since done in that line. All other murders look pale by the deep crimson of his: and, as an amateur once said to me in a querulous tone, 'There has been absolutely nothing *doing* since his time, or nothing that's worth speaking of.' But this is wrong: for it is unreasonable to expect all men to be great artists, and born with the genius of Mr Williams.—Now it will be remembered that in the first of these murders (that of the Marrs*) the same incident (of a knocking at the door soon after the work of extermination was complete) did actually occur which the genius of Shakspeare had invented: and all good judges and the most eminent dilettanti acknowledged the felicity of Shakspeare's suggestion as soon as it was actually realized. Here then was a fresh proof that I had been right in relying on my own feeling in opposition to my understanding; and again I set myself to study the problem: at length I solved it to my own satisfaction; and my solution is this. Murder in ordinary cases, where the sympathy is wholly directed to the case of the murdered person, is an incident of coarse and vulgar horror; and for this reason—that it flings the interest exclusively upon the natural but ignoble instinct by which we cleave to life; an instinct which, as being indispensable to the primal law of self-preservation, is the same in kind (though different in degree) amongst all living creatures; this instinct therefore, because it annihilates all distinctions, and degrades the greatest of men to the level of 'the poor beetle that we tread on,'* exhibits human nature in its most abject and humiliating attitude. Such an attitude would little suit the purposes of the poet. What then must he do? He must throw the interest on the murderer: our sympathy must be with *him*; (of course I mean a sympathy of comprehension, a sympathy by which we enter into his feelings, and are made to understand them,—not a sympathy[1] of pity or approbation:) in the murdered person all strife of thought, all flux and reflux of passion and of purpose, are crushed by one overwhelming panic: the fear of instant death smites him 'with its petrific mace.'* But in the murderer, such a murderer as a poet will condescend to, there must be raging some great storm of passion,—jealousy, ambition, vengeance, hatred,—which will create a hell within him;* and into this hell we are to look. In Macbeth, for the sake of gratifying his own enormous and teeming faculty of creation, Shakspeare has introduced two murderers: and, as usual in his hands, they are remarkably discriminated: but, though in Macbeth the strife of mind is greater than in his wife, the tiger spirit not so awake, and his feelings caught chiefly by contagion from her,—yet, as both were finally involved in the guilt of murder, the murderous mind of necessity is finally to be presumed in both. This was to be expressed; and on its own account, as well as to make it a more proportionable antagonist to the unoffending nature of their victim, 'the gracious Duncan,'* and adequately to expound 'the deep damnation of his taking off,'* this was to be expressed with peculiar energy. We were to be made to feel that the human nature, *i.e.* the divine nature of love and mercy, spread through the hearts of all creatures, and seldom utterly withdrawn from man,—was gone, vanished, extinct; and that the fiendish nature had taken its place. And, as this effect is marvellously accomplished in the dialogues and soliloquies themselves, so it is finally consummated by the expedient under consideration; and it is to this that I now solicit the reader's attention. If the reader has ever wit-

---

[1] It seems almost ludicrous to guard and explain my use of a word in a situation where it should naturally explain itself. But it has become necessary to do so, in consequence of the unscholarlike use of the word sympathy, at present so general, by which, instead of taking it in its proper sense, as the act of reproducing in our minds the feelings of another, whether for hatred, indignation, love, pity, or approbation, it is made a mere synonyme of the word *pity*; and hence, instead of saying, 'sympathy *with* another,' many writers adopt the monstrous barbarism of 'sympathy *for* another.'

nessed a wife, daughter, or sister, in a fainting fit, he may chance to have observed that the most affecting moment in such a spectacle, is *that* in which a sigh and a stirring announce the recommencement of suspended life. Or, if the reader has ever been present in a vast metropolis on the day when some great national idol was carried in funeral pomp to his grave, and chancing to walk near to the course through which it passed, has felt powerfully, in the silence and desertion of the streets and in the stagnation of ordinary business, the deep interest which at that moment was possessing the heart of man,—if all at once he should hear the death-like stillness broken up by the sound of wheels rattling away from the scene, and making known that the transitory vision was dissolved, he will be aware that at no moment was his sense of the complete suspension and pause in ordinary human concerns so full and affecting as at that moment when the suspension ceases, and the goings-on of human life* are suddenly resumed. All action in any direction is best expounded, measured, and made apprehensible, by reaction. Now apply this to the case in Macbeth. Here, as I have said, the retiring of the human heart and the entrance of the fiendish heart was to be expressed and made sensible. Another world has stepped in; and the murderers are taken out of the region of human things, human purposes, human desires. They are transfigured: Lady Macbeth is 'unsexed;'* Macbeth has forgot that he was born of woman;* both are conformed to the image of devils; and the world of devils is suddenly revealed. But how shall this be conveyed and made palpable? In order that a new world may step in, this world must for a time disappear. The murderers, and the murder, must be insulated—cut off by, an immeasurable gulph from the ordinary tide and succession of human affairs—locked up and sequestered in some deep recess: we must be made sensible that the world of ordinary life is suddenly arrested— laid asleep—tranced—racked into a dread armistice: time must be annihilated; relation to things without abolished; and all must pass self-withdrawn into a deep syncope and suspension of earthly passion. Hence it is that when the deed is done—when the work of darkness is perfect, then the world of darkness passes away like a pageantry in the clouds: the knocking at the gate is heard; and it makes known audibly that the reaction has commenced: the human has made its reflux upon the fiendish: the pulses of life are beginning to beat again: and the re-establishment of the goings-on of the world in which we live, first makes us profoundly sensible of the awful parenthesis that had suspended them.

Oh! mighty poet!—Thy works are not as those of other men, simply and merely great works of art; but are also like the phenomena of nature, like the sun and the sea, the stars and the flowers,—like frost and snow, rain and dew, hail-storm and thunder, which are to be studied with entire submission of our own faculties, and in the perfect faith that in them there can be no too much or too little, nothing useless or inert—but that, the further we press in our discoveries, the more we shall see proofs of design and self-supporting arrangement where the careless eye had seen nothing but accident!

N.B. In the above specimen of psychological criticism, I have purposely omitted to notice another use of the knocking at the gate, viz. the opposition and contrast which it produces in the porter's comments to the scenes immediately preceding; because this use is tolerably obvious to all who are accustomed to reflect on what they read. A third use also, subservient to the scenical illusion, has been lately noticed by a critic in the LONDON MAGAZINE:* I fully agree with him; but it did not fall in my way to insist on this.

X.Y.Z.*

ON MURDER CONSIDERED AS ONE OF THE FINE ARTS

*To the Editor of Blackwood's Magazine**

SIR,

WE have all heard of a Society for the Promotion of Vice,* of the Hell-Fire Club,* &c. At Brighton I think it was that a Society was formed for the Suppression of Virtue.* That Society was itself suppressed—but I am sorry to say that another exists in London, of a character still more atrocious. In tendency, it may be denominated a Society for the Encouragement of Murder; but, according to their own delicate ευφημισμὸς,* it is styled—The Society of Connoisseurs in Murder. They profess to be curious in homicide; amateurs and dilettanti in the various modes of bloodshed; and, in short, Murder-Fanciers. Every fresh atrocity of that class, which the police annals of Europe bring up, they meet and criticise as they would a picture, statue, or other work of art. But I need not trouble myself with any attempt to describe the spirit of their proceedings, as you will collect *that* much better from one of the Monthly Lectures read before the Society last year. This has fallen into my hands accidentally, in spite of all the vigilance exercised to keep their transactions from the public eye. The publication of it will alarm them; and my purpose is that it should. For I would much rather put them down quietly, by an appeal to public opinion through you, than by such an exposure of names as would follow an appeal to Bow-street;* which last appeal, however, if this should fail, I must positively resort to. For it is scandalous that such things should go on in a Christian land. Even in a heathen land, the public toleration of murder was felt by a Christian writer to be the most crying reproach of the public morals. This writer was Lactantius;* and with his words, as singularly applicable to the present occasion, I shall conclude:—'Quid tam horribile,' says he, 'tam tetrum, quam hominis trucidatio? Ideo severissimis legibus vita nostra munitur; ideo bella execrabilia sunt. Invenit tamen consuetudo quatenus homicidium sine bello ac sine legibus faciat: et hoc sibi voluptas quod scelus vindicavit. Quod si interesse homicidio sceleris conscientia est,—et eidem facinori spectator obstrictus est cui et admissor; ergo et in his gladiatorum caedibus non minus cruore profunditur qui spectat, quam ille qui facit: nec potest esse immunis à sanguine qui voluit effundi; aut videri non interfecisse, qui interfectori et favit et proemium postu- lavit.' 'Human life,' says he, 'is guarded by laws of the uttermost rigour, yet custom has devised a mode of evading them in behalf of murder; and the demands of taste (voluptas) are now become the same as those of abandoned guilt.' Let the Society of Gentlemen Amateurs consider this; and let me call their especial attention to the last sentence, which is so weighty, that I shall attempt to convey it in English:—'Now, if merely to be present at a murder fastens on a man the character of an accomplice,—if barely to be a spectator involves us in one common guilt with the perpetrator; it follows of necessity, that, in these murders of the amphitheatre, the hand which inflicts the fatal blow is not more deeply imbrued in blood than his who sits and looks on; neither can *he* be clear of blood who has countenanced its shedding; nor that man seem other than a participator in murder who gives his applause to the murderer, and calls for prizes in his behalf.' The '*proemia postulavit*'* I have not yet heard charged upon the Gentlemen Amateurs of London, though undoubtedly their proceedings tend to that; but the '*interfectori favit*'* is implied in the very title of this association, and expressed in every line of the lecture which I send you.—I am, &c.

X.Y.Z.*

(*Note of the Editor.*—We thank our correspondent for his communi- cation, and also for the quotation from Lactantius, which is very pertinent to *his* view of the case; our own, we confess, is different. We cannot suppose the lecturer to be in earnest, any more than Erasmus in his Praise of Folly,* or Dean Swift in his proposal for eating children.* However, either on his view or on ours, it is equally fit that the lecture should be made public.)

LECTURE

GENTLEMEN,—I have had the honour to be appointed by your committee to the trying task of reading the Williams'* Lecture on Murder, considered as one of the Fine Arts—a task which might be easy enough three or four centuries ago, when the art was little understood, and few great models had been exhibited; but in this

age, when masterpieces of excellence have been executed by professional men, it must be evident, that in the style of criticism applied
to them, the public will look for something of a corresponding
improvement. Practice and theory must advance *pari passu.** People
begin to see that something more goes to the composition of a fine
murder than two blockheads to kill and be killed—a knife—a purse—
and a dark lane. Design, gentlemen, grouping, light and shade,
poetry, sentiment, are now deemed indispensable to attempts of this
nature. Mr Williams has exalted the ideal of murder to all of us; and
to me, therefore, in particular, has deepened the arduousness of my
task. Like Aeschylus or Milton in poetry, like Michael Angelo* in
painting, he has carried his art to a point of colossal sublimity; and,
as Mr Wordsworth observes, has in a manner 'created the taste by
which he is to be enjoyed.'* To sketch the history of the art, and to
examine its principles critically, now remains as a duty for the connoisseur, and for judges of quite another stamp from his Majesty's
Judges of Assize.*

Before I begin, let me say a word or two to certain prigs, who
affect to speak of our society as if it were in some degree immoral in
its tendency. Immoral!—God bless my soul, gentlemen, what is it
that people mean? I am for morality, and always shall be, and for
virtue and all that; and I do affirm, and always shall, (let what will
come of it,) that murder is an improper line of conduct—highly
improper; and I do not stick to assert, that any man who deals
in murder, must have very incorrect ways of thinking, and truly
inaccurate principles; and so far from aiding and abetting him by
pointing out his victim's hiding-place, as a great moralist[1] of Germany
declared it to be every good man's duty to do, I would subscribe one
shilling and sixpence to have him apprehended, which is more by
eighteen-pence than the most eminent moralists have subscribed for
that purpose. But what then? Everything in this world has two
handles.* Murder, for instance, may be laid hold of by its moral
handle, (as it generally is in the pulpit, and at the Old Bailey;)* and

---

[1] Kant—who carried his demands of unconditional veracity to so extravagant
a length as to affirm, that, if a man were to see an innocent person escape from a
murderer, it would be his duty, on being questioned by the murderer, to tell the truth,
and to point out the retreat of the innocent person, under any certainty of causing
murder. Lest this doctrine should be supposed to have escaped him in any heat of
dispute, on being taxed with it by a celebrated French writer, he solemnly reaffirmed it,
with his reasons.*

that, I confess, is its weak side; or it may also be treated *aesthetically*, as the Germans call it, that is, in relation to good taste.

To illustrate this, I will urge the authority of three eminent persons, viz. S. T. Coleridge, Aristotle, and Mr Howship* the surgeon. To begin with S.T.C.—One night, many years ago, I was drinking tea with him in Berners' Street, (which, by the way, for a short street, has been uncommonly fruitful in men of genius.)* Others were there besides myself; and amidst some carnal considerations of tea and toast, we were all imbibing a dissertation on Plotinus from the attic lips* of S.T.C. Suddenly a cry arose of '*Fire—fire!*'—upon which all of us, master and disciples, Plato and οἱ περί τον Πλάτωνα,* rushed out, eager, for the spectacle.* The fire was in Oxford Street, at a piano-forte maker's; and, as it promised to be a conflagration of merit, I was sorry that my engagements forced me away from Mr Coleridge's party before matters were come to a crisis. Some days after, meeting with my Platonic host, I reminded him of the case, and begged to know how that very promising exhibition had terminated. 'Oh, sir,' said he, 'it turned out so ill, that we damned it unanimously.' Now, does any man suppose that Mr Coleridge,—who, for all he is too fat to be a person of active virtue, is undoubtedly a worthy Christian,—that this good S.T.C., I say, was an incendiary, or capable of wishing any ill to the poor man and his piano-fortes (many of them, doubtless, with the additional keys)?* On the contrary, I know him to be that sort of man that I durst stake my life upon it he would have worked an engine in a case of necessity, although rather of the fattest for such fiery trials of his virtue. But how stood the case? Virtue was in no request. On the arrival of the fire-engines, morality had devolved wholly on the insurance office.* This being the case, he had a right to gratify his taste. He had left his tea. Was he to have nothing in return?

I contend that the most virtuous man, under the premises stated, was entitled to make a luxury of the fire, and to hiss it, as he would any other performance that raised expectations in the public mind, which afterwards it disappointed. Again, to cite another great authority, what says the Stagyrite? He (in the Fifth Book, I think it is, of his Metaphysics,) describes what he calls κλεπτὴν τέλειον, i.e. *a perfect thief*;* and, as to Mr Howship, in a work of his on Indigestion, he makes no scruple to talk with admiration of a certain ulcer which he had seen, and which he styles 'a beautiful ulcer.'*

Now will any man pretend, that, abstractedly considered, a thief could appear to Aristotle a perfect character, or that Mr Howship could be enamoured of an ulcer? Aristotle, it is well known, was himself so very moral a character, that, not content with writing his Nichomachéan Ethics, in one volume octavo, he also wrote another system, called *Magna Moralia*, or Big Ethics.* Now, it is impossible that a man who composes any ethics at all, big or little, should admire a thief *per se*, and, as to Mr Howship, it is well known that he makes war upon all ulcers; and, without suffering himself to be seduced by their charms, endeavours to banish them from the county of Middlesex. But the truth is, that, however objectionable *per se*, yet, relatively to others of their class, both a thief and an ulcer may have infinite degrees of merit. They are both imperfections, it is true; but to be imperfect being their essence, the very greatness of their imperfection becomes their perfection. *Spartam nactus es, hanc exorna.** A thief like Autolycus or Mr Barrington,* and a grim phagedaenic ulcer,* superbly defined, and running regularly through all its natural stages, may no less justly be regarded as ideals after *their* kind, than the most faultless moss-rose amongst flowers, in its progress from bud to 'bright consummate flower;'* or, amongst human flowers, the most magnificent young female, apparelled in the pomp of womanhood. And thus not only the ideal of an inkstand may be imagined, (as Mr Coleridge demonstrated in his celebrated correspondence with Mr Blackwood,)* in which, by the way, there is not so much, because an inkstand is a laudable sort of thing, and a valuable member of society; but even imperfection itself may have its ideal or perfect state.

Really, gentlemen, I beg pardon for so much philosophy at one time, and now, let me apply it. When a murder is in the paulo-post-futurum* tense, and a rumour of it comes to our ears, by all means let us treat it morally. But suppose it over and done, and that you can say of it, Τετέλεσαι, or (in that adamantine molossus of Medea) εἴργασαι;* Suppose the poor murdered man to be out of his pain, and the rascal that did it off like a shot, nobody knows whither; suppose, lastly, that we have done our best, by putting out our legs to trip up the fellow in his flight, but all to no purpose—'abiit, evasit,'* &c.—why, then, I say, what's the use of any more virtue? Enough has been given to morality; now comes the turn of Taste and the Fine Arts. A sad thing it was, no doubt, very sad; but *we* can't mend it.

Therefore let us make the best of a bad matter; and, as it is impossible to hammer anything out of it for moral purposes, let us treat it aesthetically, and see if it will turn to account in that way. Such is the logic of a sensible man, and what follows? We dry up our tears, and have the satisfaction perhaps to discover, that a transaction, which, morally considered, was shocking, and without a leg to stand upon, when tried by principles of Taste, turns out to be a very meritorious performance. Thus all the world is pleased; the old proverb is justified, that it is an ill wind which blows nobody good; the amateur, from looking bilious and sulky, by too close an attention to virtue, begins to pick up his crumbs, and general hilarity prevails. Virtue has had her day; and henceforward, *Vertu** and Connoisseurship have leave to provide for themselves. Upon this principle, gentlemen, I propose to guide your studies, from Cain to Mr Thurtell.* Through this great gallery of murder, therefore, together let us wander hand in hand, in delighted admiration, while I endeavour to point your attention to the objects of profitable criticism.

The first murder is familiar to you all. As the inventor of murder, and the father of the art,* Cain must have been a man of first-rate genius. All the Cains were men of genius. Tubal Cain* invented tubes, I think, or some such thing. But, whatever were the originality and genius of the artist, every art was then in its infancy; and the works must be criticised with a recollection of that fact. Even Tubal's work would probably be little approved at this day in Sheffield;* and therefore of Cain (Cain senior, I mean,) it is no disparagement to say, that his performance was but so so. Milton, however, is supposed to have thought differently. By his way of relating the case, it should seem to have been rather a pet murder with him, for he retouches it with an apparent anxiety for its picturesque effect:—

> Whereat he inly raged; and, as they talk'd,
> Smote him into the midriff with a stone
> That beat out life: he fell; and, deadly pale,
> Groan'd out his soul *with gushing blood effus'd.*
>   *Par. Lost, B. XI.**

Upon this, Richardson the painter, who had an eye for effect, remarks as follows, in his Notes on Paradise Lost, p. 497:—'It has been thought,' says he, 'that Cain beat (as the common saying is,) the breath out of his brother's body with a great stone; Milton gives in to this, with the addition, however, of a large wound.'* In this place it was a judicious addition; for the rudeness of the weapon, unless raised and enriched by a warm, sanguinary colouring, has too much of the naked air of the savage school; as if the deed were perpetrated by a Polypheme* without science, premeditation, or anything but a mutton bone. However, I am chiefly pleased with the improvement, as it implies that Milton was an amateur. As to Shakspeare, there never was a better; as his description of the murdered Duke of Gloucester, in Henry VI.,* of Duncan's, Banquo's,* &c. sufficiently proves.

The foundation of the art having been once laid, it is pitiable to see how it slumbered without improvement for ages. In fact, I shall now be obliged to leap over all murders, sacred and profane, as utterly unworthy of notice, until long after the Christian era. Greece, even in the age of Pericles,* produced no murder of the slightest merit; and Rome had too little originality of genius in any of the arts to succeed, where her model failed her. In fact, the Latin language sinks under the very idea of murder. 'The man was murdered;'— how will this sound in Latin? *Interfectus est, interemptus est*—which simply expresses a homicide; and hence the Christian Latinity of the middle ages was obliged to introduce a new word, such as the feebleness of classic conceptions never ascended to. *Murdratus est,** says the sublimer dialect of Gothic ages. Meantime, the Jewish school of murder kept alive whatever was yet known in the art, and gradually transferred it to the Western World. Indeed the Jewish school was always respectable, even in the dark ages, as the case of Hugh of Lincoln shows, which was honoured with the approbation of Chaucer, on occasion of another performance from the same school, which he puts into the mouth of the Lady Abbess.*

Recurring, however, for one moment to classical antiquity, I cannot but think that Catiline, Clodius, and some of that coterie, would have made first-rate artists; and it is on all accounts to be regretted, that the priggism of Cicero* robbed his country of the only chance she had for distinction in this line. As the *subject* of a murder, no person could have answered better than himself. Lord! how he would have howled with panic, if he had heard Cethegus* under his bed. It would have been truly diverting to have listened to him; and satisfied I am, gentlemen, that he would have preferred the *utile* of creeping into a closet, or even into a *cloaca*, to the *honestum** of facing the bold artist.

To come now to the dark ages—(by which we, that speak with precision, mean, *par excellence*, the tenth century, and the times immediately before and after)—these ages ought naturally to be favourable to the art of murder, as they were to church-architecture, to stained-glass, &c.; and, accordingly, about the latter end of this period, there arose a great character in our art, I mean the Old Man of the Mountains. He was a shining light, indeed, and I need not tell you, that the very word 'assassin'* is deduced from him. So keen an amateur was he, that on one occasion, when his own life was attempted by a favourite assassin, he was so much pleased with the talent shown, that notwithstanding the failure of the artist, he created him a Duke upon the spot, with remainder to the female line, and settled a pension on him for three lives.* Assassination is a branch of the art which demands a separate notice; and I shall devote an entire lecture to it. Meantime, I shall only observe how odd it is, that this branch of the art has flourished by fits. It never rains, but it pours. Our own age can boast of some fine specimens; and, about two centuries ago, there was a most brilliant constellation of murders in this class. I need hardly say, that I allude especially to those five splendid works,—the assassinations of William I. of Orange, of Henry IV. of France,* of the Duke of Buckingham, (which you will find excellently described in the letters published by Mr Ellis,* of the British Museum,) of Gustavus Adolphus, and of Wallenstein.* The King of Sweden's assassination, by the by, is doubted by many writers, Harte amongst others;* but they are wrong. He was murdered; and I consider his murder unique in its excellence; for he was murdered at noon-day, and on the field of battle,—a feature of original conception, which occurs in no other work of art that I remember. Indeed, all of these assassinations may be studied with profit by the advanced connoisseur. They are all of them *exemplaria*,* of which one may say,—

Nocturnâ versatâ manu, versate diurne;*

Especially *nocturnâ*.

In these assassinations of princes and statesmen, there is nothing to excite our wonder: important changes often depend on their deaths; and, from the eminence on which they stand, they are peculiarly exposed to the aim of every artist who happens to be possessed by the craving for scenical effect. But there is another class of assassinations, which has prevailed from an early period of the seventeenth century, that really *does* surprise me; I mean the assassination of philosophers. For, gentlemen, it is a fact, that every philosopher of eminence for the two last centuries has either been murdered, or, at the least, been very near it; insomuch, that if a man calls himself a philosopher, and never had his life attempted, rest assured there is nothing in him; and against Locke's* philosophy in particular, I think it an unanswerable objection, (if we needed any) that, although he carried his throat about with him in this world for seventy-two years, no man ever condescended to cut it. As these cases of philosophers are not much known, and are generally good and well composed in their circumstances, I shall here read an excursus on that subject, chiefly by way of showing my own learning.

The first great philosopher of the seventeenth century (if we except Galileo,) was Des Cartes;* and if ever one could say of a man that he was all *but* murdered—murdered within an inch, one must say it of him. The case was this, as reported by Baillet in his *Vie De M. Des Cartes*, tom. I. p. 102–3.* In the year 1621, when Des Cartes might be about twenty-six years old, he was touring about as usual, (for he was as restless as a hyaena,) and, coming to the Elbe, either at Gluckstadt or at Hamburg,* he took shipping for East Friezland: what he could want in East Friezland no man has ever discovered; and perhaps he took this into consideration himself; for, on reaching Embden, he resolved to sail instantly for *West* Friezland;* and being very impatient of delay, he hired a bark, with a few mariners to navigate it. No sooner had he got out to sea than he made a pleasing discovery, viz. that he had shut himself up in a den of murderers. His crew, says M. Baillet, he soon found out to be 'des scélérats,'*—not *amateurs*, gentlemen, as we are, but professional men—the height of whose ambition at that moment was to cut his throat. But the story is too pleasing to be abridged—I shall give it, therefore, accurately, from the French of his biographer: 'M. Des Cartes had no company but that of his servant, with whom he was conversing in French. The sailors, who took him for a foreign merchant, rather than a cavalier, concluded that he must have money about him. Accordingly they came to a resolution by no means advantageous to his purse. There is this difference, however, between sea-robbers and the robbers in forests, that the latter may, without hazard, spare the lives of their victims; whereas the other cannot put a passenger on shore in such a case without running the risk of being apprehended. The crew of M. Des Cartes arranged their measures with a view to evade any danger of that sort. They observed that he was a stranger from a distance, without acquaintance in the country, and that nobody would take any trouble to inquire about him, in case he should never come to hand, (*quand il viendroit à manquer.*)'* Think, gentlemen, of these Friezland dogs discussing a philosopher as if he were a puncheon of rum. 'His temper, they remarked, was very mild and patient; and, judging from the gentleness of his deportment, and the courtesy with which he treated themselves, that he could be nothing more than some green young man, they concluded that they should have all the easier task in disposing of his life. They made no scruple to discuss the whole matter in his presence, as not supposing that he understood any other language than that in which he conversed with his servant; and the amount of their deliberation was—to murder him, then to throw him into the sea, and to divide his spoils.'

Excuse my laughing, gentlemen, but the fact is, I always *do* laugh when I think of this case—two things about it seem so droll. One is, the horrid panic or 'funk,' (as the men of Eton call it,)* in which Des Cartes must have found himself upon hearing this regular drama sketched for his own death—funeral—succession and administration to his effects. But another thing, which seems to me still more funny about this affair is, that if these Friezland hounds had been 'game,'* we should have no Cartesian philosophy; and how we could have done without *that*, considering the worlds of books it has produced, I leave to any respectable trunk-maker to declare.*

However, to go on; spite of his enormous funk, Des Cartes showed fight, and by that means awed these Anti-Cartesian rascals. 'Finding,' says M. Baillet, 'that the matter was no joke, M. Des Cartes leaped upon his feet in a trice, assumed a stern countenance that these cravens had never looked for, and addressing them in their own language, threatened to run them through on the spot if they dared to offer him any insult.' Certainly, gentlemen, this would have been an honour far above the merits of such inconsiderable rascals—to be spitted like larks upon a Cartesian sword; and therefore I am glad M. Des Cartes did not rob the gallows by executing his threat, especially as he could not possibly have brought his vessel to port, after he had murdered his crew; so that he must have continued to cruise for ever in the Zuyder Zee,* and would probably have been mistaken by sailors for the *Flying Dutchman*,* homeward-bound. 'The spirit which M. Des Cartes manifested,' says his biographer, 'had the effect of magic on these wretches. The suddenness of their consternation struck their minds with a confusion which blinded them to their advantage, and they conveyed him to his destination as peaceably as he could desire.'

Possibly, gentlemen, you may fancy that, on the model of Caesar's address to his poor ferryman,—'*Caesarem vehis et fortunas ejus*,'*—M. Des Cartes needed only to have said,—'Dogs, you cannot cut my throat, for you carry Des Cartes and his philosophy,' and might safely have defied them to do their worst. A German emperor* had the same notion, when, being cautioned to keep out of the way of a cannonading, he replied, 'Tut! man. Did you ever hear of a cannon-ball that killed an emperor?' As to an emperor I cannot say, but a less thing has sufficed to smash a philosopher; and the next great philosopher of Europe undoubtedly *was* murdered. This was Spinosa.*

I know very well the common opinion about him is, that he died in his bed.* Perhaps he did, but he was murdered for all that; and this I shall prove by a book published at Brussels, in the year 1731, entitled, *La Via de Spinosa; par M. Jean Colerus*,* with many additions, from a MS. life, by one of his friends. Spinosa died on the 21st February 1677, being then little more than forty-four years old. This of itself looks suspicious; and M. Jean admits, that a certain expression in the MS. life of him would warrant the conclusion, 'que sa mort n'a pas été tout-à-fait naturelle.'* Living in a damp country, and a sailor's country, like Holland, he may be thought to have indulged a good deal in grog, especially in punch,[2] which was then newly discovered. Undoubtedly he might have done so; but the fact is that he did not. M. Jean calls him 'extrêmement sobre en son boire et en son

---

[2] 'June 1, 1675.—Drinke part of 3 boules of punch, (a liquor very strainge to me,)' says the Rev. Mr Henry Teonge,* in his Diary lately published. In a note on this passage, a reference is made to Fryer's Travels to the East Indies, 1672,* who speaks of 'that enervating liquor called *Paunch*, (which is Indostan for five,) from five ingredients.' Made thus, it seems the medical men called it Diapente; if with four only, Diatessaron. No doubt, it was its Evangelical* name that recommended it to the Rev. Mr Teonge.

manger.'* And though some wild stories were afloat about his using the juice of mandragora (p. 140,) and opium,* (p. 144,) yet neither of these articles appeared in his druggist's bill. Living, therefore, with such sobriety, how was it possible that he should die a natural death at forty-four? Hear his biographer's account:—'Sunday morning the 21st of February, before it was church-time, Spinosa came down stairs and conversed with the master and mistress of the house.' At this time, therefore, perhaps ten o'clock on Sunday morning, you see that Spinosa was alive, and pretty well. But it seems 'he had summoned from Amsterdam a certain physician, whom,' says the biographer, 'I shall not otherwise point out to notice than by these two letters, L. M.* This L. M. had directed the people of the house to purchase an ancient cock, and to have him boiled forthwith, in order that Spinosa might take some broth about noon, which in fact he did, and ate some of the *old cock* with a good appetite, after the landlord and his wife had returned from church.'

'In the afternoon, L. M. staid alone with Spinosa, the people of the house having returned to church; on coming out from which they learnt, with much surprise, that Spinosa had died about three o'clock, in the presence of L. M., who took his departure for Amsterdam the same evening, by the night-boat, without paying the least attention to the deceased. No doubt he was the readier to dispense with these duties, as he had possessed himself of a ducatoon* and a small quantity of silver, together with a silver-hafted knife, and had absconded with his pillage.' Here you see, gentlemen, the murder is plain, and the manner of it. It was L. M. who murdered Spinosa for his money. Poor S. was an invalid, meagre, and weak: as no blood was observed, L. M., no doubt, threw him down and smothered him with pillows,— the poor man being already half suffocated by his infernal dinner.— But who was L. M.? It surely never could be Lindley Murray;* for I saw him at York in 1825; and besides, I do not think he would do such a thing; at least, not to a brother grammarian: for you know, gentlemen, that Spinosa wrote a very respectable Hebrew grammar.*

Hobbes,* but why, or on what principle, I never could understand, was not murdered. This was a capital oversight of the professional men in the seventeenth century; because in every light he was a fine subject for murder, except, indeed, that he was lean and skinny; for I can prove that he had money, and (what is very funny,) he had no right to make the least resistance; for, according to himself, irresistible power creates the very highest species of right,* so that it is rebellion of the blackest die to refuse to be murdered, when a competent force appears to murder you. However, gentlemen, though he was not murdered, I am happy to assure you that (by his own account,) he was three times very near being murdered.—The first time was in the spring of 1640, when he pretends to have circulated a little MS. on the king's behalf,* against the Parliament; he never could produce this MS., by the by; but he says that, 'had not his Majesty dissolved the Parliament,' (in May,) 'it had brought him into danger of his life.'* Dissolving the Parliament, however, was of no use; for, in November of the same year, the Long Parliament* assembled, and Hobbes, a second time, fearing he should be murdered, ran away to France. This looks like the madness of John Dennis, who thought that Louis XIV. would never make peace with Queen Anne,* unless he were given up to his vengeance; and actually ran away from the sea-coast in that belief. In France, Hobbes managed to take care of his throat pretty well for ten years; but at the end of that time, by way of paying court to Cromwell, he published his Leviathan.* The old coward now began to 'funk' horribly for the third time; he fancied the swords of the cavaliers were constantly at his throat, recollecting how they had served the Parliament ambassadors at the Hague and Madrid.* 'Tum,' says he, in his dog-Latin life of himself,

> Tum venit in mentem mihi Dorislaus et Ascham;
> Tanquam proscripto terror ubique aderat.*

And accordingly he ran home to England. Now, certainly, it is very true that a man deserved a cudgelling for writing Leviathan; and two or three cudgellings for writing a pentameter ending so villainously as—'terror ubique aderat!'* But no man ever thought him worthy of any thing beyond cudgelling. And, in fact, the whole story is a bounce* of his own. For, in a most abusive letter which he wrote 'to a learned person,' (meaning Wallis the mathematician,*) he gives quite another account of the matter, and says (p. 8.), he ran home 'because he would not trust his safety with the French clergy;'* insinuating that he was likely to be murdered for his religion, which would have been a high joke indeed—Tom's being brought to the stake for religion.*

Bounce or not bounce, however, certain it is, that Hobbes, to the end of his life, feared that somebody would murder him. This is

proved by the story I am going to tell you: it is not from a manuscript, but, (as Mr Coleridge says), it is as good as manuscript;* for
it comes from a book now entirely forgotten, viz.—'The Creed of
Mr Hobbes Examined; in a Conference between him and a Student
in Divinity,' (published about ten years before Hobbes's death.)
The book is anonymous, but it was written by Tennison, the same
who, about thirty years after, succeeded Tillotson* as Archbishop of
Canterbury. The introductory anecdote is as follows:*—'A certain
divine, it seems, (no doubt Tennison himself,) took an annual tour
of one month to different parts of the island. In one of these excur-
sions (1670) he visited the Peak in Derbyshire, partly in consequence
of Hobbes's description of it.* Being in that neighbourhood, he
could not but pay a visit to Buxton; and at the very moment of his
arrival, he was fortunate enough to find a party of gentlemen dis-
mounting at the inn door, amongst whom was a long thin fellow, who
turned out to be no less a person than Mr Hobbes, who probably had
ridden over from Chattsworth.* Meeting so great a lion,—a tourist,
in search of the picturesque, could do no less than present himself in
the character of bore. And luckily for this scheme, two of Mr
Hobbes's companions were suddenly summoned away by express;
so that, for the rest of his stay at Buxton, he had Leviathan entirely
to himself, and had the honour of bowsing with him in the evening.
Hobbes, it seems, at first showed a good deal of stiffness, for he was
shy of divines; but this wore off, and he became very sociable and
funny, and they agreed to go into the bath together. How Tennison
could venture to gambol in the same water with Leviathan,* I cannot
explain; but so it was: they frolicked about like two dolphins, though
Hobbes must have been as old as the hills; and 'in those intervals
wherein they abstained from swimming and plunging themselves,'
(i.e. diving) 'they discoursed of many things relating to the Baths of
the Ancients, and the Origine of Springs. When they had in this
manner passed away an hour, they stepped out of the bath; and,
having dried and cloathed themselves, they sate down in expectation
of such a supper as the place afforded; designing to refresh themselves like the *Deipnosophilae*,* and rather to reason than to drink
profoundly. But in this innocent intention they were interrupted by
the disturbance arising from a little quarrel, in which some of the
ruder people in the house were for a short time engaged. At this Mr
Hobbes seemed much concerned, though he was at some distance

from the persons.'—And why was he concerned, gentlemen? No doubt you fancy, from some benign and disinterested love of peace and harmony, worthy of an old man and a philosopher. But listen— 'For a while he was not composed, but related it once or twice as to himself, with a low and careful tone, how Sextus Roscius was murthered after supper by the Balneae Palatinae.* Of such general extent is that remark of Cicero, in relation to Epicurus the Atheist, of whom he observed that he of all men dreaded most those things which he contemned—Death and the Gods.'*—Merely because it was supper-time, and in the neighbourhood of a bath, Mr Hobbes must have the fate of Sextus Roscius. What logic was there in this, unless to a man who was always dreaming of murder?—Here was Leviathan, no longer afraid of the daggers of English cavaliers or French clergy, but 'frightened from his propriety'* by a row in an ale-house between some honest clod-hoppers of Derbyshire, whom his own gaunt scare-crow of a person that belonged to quite another century, would have frightened out of their wits.

Malebranche,* it will give you pleasure to hear, was murdered. The man who murdered him is well known: it was Bishop Berkeley.* The story is familiar, though hitherto not put in a proper light. Berkeley, when a young man, went to Paris and called on Père Malebranche. He found him in his cell cooking. Cooks have ever been a *genus irritabile*;* authors still more so: Malebranche was both: a dispute arose; the old Father, warm already, became warmer; culinary and metaphysical irritations united to derange his liver: he took to his bed, and died. Such is the common version of the story: 'So the whole ear of Denmark is abused.'*—The fact is, that the matter was hushed up, out of consideration for Berkeley, who (as Pope remarked) had 'every virtue under heaven:'* else it was well known that Berkeley, feeling himself nettled by the waspishness of the old Frenchman, squared at him; a *turn-up** was the consequence: Malebranche was floored in the first round; the conceit was wholly taken out of him; and he would perhaps have given in; but Berkeley's blood was now up, and he insisted on the old Frenchman's retracting his doctrine of Occasional Causes.* The vanity of the man was too great for this; and he fell a sacrifice to the impetuosity of Irish youth, combined with his own absurd obstinacy.

Leibnitz,* being every way superior to Malebranche, one might, *a fortiori*,* have counted on *his* being murdered; which, however, was not the case. I believe he was nettled at this neglect, and felt himself insulted by the security in which he passed his days. In no other way can I explain his conduct at the latter end of his life, when he chose to grow very avaricious, and to hoard up large sums of gold, which he kept in his own house. This was at Vienna, where he died; and letters are still in existence, describing the immeasurable anxiety which he entertained for his throat.* Still his ambition, for being *attempted* at least, was so great, that he would not forego the danger. A late English pedagogue, of Birmingham manufacture, viz. Dr Parr,* took a more selfish course, under the same circumstances. He had amassed a considerable quantity of gold and silver plate, which was for some time deposited in his bed-room at his parsonage house, Hatton. But growing every day more afraid of being murdered, which he knew that he could not stand, (and to which, indeed, he never had the slightest pretension,) he transferred the whole to the Hatton blacksmith; conceiving, no doubt, that the murder of a black-smith would fall more lightly on the *salus reipublicae*,* than that of a pedagogue. But I have heard this greatly disputed; and it seems now generally agreed, that one good horse-shoe is worth about 2¼ Spital sermons.*

As Leibnitz, though not murdered, may be said to have died, partly of the fear that he should be murdered, and partly of vexation that he was not,—Kant, on the other hand—who had no ambition in that way—had a narrower escape from a murderer than any man we read of, except Des Cartes. So absurdly does Fortune throw about her favours! The case is told, I think, in an anonymous life of this very great man.* For health's sake, Kant imposed upon himself, at one time, a walk of six miles every day along a highroad. This fact becoming known to a man who had his private reasons for commit-ting murder, at the third milestone from Königsberg,* he waited for his 'intended,' who came up to time as duly as a mail-coach. But for an accident, Kant was a dead man. However, on considerations of 'morality,' it happened that the murderer preferred a little child, whom he saw playing in the road, to the old transcendentalist: this child he murdered; and thus it happened that Kant escaped.* Such is the German account of the matter; but my opinion is—that the murderer was an amateur, who felt how little would be gained to the cause of good taste by murdering an old, arid, and adust metaphysician; there was no room for display, as the man could not possibly look more like a mummy when dead, than he had done alive.

Thus, gentlemen, I have traced the connexion between philosophy and our art, until insensibly I find that I have wandered into our own era. This I shall not take any pains to characterise apart from that which preceded it, for, in fact, they have no distinct character. The 17th and 18th centuries, together with so much of the 19th as we have yet seen, jointly compose the Augustan age of murder. The finest work of the 17th century is, unquestionably, the murder of Sir Edmondbury Godfrey,* which has my entire approbation. At the same time, it must be observed, that the quantity of murder was not great in this century, at least amongst our own artists; which, perhaps, is attributable to the want of enlightened patronage. *Sint Maecenates, non deerunt, Flacce, Marones.** Consulting Grant's 'Observations on the Bills of Mortality,' (4th edition, Oxford, 1665,) I find, that out of 229,250, who died in London during one period of twenty years in the 17th century, not more than eighty-six were murdered; that is, about 4 three-tenths per annum.* A small number this, gentlemen, to found an academy upon; and certainly, where the quantity is so small, we have a right to expect that the quality should be first-rate. Perhaps it was; yet, still I am of opinion that the best artist in this century was not equal to the best in that which followed. For instance, however praiseworthy the case of Sir Edmondbury Godfrey may be (and nobody can be more sensible of its merits than I am,) still I cannot consent to place it on a level with that Mrs Ruscombe* of Bristol, either as to originality of design, or boldness and breadth of style. This good lady's murder took place early in the reign of George III.*—a reign which was notoriously favourable to the arts generally. She lived in College Green,* with a single maid-servant, neither of them having any pretension to the notice of history but what they derived from the great artist whose workmanship I am recording. One fine morning, when all Bristol was alive and in motion, some suspicion arising, the neighbours forced an entrance into the house, and found Mrs Ruscombe murdered in her bed-room, and the servant murdered on the stairs: this was at noon; and, not more than two hours before, both mistress and servant had been seen alive. To the best of my remembrance, this was in 1764;

upwards of sixty years, therefore, have now elapsed, and yet the artist is still undiscovered. The suspicions of posterity have settled upon two pretenders—a baker and a chimney-sweeper. But posterity is wrong; no unpractised artist could have conceived so bold an idea as that of a noon-day murder in the heart of a great city. It was no obscure baker, gentlemen, or anonymous chimney-sweeper, be assured, that executed this work. I know who it was. (*Here there was a general buzz, which at length broke out into open applause; upon which the lecturer blushed, and went on with much earnestness.*) For Heaven's sake, gentlemen, do not mistake me; it was not I that did it. I have not the vanity to think myself equal to any such achievement; be assured that you greatly overrate my poor talents; Mrs Ruscombe's affair was far beyond my slender abilities. But I came to know who the artist was, from a celebrated surgeon, who assisted at his dissection.* This gentleman had a private museum in the way of his profession, one corner of which was occupied by a cast from a man of remarkably fine proportions.

'That,' said the surgeon, 'is a cast from the celebrated Lancashire highwayman, who concealed his profession for some time from his neighbours, by drawing woollen stockings over his horse's legs, and in that way muffling the clatter which he must else have made in riding up a flagged alley that led to his stable. At the time of his execution for highway robbery, I was studying under Cruickshank:* and the man's figure was so uncommonly fine, that no money or exertion was spared to get into possession of him with the least possible delay. By the connivance of the under-sheriff he was cut down within the legal time, and instantly put into a chaise and four; so that, when he reached Cruickshank's, he was positively not dead. Mr ——, a young student at that time, had the honour of giving him the *coup de grace**—and finishing the sentence of the law.' This remarkable anecdote, which seemed to imply that all the gentlemen in the dissecting-room were amateurs of our class, struck me a good deal; and I was repeating it one day to a Lancashire lady, who thereupon informed me, that she had herself lived in the neighbourhood of that highwayman, and well remembered two circumstances, which combined in the opinion of all his neighbours, to fix upon him the credit of Mrs Ruscombe's affair. One was, the fact of his absence for a whole fortnight at the period of that murder: the other, that, within a very little time after, the neighbourhood of this highwayman was deluged with dollars: now Mrs Ruscombe was known to have hoarded about two thousand of that coin. Be the artist, however, who he might, the affair remains a durable monument of his genius; for such was the impression of awe, and the sense of power left behind, by the strength of conception manifested in this murder, that no tenant (as I was told in 1810) had been found up to that time for Mrs Ruscombe's house.

But, whilst I thus eulogize the Ruscombian case, let me not be supposed to overlook the many other specimens of extraordinary merit spread over the face of this century. Such cases, indeed, as that of Miss Bland,* or of Captain Donnellan, and Sir Theophilus Boughton,* shall never have any countenance from me. Fie on these dealers in poison, say I: can they not keep to the old honest way of cutting throats, without introducing such abominable innovations from Italy?* I consider all these poisoning cases, compared with the legitimate style, as no better than wax-work by the side of sculpture, or a lithographic print by the side of a fine Volpato.* But, dismissing these, there remain many excellent works of art in a pure style, such as nobody need be ashamed to own, as every candid connoisseur will admit. *Candid*,* observe, I say; for great allowances must be made in these cases; no artist can ever be sure of carrying through his own fine preconception. Awkward disturbances will arise; people will not submit to have their throats cut quietly; they will run, they will kick, they will bite; and, whilst the portrait painter often has to complain of too much torpor in his subject, the artist, in our line, is generally embarrassed by too much animation. At the same time, however disagreeable to the artist, this tendency in murder to excite and irritate the subject, is certainly one of its advantages to the world in general, which we ought not to overlook, since it favours the developement of latent talent. Jeremy Taylor notices with admiration, the extraordinary leaps which people will take under the influence of fear.* There was a striking instance of this in the recent case of the M'Keands;* the boy cleared a height, such as he will never clear again to his dying day. Talents also of the most brilliant description for thumping, and indeed for all the gymnastic exercises, have sometimes been developed by the panic which accompanies our artists; talents else buried and hid under a bushel to the possessors, as much as to their friends. I remember an interesting illustration of this fact, in a case which I learned in Germany.

Riding one day in the neighbourhood of Munich, I overtook a distinguished amateur of our society, whose name I shall conceal. This gentleman informed me that, finding himself wearied with the frigid pleasures (so he called them) of mere amateurship, he had quitted England for the continent—meaning to practise a little professionally. For this purpose he resorted to Germany, conceiving the police in that part of Europe to be more heavy and drowsy than elsewhere. His *debut* as a practitioner took place at Mannheim;* and, knowing me to be a brother amateur, he freely communicated the whole of his maiden adventure. 'Opposite to my lodging,' said he, 'lived a baker: he was somewhat of a miser, and lived quite alone. Whether it were his great expanse of chalky face, or what else, I know not—but the fact was, I "fancied"* him, and resolved to commence business upon his throat, which by the way he always carried bare—a fashion which is very irritating to my desires. Precisely at eight o'clock in the evening, I observed that he regularly shut up his windows. One night I watched him when thus engaged—bolted in after him—locked the door—and, addressing him with great suavity, acquainted him with the nature of my errand; at the same time advising him to make no resistance, which would be mutually unpleasant. So saying, I drew out my tools; and was proceeding to operate. But at this spectacle, the baker, who seemed to have been struck by catalepsy at my first announce, awoke into tremendous agitation. "I will *not* be murdered!" he shrieked aloud; "what for will I lose my precious throat?"—"What for?" said I; "if for no other reason, for this—that you put alum into your bread. But no matter, alum or no alum, (for I was resolved to forestall any argument on that point) know that I am a virtuoso in the art of murder—am desirous of improving myself in its details—and am enamoured of your vast surface of throat, to which I am determined to be a customer." "Is it so?" said he, "but I'll find you custom in another line;" and so saying, he threw himself into a boxing attitude. The very idea of his boxing struck me as ludicrous. It is true, a London baker had distinguished himself in the ring, and became known to fame under the title of the Master of the Rolls;* but he was young and unspoiled: whereas this man was a monstrous feather-bed in person, fifty years old, and totally out of condition. Spite of all this, however, and contending against me, who am a master in the art, he made so desperate a defence, that many times I feared he might turn the tables upon me;

and that I, an amateur, might be murdered by a rascally baker. What a situation! Minds of sensibility will sympathize with my anxiety. How severe it was, you may understand by this, that for the first 13 rounds the baker had the advantage. Round the 14th,* I received a blow on the right eye, which closed it up; in the end, I believe, this was my salvation: for the anger it roused in me was so great that, in this and every one of the three following rounds, I floored the baker.

'Round 18th. The baker came up piping, and manifestly the worse for wear. His geometrical exploits* in the four last rounds had done him no good. However, he showed some skill in stopping a message which I was sending to his cadaverous mug;* in delivering which, my foot slipped, and I went down.

'Round 19th. Surveying the baker, I became ashamed of having been so much bothered by a shapeless mass of dough; and I went in fiercely, and administered some severe punishment. A rally took place—both went down—Baker undermost—ten to three on Amateur.

'Round 20th.—The baker jumped up with surprising agility; indeed, he managed his pins* capitally, and fought wonderfully, considering that he was drenched in perspiration; but the shine was now taken out of him, and his game was the mere effect of panic. It was now clear that he could not last much longer. In the course of this round we tried the weaving system, in which I had greatly the advantage, and hit him repeatedly on the conk.* My reason for this was, that his conk was covered with carbuncles; and I thought I should vex him by taking such liberties with his conk, which in fact I did.

'The three next rounds, the master of the rolls staggered about like a cow on the ice. Seeing how matters stood, in round 24th I whispered something into his ear, which sent him down like a shot. It was nothing more than my private opinion of the value of his throat at an annuity office. This little confidential whisper affected him greatly; the very perspiration was frozen on his face, and for the next two rounds I had it all my own way. And when I called *time* for the twenty-seventh round, he lay like a log on the floor.'

After which, said I to the amateur, 'It may be presumed that you accomplished your purpose.'—'You are right,' said he mildly, 'I did; and a great satisfaction, you know, it was to my mind, for by this means I killed two birds with one stone;' meaning that he had both thumped the baker and murdered him. Now, for the life of me, I could not see *that*; for, on the contrary, to my mind it appeared that he had taken two stones to kill one bird, having been obliged to take the conceit out of him first with his fists, and then with his tools. But no matter for his logic. The moral of his story was good, for it showed what an astonishing stimulus to latent talent is contained in any reasonable prospect of being murdered. A pursy, unwieldy, half cata-leptic baker of Mannheim had absolutely fought six-and-twenty rounds with an accomplished English boxer merely upon this inspir-ation; so greatly was natural genius exalted and sublimed by the genial presence of his murderer.

Really, gentlemen, when one hears of such things as these, it becomes a duty, perhaps, a little to soften that extreme asperity with which most men speak of murder. To hear people talk, you would suppose that all the disadvantages and inconveniences were on the side of being murdered, and that there were none at all in *not* being murdered. But considerate men think otherwise. 'Certainly,' says Jer. Taylor, 'it is a less temporal evil to fall by the rudeness of a sword than the violence of a fever: and the axe' (to which he might have added the ship-carpenter's mallet and the crow-bar) 'a much less affliction than a strangury.'* Very true; the Bishop talks like a wise man and an amateur, as he is; and another great philosopher, Marcus Aurelius, was equally above the vulgar prejudices on this subject. He declares it to be one of 'the noblest functions of reason to know whether it is time to walk out of the world or not.' (Book III. Collers' Translation.)* No sort of knowledge being rarer than this, surely *that* man must be a most philanthropic character, who undertakes to instruct people in this branch of knowledge gratis, and at no little hazard to himself. All this, however, I throw out only in the way of speculation to future moralists; declaring in the meantime my own private conviction, that very few men commit murder upon philan-thropic or patriotic principles, and repeating what I have already said once at least—that, as to the majority of murderers, they are very incorrect characters.

With respect to Williams's murders, the sublimest and most entire in their excellence that ever were committed, I shall not allow myself to speak incidentally. Nothing less than an entire lecture, or even an entire course of lectures, would suffice to expound their merits.* But one curious fact, connected with his case, I shall mention, because it seems to imply that the blaze of his genius absolutely dazzled the eye of criminal justice. You all remember, I doubt not, that the instruments with which he executed his first great work (the murder of the Marrs), were a ship-carpenter's mallet and a knife. Now the mallet belonged to an old Swede, one John Petersen,* and bore his initials. This instrument Williams left behind him, in Marr's house, and it fell into the hands of the Magistrates. Now, gentlemen, it is a fact that the publication of this circumstance of the initials led immediately to the apprehension of Williams, and, if made earlier, would have prevented his second great work, (the murder of the Williamsons,*) which took place precisely twelve days after. But the Magistrates kept back this fact from the public for the entire twelve days, and until that second work was accomplished. That finished, they published it, apparently feeling that Williams had now done enough for his fame, and that his glory was at length placed beyond the reach of accident.

As to Mr Thurtell's case, I know not what to say. Naturally, I have every disposition to think highly of my predecessor in the chair of this society; and I acknowledge that his lectures were unexceptionable. But, speaking ingenuously, I do really think that his principal performance, as an artist, has been much overrated. I admit that at first I was myself carried away by the general enthusiasm. On the morning when the murder was made known in London, there was the fullest meeting of amateurs that I have ever known since the days of Williams; old bed-ridden connoisseurs, who had got into a peevish way of sneering and complaining 'that there was nothing doing,' now hobbled down to our club-room: such hilarity, such benign expression of general satisfaction, I have rarely witnessed. On every side you saw people shaking hands, congratulating each other, and forming dinner-parties for the evening; and nothing was to be heard but triumphant challenges of—'Well! will *this* do?' 'Is *this* the right thing?' 'Are you satisfied at last?' But, in the midst of this, I remember we all grew silent on hearing the old cynical amateur, L. S——,* that *laudator temporis acti*,* stumping along with his wooden leg; he entered the room with his usual scowl, and, as he advanced, he continued to growl and stutter the whole way—'Not an original idea in the whole piece—mere plagiarism,—base plagiarism from hints that I threw out! Besides, his style is as hard as Albert Durer, and as coarse as Fuseli.'* Many thought that this was mere jealousy, and general waspishness; but I confess that, when the first glow of enthusiasm had subsided, I have found most judicious critics to agree that there was something *falsetto** in the style of Thurtell. The fact is, he was a member of our society, which naturally gave a friendly bias to our judgments; and his person was universally familiar to the cockneys, which gave him, with the whole London public, a temporary popularity, that his pretensions are not capable of supporting; for *opinionum commenta delet dies, naturae judicia confirmat.**—There was, however, an unfinished design of Thurtell's for the murder of a man with a pair of dumb-bells,* which I admired greatly; it was a mere outline, that he never completed; but to my mind it seemed every way superior to his chief work. I remember that there was great regret expressed by some amateurs that this sketch should have been left in an unfinished state: but there I cannot agree with them; for the fragments and first bold outlines of original artists have often a felicity about them which is apt to vanish in the management of the details.

The case of the M'Keands I consider far beyond the vaunted performance of Thurtell,—indeed above all praise; and bearing that relation, in fact, to the immortal works of Williams, which the Aeneid bears to the Iliad.*

But it is now time that I should say a few words about the principles of murder, not with a view to regulate your practice, but your judgment: as to old women, and the mob of newspaper readers, they are pleased with anything, provided it is bloody enough. But the mind of sensibility requires something more. *First*, then, let us speak of the kind of person who is adapted to the purpose of the murderer; *secondly*, of the place where; *thirdly*, of the time when,* and other little circumstances.

As to the person, I suppose it is evident that he ought to be a good man;* because, if he were not, he might himself, by possibility, be contemplating murder at the very time; and such 'diamond-cut-diamond'* tussles, though pleasant enough where nothing better is stirring, are really not what a critic can allow himself to call murders. I could mention some people (I name no names) who have been murdered by other people in a dark lane; and so far all seemed correct enough; but, on looking farther into the matter, the public have become aware that the murdered party was himself, at the moment, planning to rob his murderer, at the least, and possibly to murder him, if he had been strong enough. Whenever that is the case, or may be thought to be the case, farewell to all the genuine effects of the art. For the final purpose of murder, considered as a fine art, is precisely the same as that of Tragedy, in Aristotle's account of it, viz. 'to cleanse the heart by means of pity and terror.'* Now, terror there may be, but how can there be any pity for one tiger destroyed by another tiger?

It is also evident that the person selected ought not to be a public character. For instance, no judicious artist would have attempted to murder Abraham Newland.* For the case was this: everybody read so much about Abraham Newland, and so few people ever saw him, that there was a fixed belief that he was an abstract idea. And I remember that once, when I happened to mention that I had dined at a coffee-house in company with Abraham Newland, everybody looked scornfully at me, as though I had pretended to have played at billiards with Prester John,* or to have had an affair of honour* with the Pope. And, by the way, the Pope would be a very improper person to murder: for he has such a virtual ubiquity as the Father of Christendom, and, like the cuckoo, is so often heard but never seen, that I suspect most people regard *him* also as an abstract idea. Where, indeed, a public character is in the habit of giving dinners, 'with every delicacy of the season,'* the case is very different: every person is satisfied that *he* is no abstract idea; and, therefore, there can be no impropriety in murdering him; only that his murder will fall into the class of assassinations, which I have not yet treated.

Thirdly, The subject chosen ought to be in good health: for it is absolutely barbarous to murder a sick person, who is usually quite unable to bear it. On this principle, no Cockney* ought to be chosen who is above twenty-five, for after that age he is sure to be dyspeptic. Or at least, if a man will hunt in that warren, he ought to murder a couple at one time; if the Cockneys chosen should be tailors, he will of course think it his duty, on the old established equation, to murder eighteen*—And, here, in this attention to the comfort of sick people, you will observe the usual effect of a fine art to soften and refine the feelings. The world in general, gentlemen, are very bloody-minded; and all they want in a murder is a copious effusion of blood; gaudy display in this point is enough for *them*. But the enlightened connoisseur is more refined in his taste; and from our art, as from all the other liberal arts when thoroughly cultivated, the result is—to improve and to humanize the heart; so true is it, that—

—Ingenuas didicisse fideliter artes,
Emollit mores, nec sinit esse feros.*

A philosophic friend, well-known for his philanthropy and general
benignity, suggests that the subject chosen ought also to have a family of young children wholly dependent on his exertions, by way of
deepening the pathos. And, undoubtedly, this is a judicious caution.
Yet I would not insist too keenly on this condition. Severe good taste
unquestionably demands it; but still, where the man was otherwise
unobjectionable in point of morals and health, I would not look with
too curious a jealousy to a restriction which might have the effect of
narrowing the artist's sphere.

So much for the person. As to the time, the place, and the tools, I
have many things to say, which at present I have no room for. The good
sense of the practitioner has usually directed him to night and privacy.
Yet there have not been wanting cases where this rule was departed
from with excellent effect. In respect to time, Mrs Ruscombe's case
is a beautiful exception, which I have already noticed; and in respect
both to time and place, there is a fine exception in the Annals of
Edinburgh, (year 1805), familiar to every child in Edinburgh, but
which has unaccountably been defrauded of its due portion of fame
amongst English amateurs. The case I mean is that of a porter to
one of the Banks, who was murdered whilst carrying a bag of money,
in broad daylight, on turning out of the High Street, one of the
most public streets in Europe, and the murderer is to this hour
undiscovered.*

Sed fugit interea, fugit irreparabile tempus,
Singula dum capti circumvectamur amore.*

And now, gentlemen, in conclusion, let me again solemnly disclaim
all pretensions on my own part to the character of a professional
man. I never attempted any murder in my life, except in the year
1801, upon the body of a tom-cat; and *that* turned out differently
from my intention. My purpose, I own, was downright murder.
'Semper ego auditor tantum?' said I, 'nunquamne reponam?'* And I
went down stairs in search of Tom at one o'clock on a dark night,
with the 'animus,'* and no doubt with the fiendish looks, of a murderer. But when I found him, he was in the act of plundering the
pantry of bread and other things. Now this gave a new turn to the

affair; for the time being one of general scarcity, when even Christians were reduced to the use of potato-bread, rice-bread, and all sorts of things, it was downright treason in a tom-cat to be wasting good wheaten-bread in the way he was doing. It instantly became a patriotic duty to put him to death; and as I raised aloft and shook the glittering steel, I fancied myself rising like Brutus,* effulgent from a crowd of patriots, and, as I stabbed him, I

> called aloud on Tully's name,
> And bade the father of his country hail!*

Since then, what wandering thoughts I may have had of attempting the life of an ancient ewe, of a superannuated hen, and such 'small deer,'* are locked up in the secrets of my own breast; but for the higher departments of the art, I confess myself to be utterly unfit. My ambition does not rise so high. No, gentlemen, in the words of Horace,

> ——fungar vice cotis, acutum
> Reddere quae ferrum valet, exsors ipsa secandi.*

THE AVENGER

Why callest thou me murderer, and not rather the wrath of God
burning after the steps of the oppressor, and cleansing the earth
when it is wet with blood?*

THAT series of terrific events by which our quiet city and university
in the north-eastern quarter of Germany were convulsed during the
year 1816, has in itself, and considered merely as a blind movement
of human tiger-passion ranging unchained amongst men, something
too memorable to be forgotten or left without its own separate
record; but the moral lesson, impressed by these events, is yet more
memorable, and deserves the deep attention of coming generations
in their struggle after human improvement, not merely in its own
limited field of interest directly awakened, but in all analogous fields
of interest; as in fact already, and more than once, in connexion with
these very events, *this lesson has* obtained the effectual attention of
Christian kings and Princes assembled in Congress. No tragedy,
indeed, amongst all the sad ones by which the charities of the human
heart or of the fire-side, have ever been outraged, can better merit a
separate chapter in the private history of German manners or social
life than this unparalleled case. And, on the other hand, no one can
put in a better claim to be the historian than myself.

I was at the time, and still am, a Professor in that city and university which had the melancholy distinction of being its theatre. I
knew familiarly all the parties who were concerned in it—either as
sufferers or as agents. I was present from first to last, and watched
the whole course of the mysterious storm which fell upon our
devoted city in a strength like that of a West Indian hurricane, and
which did seriously threaten at one time to depopulate our university, through the dark suspicions which settled upon its members,
and the natural reaction of generous indignation in repelling them—
whilst the city in its more stationary and native classes would very
soon have manifested *their* awful sense of things, of the hideous
insecurity for life, and of the unfathomable dangers which had
undermined their hearths below their very feet, by sacrificing, whenever circumstances allowed them, their houses and beautiful gardens
in exchange for days uncursed by panic, and nights unpolluted by

blood. Nothing, I can take upon myself to assert, was left undone of
all that human foresight could suggest, or human ingenuity could
accomplish. But observe the melancholy result; the more certain did
these arrangements strike people as remedies for the evil, so much
the more effectually did they aid the terror, but above all, the awe—
the sense of mystery, when ten cases of total extermination, applied
to separate households, had occurred, in every one of which these
precautionary aids had failed to yield the slightest assistance. The
horror, the perfect frenzy of fear, which seized upon the town after
that experience, baffles all attempt at description. Had these various
contrivances failed merely in some human and intelligible way, as by
bringing the aid too tardily—still in such cases, though the danger
would no less have been evidently deepened, nobody would have felt
any further mystery than what, from the very first, rested upon the
persons and the motives of the murderers. But, as it was, when in ten
separate cases of exterminating carnage, the astounded police, after
an examination the most searching, pursued from day to day, and
almost exhausting the patience by the minuteness of the investigation, had finally pronounced that no attempt apparently had been
made to benefit by any of the signals preconcerted, that no footstep
apparently had moved in that direction—then, and after that result,
a blind misery of fear fell upon the population, so much the worse
than any anguish of a beleaguered city that is awaiting the storming
fury of a victorious enemy, by how much the shadowy—the uncertain
—the infinite is at all times more potent in mastering the mind than
a danger that is known—measurable—palpable—and human.* The
very police, instead of offering protection or encouragement, were
seized with terror for themselves. And the general feeling, as it was
described to me by a grave citizen whom I met in a morning walk
(for the overmastering sense of a public calamity broke down every
barrier of reserve, and all men talked freely to all men in the streets,
as they would have done during the rockings of an earthquake),
was, even amongst the boldest, like that which sometimes takes
possession of the mind in dreams—when one feels oneself sleeping
alone, utterly divided from all call or hearing of friends, doors
open that should be shut, or unlocked that should be triply secured,
the very walls gone, barriers swallowed up by unknown abysses,
nothing around one but frail curtains, and a world of illimitable
night, whisperings at a distance, correspondence going on between

darkness and darkness, like one deep calling to another,* and the dreamer's own heart the centre from which the whole net-work of this unimaginable chaos radiates, by means of which the blank *privations* of silence and darkness become powers the most *positive* and awful.

Agencies of fear, as of any other passion, and above all, of passion felt in communion with thousands, and in which the heart beats in conscious sympathy with an entire city, through all its regions of high and low, young and old, strong and weak; such agencies avail to raise and transfigure the natures of men; mean minds become elevated; dull men become eloquent; and when matters came to this crisis, the public feeling, as made known by voice, gesture, manner, or words, was such that no stranger could represent it to his fancy. In that respect, therefore, I had an advantage, being upon the spot through the whole course of the affair, for giving a faithful narrative; as I had still more eminently, from the sort of central station which I occupied, with respect to all the movements of the case. I may add, that I had another advantage, not possessed, or not in the same degree, by any other inhabitant of the town. I was personally acquainted with every family of the slightest account, belonging to the resident population; whether amongst the old local gentry, or the new settlers whom the late wars had driven to take refuge within our walls.

It was in September, 1815, that I received a letter from the Chief Secretary to the Prince of M——, a nobleman connected with the diplomacy of Russia, from which I quote an extract:—'I wish, in short, to recommend to your attentions, and in terms stronger than I know how to devise, a young man on whose behalf the Czar himself is privately known to have expressed the very strongest interest. He was at the battle of Waterloo* as an aide-de-camp to a Dutch general officer, and is decorated with distinctions won upon that awful day. However, though serving in that instance under English orders, and although an Englishman of rank, he does not belong to the English military service. He has served, young as he is, under *various* banners, and under ours, in particular, in the cavalry of our Imperial Guard. He is English by birth, nephew to the Earl of E., and heir presumptive to his immense estates. There is a wild story current— that his mother was a gipsy of transcendent beauty, which may account for his somewhat Moorish complexion, though, after all, *that* is not of a deeper tinge than I have seen amongst many an Englishman. He is himself one of the noblest looking of God's creatures. Both father and mother, however, are now dead; since then, he has become the favourite of his uncle, who detained him in England after the Emperor had departed—and, as this uncle is now in the last stage of infirmity, Mr Wyndham's succession to the vast family estates is inevitable, and probably near at hand. Mean-time, he is anxious for some assistance in his studies. Intellectually he stands in the very first rank of men, as I am sure you will not be slow to discover; but his long military service, and the unparalleled tumult of our European history since 1805, have interfered (as you may suppose) with the cultivation of his mind; for he entered the cavalry service of a German power when a mere boy, and shifted about from service to service as the hurricane of war blew from this point or from that. During the French anabasis to Moscow* he entered our service, made himself a prodigious favourite with the whole Imperial family, and even now is only in his twenty-second year. As to his accomplishments, they will speak for themselves; they are infinite, and applicable to every situation of life. Greek is what he wants from you; never ask about terms. He will acknowledge any trouble he may give you, as he acknowledges all trouble, *en prince*.* And ten years hence you will look back with pride upon having contributed your part to the formation of one whom all here at St Petersburg, not soldiers only, but we *diplomates*, look upon as certain to prove a great man, and a leader amongst the intellects of Christendom.'

Two or three other letters followed; and at length it was arranged that Mr Maximilian Wyndham should take up his residence at my monastic abode for one year. He was to keep a table, and an establishment of servants, at his own cost; was to have an apartment of some dozen or so of rooms; the unrestricted use of the library; with some other public privileges willingly conceded by the magistracy of the town; in return for all which he was to pay me a thousand guineas: and already beforehand, by way of acknowledgment for the public civilities of the town, he sent, through my hands, a contribution of three hundred guineas to the various local institutions for education of the poor, or for charity.

The Russian Secretary had latterly corresponded with me from a little German town not more than ninety miles distant: and, as he had special couriers at his service, the negotiation advanced so rapidly, that all was closed before the end of September. And, when once that consummation was attained, I, that previously had breathed no syllable of what was stirring, now gave a loose to the interesting tidings, and suffered them to spread through the whole compass of the town. It will be easily imagined that such a story, already romantic enough in its first outline, would lose nothing in the telling. An Englishman to begin with, which name of itself, and at all times, is a passport into German favour, but much more since the late memorable wars that, but for Englishmen, would have drooped into disconnected efforts—next, an Englishman of rank and of the *haute noblesse*,*—then a soldier covered with brilliant distinctions, and in the most brilliant arm of the service; young, moreover, and yet a veteran by his experience,—fresh from the most awful battle of this planet since the day of Pharsalia,*—radiant with the favour of courts and of Imperial ladies,—finally (which alone would have given him an interest in all female hearts), an Antinous* of faultless beauty, a Grecian statue, as it were, into which the breath of life had been breathed by some modern Pygmalion,*—such a pomp of gifts and endowments settling upon one man's head, should not have required for its effect the vulgar consummation (and yet to many it *was* the consummation and crest of the whole) that he was reputed to be rich beyond the dreams of romance or the necessities of a fairy tale. Unparalleled was the impression made upon our stagnant society; every tongue was busy in discussing the marvellous young Englishman from morning to night; every female fancy was busy in depicting the personal appearance of this gay apparition.

On his arrival at my house, I became sensible of a truth which I had observed some years before. The commonplace maxim is—that it is dangerous to raise expectations too high. This, which is thus generally expressed, and without limitation, is true only conditionally; it is true then and there only where there is but little merit to sustain and justify the expectation. But in any case where the merit is transcendent of its kind, it is always useful to rack the expectation up to the highest point; in any thing which partakes of the infinite, the most unlimited expectations will find ample room for gratification; whilst it is certain that ordinary observers, possessing little sensibility, unless where they have been warned to expect, will often fail to see what exists in the most conspicuous splendour. In this instance it certainly did no harm to the subject of expectation, that I had been warned to look for so much. The warning, at any rate, put me on the look-out for whatever eminence there might be of grandeur in his personal appearance; whilst, on the other hand, this existed in such excess, so far transcending any thing I had ever met with in my experience, that no expectation which it is in words to raise could have been disappointed.

These thoughts travelled with the rapidity of light through my brain as at one glance my eye took in the supremacy of beauty and power which seemed to have alighted from the clouds before me. Power, and the contemplation of power, in any absolute incarnation of grandeur or excess, necessarily have the instantaneous effect of quelling all perturbation. My composure was restored in a moment. I looked steadily at him. We both bowed. And, at the moment when he raised his head from that inclination, I caught the glance of his eye; an eye such as might have been looked for in a face of such noble lineaments—

> Blending the nature of the star
> With that of summer skies;*

and, therefore, meant by nature for the residence and organ of serene and gentle emotions; but it surprised, and at the same time filled me more almost with consternation than with pity, to observe, that in those eyes a light of sadness had settled more profound than seemed possible for youth, or almost commensurate to a human sorrow; a sadness that might have become a Jewish prophet, when laden with inspirations of wo.*

Two months had now passed away since the arrival of Mr Wyndham. He had been universally introduced to the superior society of the place; and, as I need hardly say, universally received with favour and distinction. In reality, his wealth and importance, his military honours, and the dignity of his character as expressed in his manners and deportment, were too eminent to allow of his being treated with less than the highest attention in any society whatever. But the effect of these various advantages, enforced and recommended as they were by a personal beauty so rare, was somewhat too potent for the comfort and self-possession of ordinary people; and really exceeded in a painful degree the standard of pretensions under which such people could feel themselves at their ease. He was not naturally of a reserved turn; far from it. His disposition had been open, frank, and confiding originally; and his roving, adventurous life, of which considerably more than one-half had been passed in camps, had communicated to his manners a more than military frankness. But the profound melancholy which possessed him, from whatever cause it arose, necessarily chilled the native freedom of his demeanour, unless when it was revived by strength of friendship or of love. The effect was awkward and embarrassing to all parties. Every voice paused or faltered when he entered a room—dead silence ensued—not an eye but was directed upon him, or else, sunk in timidity, settled upon the floor; and young ladies seriously lost the power, for a time, of doing more than murmuring a few confused, half-inarticulate syllables, or half-inarticulate sounds. The solemnity, in fact, of a first presentation, and the utter impossibility of soon recovering a free unembarrassed movement of conversation, made such scenes really distressing to all who participated in them, either as actors or spectators. Certainly this result was not a pure effect of manly beauty, however heroic, and in whatever excess; it arose in part from the many and extraordinary endowments which had centered in his person, not less from fortune than from nature; in part also, as I have said, from the profound sadness and freezing gravity of Mr Wyndham's manner; but still more from the perplexing mystery which surrounded that sadness.

Were there, then, no exceptions to this condition of awe-struck admiration? Yes: One at least there was in whose bosom the spell of all-conquering passion soon thawed every trace of icy reserve. Whilst the rest of the world retained a dim sentiment of awe towards Mr Wyndham, Margaret Liebenheim* only heard of such a feeling to wonder that it could exist towards *him*. Never was there so victorious a conquest interchanged between two youthful hearts—never before such a rapture of instantaneous sympathy. I did not witness the first meeting of this mysterious Maximilian and this magnificent Margaret, and do not know whether Margaret manifested that trepidation and embarrassment which distressed so many of her youthful co-rivals; but if she did, it must have fled before the first glance of the young man's eye, which would interpret, past all misunderstanding, the homage of his soul and the surrender of his heart. Their third meeting I *did* see; and there all shadow of embarrassment had vanished, except, indeed, of that delicate embarrassment which clings to impassioned admiration. On the part of Margaret, it seemed as if a new world had dawned upon her that she had not so much as suspected amongst the capacities of human experience. Like some bird she seemed, with powers unexercised for soaring and flying, not understood even as yet, and that never until now had found an element of air capable of sustaining her wings, or tempting her to put forth her buoyant instincts. He, on the other hand, now first found the realization of his dreams, and for a mere possibility which he had long too deeply contemplated, fearing, however, that in his own case it might prove a chimera, or that he might never meet a woman answering the demands of his heart, he now found a corresponding reality that left nothing to seek.

Here, then, and thus far, nothing but happiness had resulted from the new arrangement. But, if this had been little anticipated by many, far less had I, for my part, anticipated the unhappy revolution which was wrought in the whole nature of Ferdinand von Harrelstein. He was the son of a German baron; a man of good family, but of small estate, who had been pretty nearly a soldier of fortune in the Prussian service, and had, late in life, won sufficient favour with the king and other military superiors, to have an early prospect of obtaining a commission, under flattering auspices, for this only son—a son endeared to him as the companion of unprosperous years, and as a dutifully affectionate child. Ferdinand had yet another hold upon his father's affections: his features preserved to the Baron's unclouded remembrance a most faithful and living memorial of that angelic wife who had died in giving birth to this third child—the only one who had long survived her. Anxious that his son should go through a regular course of mathematical instruction, now becoming annually more important in all the artillery services throughout Europe, and that he should receive a tincture of other liberal studies which he had painfully missed in his own military career, the Baron chose to keep his son for the last seven years at our college, until he was now entering upon his twenty-third year. For the four last he had lived with me as the sole pupil whom I had, or meant to have, had not the brilliant proposals of the young Russian guardsman persuaded me to break my resolution. Ferdinand Von Harrelstein had good talents, not dazzling but respectable; and so amiable were his temper and manners, that I had introduced him every where; and every where he was a favourite; every where, indeed, except exactly there where only in this world he cared for favour. Margaret Liebenheim, she it was whom he loved, and had loved for years with the whole ardour of his ardent soul; she it was for whom, or at whose command, he would willingly have died. Early he had felt that in her hands lay his destiny; that she it was who must be his good or his evil genius.

At first, and perhaps to the last, I pitied him exceedingly. But my pity soon ceased to be mingled with respect. Before the arrival of Mr Wyndham he had shown himself generous, indeed magnanimous. But never was there so painful an overthrow of a noble nature as manifested itself in him. I believe that he had not himself suspected the strength of his passion; and the sole resource for him, as I said often, was—to quit the city; to engage in active pursuits of enterprise, of ambition, or of science. But he heard me as a somnambulist might have heard me—dreaming with his eyes open. Sometimes he had fits of reverie, starting, fearful, agitated; sometimes he broke out into maniacal movements of wrath, invoking some absent person, praying, beseeching, menacing some air-wove phantom: sometimes he slunk into solitary corners—muttering to himself, and with gestures sorrowfully significant, or with tones and fragments of expostulation that moved the most callous to compassion. Still he turned a deaf ear to the only practical counsel that had a chance for reaching his ears. Like a bird under the fascination of a rattlesnake, he would not summon up the energies of his nature to make an effort at flying away. 'Begone, whilst it is time!' said others, as well as myself; for more than I saw enough to fear some fearful catastrophe. 'Lead us not into temptation!'* said his confessor to him in my hearing (for, though Prussians, the Von Harrelsteins were Roman Catholics), 'lead us not into temptation!—that is our daily prayer to God. Then, my son, being led into temptation, do not you persist in courting, nay, almost tempting temptation! Try the effects of absence, though but for a month.' The good father even made an overture towards imposing a penance upon him, that would have involved an absence of some duration. But he was obliged to desist; for he saw that, without effecting any good, he would merely add spiritual disobedience to the other offences of the young man. Ferdinand himself drew his attention to *this*; for he said,—'Reverend father! do not you, with the purpose of removing me from temptation, be yourself the instrument for tempting me into a rebellion against the Church. Do not you weave snares about my steps; snares there are already, and but too many.' The old man sighed, and desisted.

Then came—But enough! From pity, from sympathy, from counsel, and from consolation, and from scorn—from each of these alike the poor stricken deer* 'recoiled into the wilderness;'* he fled for days together into solitary parts of the forest; fled, as I still hoped and prayed, in good earnest and for a long farewell; but, alas! no: still he returned to the haunts of his ruined happiness and his buried hopes, at each return looking more like the wreck of his former self; and once I heard a penetrating monk observe, whose convent stood near to the city gates—'There goes one ready equally for doing or suffering,* and of whom we shall soon hear that he is involved in some great catastrophe—it may be, of deep calamity—it may be, of memorable guilt.'

So stood matters amongst us; January was drawing to its close; the weather was growing more and more winterly; high winds, piercingly cold, were raving through our narrow streets; and still the spirit of social festivity bade defiance to the storms which sang through our ancient forests. From the accident of our magistracy being selected from the tradesmen of the city, the hospitalities of the place were far more extensive than would otherwise have happened; for every member of the Corporation gave two annual entertainments in his official character. And such was the rivalship which prevailed, that often one quarter of the year's income was spent upon these galas. Nor was any ridicule thus incurred; for the costliness of the entertainment was understood to be an expression of *official* pride, done in honour of the city, not as an effort of personal display. It followed, from the spirit in which these half-yearly dances originated, that, being given on the part of the city, every stranger of rank was marked out as a privileged guest, and the hospitality of the community would have been equally affronted by failing to offer or by failing to accept the invitation.

Hence it had happened the Russian guardsman had been introduced into many a family which otherwise could not have hoped for such a distinction. Upon the evening at which I am now arrived, the 22d of January, 1816, the whole city, in its wealthier classes, was assembled beneath the roof of a tradesman who had the heart of a prince. In every point our entertainment was superb; and I remarked that the music was the finest I had heard for years. Our host was in joyous spirits; proud to survey the splendid company he had gathered under his roof; happy to witness their happiness; elated in their elation. Joyous was the dance—joyous were all faces that I saw—up to midnight, very soon after which time supper was announced; and that also, I think, was the most joyous of all the banquets I ever witnessed. The accomplished guardsman outshone himself in brilliancy; even his melancholy relaxed. In fact, how could it be otherwise? near to him sate Margaret Liebenheim—hanging upon his words—more lustrous and bewitching than ever I had beheld her. There she had been placed by the host; and every body knew why. That is one of the luxuries attached to love; all men cede their places with pleasure; women make way; even she herself knew, though not obliged to know, why she was seated in that neighbourhood; and took her place—if with a rosy suffusion upon her cheeks—yet with fulness of happiness at her heart.

The guardsman pressed forward to claim Miss Liebenheim's hand for the next dance; a movement which she was quick to favour, by retreating behind one or two parties from a person who seemed coming towards her. The music again began to pour its voluptuous tides through the bounding pulses of the youthful company. Again the flying feet of the dancers began to respond to the measures; again the mounting spirit of delight began to fill the sails of the hurrying night with steady inspiration. All went happily. Already had one dance finished; some were pacing up and down, leaning on the arms of their partners; some were reposing from their exertions; when —— Oh Heavens! what a shriek! what a gathering tumult!

Every eye was bent towards the doors—every eye strained forwards to discover what was passing. But there, every moment, less and less could be seen, for the gathering crowd more and more intercepted the view; so much the more was the ear at leisure for the shrieks redoubled upon shrieks. Miss Liebenheim had moved downwards to the crowd. From her superior height she overlooked all the ladies at the point where she stood. In the centre stood a rustic girl, whose features had been familiar to her for some months. She had recently come into the city, and had lived with her uncle, a tradesman, not ten doors from Margaret's own residence, partly on the terms of a kins-woman, partly as a servant on trial. At this moment she was exhausted with excitement and the nature of the shock she had sustained. Mere panic seemed to have mastered her; and she was leaning, unconscious and weeping, upon the shoulder of some gentleman who was endeavouring to soothe her. A silence of horror seemed to possess the company, most of whom were still unacquainted with the cause of the alarming interruption. A few, however, who had heard her first agitated words, finding that they waited in vain for a fuller explanation, now rushed tumultuously out of the ball-room to satisfy themselves on the spot. The distance was not great; and within five minutes several persons returned hastily, and cried out to the crowd of ladies that all was true which the young girl had said. 'What was true?' That her uncle Mr Weishaupt's family had been murdered; that not one member of the family had been spared—viz.:—Mr Weishaupt himself and his wife, neither of them much above sixty, but both infirm beyond their years; two maiden sisters of Mr Weishaupt, from forty to forty-six years of age; and an elderly female domestic.

An incident happened during the recital of these horrors, and of the details which followed, that furnished matter for conversation even in these hours when so thrilling interest had possession of all minds. Many ladies fainted; amongst them Miss Liebenheim; and she would have fallen to the ground but for Maximilian, who sprang forward and caught her in his arms. She was long of returning to herself; and during the agony of his suspense he stooped and kissed her pallid lips. That sight was more than could be borne by one who stood a little behind the group. He rushed forward, with eyes glaring like a tiger's, and levelled a blow at Maximilian. It was poor maniacal Von Harrelstein, who had been absent in the forest for a week. Many people stepped forward and checked his arm, uplifted for a repetition of this outrage. One or two had some influence with him, and led him away from the spot; whilst, as to Maximilian, so absorbed was he that he had not so much as perceived the affront offered to himself. Margaret, on reviving, was confounded at finding herself so situated amidst a great crowd; and yet the prudes complained that there was a look of love exchanged between herself and Maximilian that ought not to have escaped her in such a situation. If they meant, by such a situation, one so public, it must be also recollected that it was a situation of excessive agitation; but if they alluded to the horrors of the moment, no situation more naturally opens the heart to affection and confiding love than the recoil from scenes of exquisite terror.

An examination went on that night before the magistrates, but all was dark; although suspicion attached to a negro, named Aaron, who had occasionally been employed in menial services by the family, and had been in the house immediately before the murder. The circumstances were such as to leave every man in utter perplexity as to the presumption for and against him. His mode of defending himself, and his general deportment, were marked by the coolest, nay, the most sneering indifference. The first thing he did, on being acquainted with the suspicions against himself, was, to laugh ferociously, and, to all appearance, most cordially and unaffectedly. He demanded whether a poor man, like himself, would have left so much wealth as lay scattered abroad in that house, gold repeaters, massy plate, gold snuff boxes, untouched? That argument, certainly, weighed much in his favour. And yet again it was turned against him—for a magistrate asked him how *he* happened to know already that nothing had been touched. True it was, and a fact which had puzzled, no less than it had awed the magistrates, that upon their examination of the premises many rich articles of *bijouterie*,* jewellery, and personal ornaments had been found lying underanged, and apparently in their usual situations; articles so portable that in the very hastiest flight some might have been carried off. In particular there was a crucifix of gold, enriched with jewels so large and rare, that of itself it would have constituted a prize of great magnitude. Yet this was left untouched, though suspended in a little oratory that had been magnificently adorned by the elder of the maiden sisters: there was an altar, in itself a splendid object, furnished with every article of the most costly material and workmanship, for the private celebration of mass. This crucifix, as well as every thing else in the little closet, must have been seen by one, at least, of the murderous party; for hither had one of the ladies fled; hither had one of the murderers pursued; she had clasped the golden pillars which supported the altar; had turned perhaps her dying looks upon the crucifix; for there, with one arm still wreathed about the altar foot, though in her agony she had turned round upon her face, did the elder sister lie when the magistrates first broke open the street-door. And upon the beautiful *parquet*, or inlaid floor which ran round the room, were still impressed the footsteps of the murderer. These, it was hoped, might furnish a clue to the discovery of one at least among the murderous band. They were rather difficult to trace accurately; those parts of

the traces which lay upon the black *tessellae** being less distinct in
the outline than the others upon the white or coloured. Most
unquestionably, so far as this went, it furnished a negative circumstance in favour of the negro, for the footsteps were very different in
outline from his, and smaller, for Aaron was a man of colossal build.
And as to his knowledge of the state in which the premises had been
found, and his having so familiarly relied upon the fact of no robbery
having taken place as an argument on his own behalf—he contended
that he had himself been amongst the crowd that pushed into the
house along with the magistrates; that, from his previous acquaintance with the rooms and their ordinary condition, a glance of the eye
had been sufficient for him to ascertain the undisturbed condition of
all the valuable property most obvious to the grasp of a robber; that,
in fact, he had seen enough for his argument before he and the rest
of the mob had been ejected by the magistrates; but finally, that,
independently of all this, he had heard both the officers, as they
conducted him, and all the tumultuous gatherings of people in the
street, arguing for the mysteriousness of the bloody transaction upon
that very circumstance of so much gold, silver, and jewels being left
behind untouched.

In six weeks or less from the date of this terrific event, the negro
was set at liberty by a majority of voices amongst the magistrates. In
that short interval other events had occurred, no less terrific and
mysterious. In this first murder, though the motive was dark and
unintelligible, yet the agency was not so; ordinary assassins apparently, and with ordinary means, had assailed a helpless and an
unprepared family; had separated them; attacked them singly in
flight (for in this first case all but one of the murdered persons
appeared to have been making for the street-door); and in all this
there was no subject for wonder, except the original one as to the
motive. But now came a series of cases destined to fling this earliest
murder into the shade. Nobody could now be unprepared; and yet
the tragedies, henceforwards, which passed before us, one by one, in
sad, leisurely, or in terrific groups, seemed to argue a lethargy like
that of apoplexy in the victims, one and all. The very midnight of
mysterious awe fell upon all minds.

Three weeks had passed since the murder at Mr Weishaupt's—
three weeks the most agitated that had been known in this sequestered city. We felt ourselves solitary, and thrown upon our own

resources; all combination with other towns being unavailing from their great distance. Our situation was no ordinary one. Had there been some mysterious robbers amongst us, the chances of a visit, divided amongst so many, would have been too small to distress the most timid; whilst to young and high-spirited people, with courage to spare for ordinary trials, such a state of expectation would have sent pulses of pleasurable anxiety amongst the nerves. But murderers! exterminating murderers!—clothed in mystery and utter darkness— these were objects too terrific for any family to contemplate with fortitude. Had these very murderers added to their functions those of robbery, they would have become less terrific; nine out of every ten would have found themselves discharged, as it were, from the roll of those who were liable to a visit; while such as knew themselves liable would have had warning of their danger in the fact of being rich; and would, from the very riches which constituted that danger, have derived the means of repelling it. But, as things were, no man could guess what it was that must make him obnoxious to the murderers. Imagination exhausted itself in vain guesses at the causes which could by possibility have made the poor Weishaupts objects of such hatred to any man. True, they were bigoted in a degree which indicated feebleness of intellect; but *that* wounded no man in particular, whilst to many it recommended them. True, their charity was narrow and exclusive, but to those of their own religious body it expanded munificently; and, being rich beyond their wants, or any means of employing wealth which their gloomy asceticism allowed, they had the power of doing a great deal of good amongst the indigent Papists of the suburbs. As to the old gentleman and his wife, their infirmities confined them to the house. Nobody remembered to have seen them abroad for years. How, therefore, or when, could they have made an enemy? And, with respect to the maiden sisters of Mr Weishaupt, they were simply weak-minded persons, now and then too censorious, but not placed in a situation to incur serious anger from any quarter, and too little heard of in society to occupy much of any body's attention.

Conceive, then, that three weeks have passed away, that the poor Weishaupts have been laid in that narrow sanctuary which no murderer's voice will ever violate. Quiet has not returned to us, but the first flutterings of panic have subsided. People are beginning to respire freely again; and such another space of time would have cicatrised

our wounds—when, hark! a church-bell rings out a loud alarm;—the
night is starlight and frosty—the iron notes are heard clear, solemn,
but agitated. What could this mean? I hurried to a room over the
porter's lodge, and, opening the window, I cried out to a man passing
hastily below—'What, in God's name, is the meaning of this?' It was
a watchman belonging to our district. I knew his voice, he knew
mine, and he replied in great agitation,—

'It is another murder, sir, at the old town councillor's, Albernass;
and this time they have made a clear house of it.'

'God preserve us! Has a curse been pronounced upon this city?
What can be done? What are the magistrates going to do?'

'I don't know, sir. I have orders to run to the Black Friars, where
another meeting is gathering. Shall I say you will attend, sir?'

'Yes—no—stop a little. No matter, you may go on; I'll follow
immediately.'

I went instantly to Maximilian's room. He was lying asleep on a
sofa, at which I was not surprised, for there had been a severe stag-
chase in the morning. Even at this moment, I found myself arrested
by two objects, and I paused to survey them. One was Maximilian
himself. A person so mysterious took precedence of other interests
even at a time like this; and especially by his features, which, composed in profound sleep, as sometimes happens, assumed a new
expression—which arrested me chiefly by awaking some confused
remembrance of the same features seen under other circumstances
and in times long past; but where? This was what I could not recollect, though once before a thought of the same sort had crossed
my mind. The other object of my interest was a miniature, which
Maximilian was holding in his hand. He had gone to sleep apparently looking at this picture; and the hand which held it had slipped
down upon the sofa, so that it was in danger of falling. I released the
miniature from his hand, and surveyed it attentively; it represented a
lady of sunny Oriental complexion, and features the most noble that
it is possible to conceive. One might have imagined such a lady, with
her raven locks and imperial eyes, to be the favourite sultana of some
Amurath or Mahomet.* What was she to Maximilian, or what *had* she
been? For, by the tear which I had once seen him drop upon this
miniature when he believed himself unobserved, I conjectured that
her dark tresses were already laid low, and her name among the list of
vanished things. Probably she was his mother, for the dress was rich

with pearls, and evidently that of a person in the highest rank of court beauties. I sighed as I thought of the stern melancholy of her son, if Maximilian were he, as connected, probably, with the fate and fortunes of this majestic beauty; somewhat haughty, perhaps, in the expression of her fine features, but still noble—generous—confiding. Laying the picture on the table, I awoke Maximilian and told him of the dreadful news. He listened attentively, made no remark, but proposed that we should go together to the meeting of our quarter at the Black Friars. He coloured upon observing the miniature on the table, and, therefore, I frankly told him in what situation I had found it, and that I had taken the liberty of admiring it for a few moments. He pressed it tenderly to his lips, sighed heavily, and we walked away together.

I pass over the frenzied state of feeling in which we found the meeting. Fear, or rather horror, did not promote harmony; many quarrelled with each other in discussing the suggestions brought forward, and Maximilian was the only person attended to; he proposed a nightly mounted patrol for every district. And, in particular, he offered, as being himself a member of the University, that the students should form themselves into a guard, and go out by rotation to keep watch and ward from sunset to sunrise. Arrangements were made towards that object by the few people who retained possession of their senses, and for the present we separated.

Never, in fact, did any events so keenly try the difference between man and man. Some started up into heroes under the excitement. Some, alas for the dignity of Man! drooped into helpless imbecility. Women, in some cases, rose superior to men, but yet not so often as might have happened under a less mysterious danger. A woman is not unwomanly, because she affronts danger boldly. But I have remarked, with respect to female courage, that it requires, more than that of men, to be sustained by hope; and that it droops more certainly in the presence of a *mysterious* danger. The fancy of women is more active, if not stronger, and it influences more directly the physical nature. In this case few were the women who made even a show of defying the danger. On the contrary, with *them* fear took the form of sadness; while with many of the men it took that of wrath.

And how did the Russian guardsman conduct himself amidst this panic? Many were surprised at his behaviour; some complained of it; I did neither. He took a reasonable interest in each separate case, listened to the details with attention, and, in the examination of persons able to furnish evidence, never failed to suggest judicious questions. But still he manifested a coolness almost amounting to carelessness, which to many appeared revolting. But these people I desired to notice that all the other military students, who had been long in the army, felt exactly in the same way. In fact, the military service of Christendom, for the last ten years, had been any thing but a parade service; and to those, therefore, who were familiar with every form of horrid butchery, the mere outside horrors of death had lost much of their terror. In the recent murder, there had not been much to call forth sympathy. The family consisted of two old bachelors, two sisters, and one grand-niece. The niece was absent on a visit, and the two old men were cynical misers, to whom little personal interest attached. Still, in this case as in that of the Weishaupts, the same two-fold mystery confounded the public mind; the mystery of the *how*, and the profounder mystery of the *why*. Here, again, no atom of property was taken, though both the misers had hordes of ducats and English guineas in the very room where they died. Their bias, again, though of an unpopular character, had rather availed to make them unknown than to make them hateful. In one point this case differed memorably from the other—that, instead of falling helpless or flying victims (as the Weishaupts had done), these old men, strong, resolute, and not so much taken by surprise, left proofs that they had made a desperate defence. The furniture was partly smashed to pieces, and the other details furnished evidence still more revolting of the *acharnement** with which the struggle had been maintained. In fact, with *them* a surprise must have been impracticable, as they admitted nobody into their house on visiting terms. It was thought singular that from each of these domestic tragedies a benefit of the same sort should result to young persons standing in nearly the same relation. The girl who gave the alarm at the ball, with two little sisters, and a little orphan nephew, their cousin, divided the very large inheritance of the Weishaupts; and in this latter case the accumulated savings of two long lives all vested in the person of the amiable grand-niece.

But now, as if in mockery of all our anxious consultations and elaborate devices, three fresh murders took place on the two consecutive nights succeeding these new arrangements. And in one case, as nearly as time could be noted, the mounted patrol must have been within call at the very moment when the awful work was going on. I shall not dwell much upon them; but a few circumstances are too interesting to be passed over. The earliest case on the first of the two nights, was that of a currier. He was fifty years old; not rich, but well off. His first wife was dead, and his daughters by her were married away from their father's house. He had married a second wife, but, having no children by her, and keeping no servants, it is probable that, but for an accident, no third person would have been in the house at the time when the murderers got admittance. About seven o'clock, a wayfaring man, a journeyman currier, who, according to our German system, was now in his *wanderjahre*,* entered the city from the forest. At the gate he made some enquiries about the curriers and tanners of our town; and, agreeably to the information he received, made his way to this Mr Heinberg's. Mr Heinberg refused to admit him, until he mentioned his errand, and pushed below the door a letter of recommendation from a Silesian* correspondent, describing him as an excellent and steady workman. Wanting such a man, and satisfied by the answers returned that he was what he represented himself, Mr Heinberg unbolted his door and admitted him. Then, after slipping the bolt into its place, he bade him sit to the fire; brought him a glass of beer; conversed with him for ten minutes; and said, 'You had better stay here to-night; I'll tell you why afterwards; but now I'll step up-stairs and ask my wife whether she can make up a bed for you; and do you mind the door whilst I'm away.' So saying, he went out of the room. Not one minute had he been gone, when there came a gentle knock at the door. It was raining heavily, and being a stranger to the city, not dreaming that in any crowded town such a state of things could exist as really did in this, the young man, without hesitation, admitted the person knocking. He has declared since—but, perhaps, confounding the feelings gained from better knowledge with the feelings of the moment—that from the moment he drew the bolt he had a misgiving that he had done wrong. A man entered in a horseman's cloak, and so muffled up that the journeyman could discover none of his features. In a low tone, the stranger said, 'Where's Heinberg?' 'Up-stairs.' 'Call him down then.' The journeyman went to the door by which Mr Heinberg had left him, and called, 'Mr Heinberg, here's one wanting you!' Mr Heinberg heard him, for the man could distinctly catch these words, 'God bless me! has the man opened the door? Oh, the traitor!

I see it.' Upon this, he felt more and more consternation, though not knowing why. Just then he heard a sound of feet behind him. On turning round, he beheld three more men in the room: one was fastening the outer door; one was drawing some arms from a cupboard; and two others were whispering together. He himself was disturbed and perplexed, and felt that all was not right. Such was his confusion, that either all the men's faces must have been muffled up, or at least he remembered nothing distinctly but one fierce pair of eyes glaring upon him. Then, before he could look round, came a man from behind and threw a sack over his head, which was drawn tight about his waist, so as to confine his arms, as well as to impede his hearing in part, and his voice altogether. He was then pushed into a room; but previously he had heard a rush up-stairs, and words like those of a person exulting, and then a door closed; once it opened, and he could distinguish the words in one voice—'and for *that*!' to which another voice replied, in tones that made his heart quake— 'Ay, for *that*, sir.' And then the same voice went on rapidly to say, 'Oh, dog! could you hope'—at which word the door closed again. Once he thought that he heard a scuffle, and he was sure that he heard the sound of feet, as if rushing from one corner of a room to another. But then all was hushed and still for about six or seven minutes, until a voice close to his ear said, 'Now, wait quietly till some persons come in to release you. This will happen within half-an-hour.' Accordingly, in less than that time, he again heard the sound of feet within the house, his own bandages were liberated, and he was brought to tell his story at the police-office. Mr Heinberg was found in his bed-room. He had died by strangulation, and the cord was still tightened about his neck. During the whole dreadful scene, his youthful wife had been locked into a closet, where she heard or saw nothing.

In the second case, the object of vengeance was again an elderly man. Of the ordinary family, all were absent at a country-house, except the master and a female servant. She was a woman of courage, and blessed with the firmest nerves; so that she might have been relied on for reporting accurately every thing seen or heard. But things took another course. The first warning that she had of the murderers' presence was from their steps and voices already in the hall. She heard her master run hastily into the hall, crying out, 'Lord Jesus!—Mary, Mary, save me!' The servant resolved to give what aid she could, seized a large poker, and was hurrying to his assistance, when she found that they had nailed up the door of communication at the head of the stairs. What passed after this she could not tell; for, when the impulse of intrepid fidelity had been balked, and she found that her own safety was provided for, by means which made it impossible to aid a poor fellow-creature who had just invoked her name, the generous-hearted creature was overcome by anguish of mind, and sank down on the stair, where she lay, unconscious of all that succeeded, until she found herself raised in the arms of a mob who had entered the house. And how came they to have entered? In a way characteristically dreadful. The night was star-lit; the patroles had perambulated the street without noticing any thing suspicious, when two foot-passengers, who were following in their rear, observed a dark-coloured stream traversing the causeway. One of them at the same instant tracing the stream backwards with his eyes, observed that it flowed from under the door of Mr Münzer, and, dipping his finger in the trickling fluid, he held it up to the lamp-light, yelling out at the moment, 'Why, this is blood!' It was so indeed, and it was yet warm. The other saw, heard, and, like an arrow, flew after the horse-patrol, then in the act of turning the corner. One cry, full of meaning, was sufficient for ears full of expectation. The horsemen pulled up, wheeled, and in another moment reined up at Mr Münzer's door. The crowd, gathering like the drifting of snow, supplied implements, which soon forced the chains of the door, and all other obstacles. But the murderous party had escaped, and all traces of their persons had vanished, as usual.

Rarely did any case occur without some peculiarity more or less interesting. In that which happened on the following night, making the fifth in the series, an impressive incident varied the monotony of horrors. In this case the parties aimed at were two elderly ladies, who conducted a female boarding-school. None of the pupils had, as yet, returned to school from their vacation; but two sisters, young girls of thirteen and sixteen, coming from a distance, had staid at school throughout the Christmas holidays. It was the youngest of these who gave the only evidence of any value, and one which added a new feature of alarm to the existing panic. Thus it was that her testimony was given:—On the day before the murder, she and her sister were sitting with the old ladies in a room fronting to the street; the elder ladies were reading, the young ones drawing. Louisa, the youngest, never had her ear inattentive to the slightest sound, and once it struck her—that she heard the creaking of a foot upon the stairs. She said nothing, but slipping out of the room, she ascertained that the two female servants were in the kitchen, and could not have been absent; that all the doors and windows, by which ingress was possible, were not only locked, but bolted and barred, a fact which excluded all possibility of invasion by means of false keys. Still she felt persuaded that she had heard the sound of a heavy foot upon the stairs. It was, however, daylight, and this gave her confidence; so that, without communicating her alarm to any body, she found courage to traverse the house in every direction, and, as nothing was either seen or heard, she concluded that her ears had been too sensitively awake. Yet that night, as she lay in bed, dim terrors assailed her, especially because she considered that, in so large a house, some closet or other might have been overlooked, and, in particular, she did not remember to have examined one or two chests, in which a man could have lain concealed. Through the greater part of the night she lay awake, but as one of the town clocks struck four, she dismissed her anxieties, and fell asleep. The next day, wearied with this unusual watching, she proposed to her sister that they should go to bed earlier than usual. This they did; and on their way up-stairs, Louisa happened to think suddenly of a heavy cloak, which would improve the coverings of her bed against the severity of the night. The cloak was hanging up in a closet within a closet, both leading off from a large room used as the young ladies' dancing-school. These closets she had examined on the previous day, and therefore she felt no particular alarm at this moment. The cloak was the first article which met her sight; it was suspended from a hook in the wall, and close to the door. She took it down, but, in doing so, exposed part of the wall and of the floor, which its folds had previously concealed. Turning away hastily, the chances were that she had gone without making any discovery. In the act of turning, however, her light fell brightly on a man's foot and leg. Matchless was her presence of mind; having previously been humming an air, she continued to do so. But now came the trial: her sister was bending her steps to the same closet. If she suffered her to do so, Lottchen would stumble on the same discovery, and expire of fright. On the other hand, if she gave her a hint, Lottchen would either fail to understand her, or, gaining but a glimpse of her meaning, would shriek aloud, or by some equally decisive expression convey the fatal news to the assassin that he had been discovered. In this torturing dilemma fear prompted an expedient, which to Lottchen appeared madness, and to Louisa herself the act of a sybil instinct with blind inspiration. 'Here,' said she, 'is our dancing-room. When shall we all meet and dance again together?' Saying which, she commenced a wild dance, whirling her candle round her head until the motion extinguished it; then, eddying round her sister in narrowing circles, she seized Lottchen's candle also, blew it out, and then interrupted her own singing to attempt a laugh. But the laugh was hysterical. The darkness, however, favoured her; and, seizing her sister's arm, she forced her along, whispering, 'Come, come, come!' Lottchen could not be so dull as entirely to misunderstand her. She suffered herself to be led up the first flight of stairs, at the head of which was a room looking into the street. In this they would have gained an asylum, for the door had a strong bolt. But as they were on the last steps of the landing, they could hear the hard breathing and long strides of the murderer ascending behind them. He had watched them through a crevice, and had been satisfied, by the hysterical laugh of Louisa, that she had seen him. In the darkness he could not follow fast, from ignorance of the localities, until he found himself upon the stairs. Louisa, dragging her sister along, felt strong as with the strength of lunacy, but Lottchen hung like a weight of lead upon her. She rushed into the room; but, at the very entrance, Lottchen fell. At that moment the assassin exchanged his stealthy pace for a loud clattering ascent. Already he was on the topmost stair—already he was throwing himself at a bound against the door, when Louisa, having dragged her sister into the room, closed the door and sent the bolt home in the very instant that the murderer's hand came into contact with the handle. Then, from the violence of her emotions, she fell down in a fit, with her arm round the sister whom she had saved.

How long they lay in this state neither ever knew. The two old ladies had rushed up stairs on hearing the tumult. Other persons had been concealed in other parts of the house. The servants found themselves suddenly locked in, and were not sorry to be saved from a collision which involved so awful a danger. The old ladies had rushed, side by side, into the very centre of those who were seeking them. Retreat was impossible; two persons at least were heard following them up-stairs. Something like a shrieking expostulation and

counter-expostulation went on between the ladies and the murderers—then came louder voices—then one heart-piercing shriek, and
then another—and then a low moaning and a dead silence. Shortly
afterwards was heard the first crashing of the door inwards by the
mob; but the murderers had fled upon the first alarm, and, to the
astonishment of the servants, had fled upwards. Examination, however, explained this: from a window in the roof, they had passed to an
adjoining house recently left empty; and here, as in other cases, we
had proof how apt people are, in the midst of elaborate provisions
against remote dangers, to neglect those which are obvious.

The reign of terror, it may be supposed, had now reached its *acmé.**
The two old ladies were both lying dead at different points on the
staircase, and, as usual, no conjecture could be made as to the nature
of the offence which they had given; but that the murder *was* a
vindictive one, the usual evidence remained behind, in the proofs
that no robbery had been attempted. Two new features, however,
were now brought forward in this system of horrors, one of which
riveted the sense of their insecurity to all families occupying extensive houses, and the other raised ill blood between the city and the
University, such as required years to allay. The first arose out of the
experience, now first obtained, that these assassins pursued the plan
of secreting themselves within the house where they meditated a
murder. All the care, therefore, previously directed to the securing of
doors and windows after nightfall appeared nugatory. The other
feature brought to light on this occasion was vouched for by one of
the servants, who declared that the moment before the door of the
kitchen was fastened upon herself and fellow-servant, she saw two
men in the hall, one on the point of ascending the stairs, the other
making towards the kitchen; that she could not distinguish the faces
of either, but that both were dressed in the academic costume
belonging to the students of the University. The consequences of
such a declaration need scarcely be mentioned. Suspicion settled
upon the students, who were more numerous since the general
peace, in a much larger proportion military, and less select or
respectable than heretofore. Still, no part of the mystery was cleared
up by this discovery; many of the students were poor enough to feel
the temptation that might be offered by any *lucrative* system of
outrage. Jealous and painful collusions were, in the mean-time, produced; and, during the latter two months of this winter, it may be

said that our city exhibited the very anarchy of evil passions. This condition of things lasted until the dawning of another spring.

It will be supposed that communications were made to the Supreme Government of the land as soon as the murders in our city were understood to be no casual occurrences, but links in a systematic series. Perhaps it might happen from some other business of a higher kind, just then engaging the attention of our governors, that our representations did not make the impression we had expected. We could not, indeed, complain of absolute neglect from the Government: they sent down one or two of their most accomplished police-officers, and they suggested some counsels, especially that we should examine more strictly into the quality of the miscellaneous population who occupied our large suburb. But they more than hinted, that no necessity was seen either for quartering troops upon us, or for arming our local magistracy with ampler powers.

This correspondence with the central Government occupied the month of March, and, before that time, the bloody system had ceased as abruptly as it began. The new police-officer flattered himself that the terror of his name had wrought this effect; but judicious people thought otherwise. All, however, was quiet until the depth of summer, when, by way of hinting to us, perhaps, that the dreadful power, which clothed itself with darkness, had not expired, but was only reposing from its labours, all at once the chief jailer of the city was missing. He had been in the habit of taking long rides in the forest, his present situation being much of a sinecure. It was on the 1st of July that he was missed. In riding through the city gates that morning he had mentioned the direction which he meant to pursue; and the last time he was seen alive was in one of the forest avenues about eight miles from the city, leading towards the point he had indicated. This jailer was not a man to be regretted on his own account; his life had been a tissue of cruelty and brutal abuse of his powers, in which he had been too much supported by the magistrates, partly on the plea that it was their duty to back their own officers against all complainers, partly, also, from the necessities created by the turbulent times for a more summary exercise of their magisterial authority. No man, therefore, on his own separate account, could more willingly have been spared than this brutal jailer; and it was a general remark, that, had the murderous band within our walls swept away this man only, they would have merited the public gratitude as purifiers from a public nuisance. But was it certain that the jailer had died by the same hands as had so deeply afflicted the peace of our city during the winter? or, indeed, that he had been murdered at all? The forest was too extensive to be searched; and it was possible that he might have met with some fatal accident. His horse had returned to the city gates in the night, and was found there in the morning. Nobody, however, for months, could give information about his rider; and it seemed probable that he would not be discovered until the autumn and the winter should again carry the sportsman into every thicket and dingle of this silvan tract. One person only seemed to have more knowledge on this subject than others, and that was poor Ferdinand von Harrelstein. He was now a mere ruin of what he had once been, both as to intellect and moral feeling; and I observed him frequently smile when the jailer was mentioned. 'Wait,' he would say, 'till the leaves begin to drop; then you will see what fine fruit our forest bears.' I did not repeat these expressions to any body except one friend, who agreed with me that the jailer had probably been hanged in some recess of the forest, which summer veiled with its luxuriant umbrage; and that Ferdinand, constantly wandering in the forest, had discovered the body: but we both acquitted him of having been an accomplice in the murder.

Mean-time, the marriage between Margaret Liebenheim and Maximilian was understood to be drawing near. Yet one thing struck every body with astonishment. As far as the young people were concerned, nobody could doubt that all was arranged; for never was happiness more perfect than that which seemed to unite them. Margaret was the impersonation of May-time and youthful rapture; even Maximilian in her presence seemed to forget his gloom; and the worm which gnawed at his heart was charmed asleep by the music of her voice, and the Paradise of her smiles. But, until the autumn came, Margaret's grandfather had never ceased to frown upon this connexion, and to support the pretensions of Ferdinand. The dislike, indeed, seemed reciprocal between him and Maximilian. Each avoided the other's company; and as to the old man, he went so far as to speak sneeringly of Maximilian. Maximilian despised him too heartily to speak of him at all. When he could not avoid meeting him, he treated him with a stern courtesy, which distressed Margaret as often as she witnessed it. She felt that her grandfather had been the aggressor; and she felt, also, that he did injustice to the merits of her lover. But she had a filial tenderness for the old man, as the father of her sainted mother, and on his own account, continually making more claims on her pity, as the decay of his memory, and a childish fretfulness growing upon him from day to day, marked his increasing imbecility.

Equally mysterious it seemed, that, about this time, Miss Lieben-heim began to receive anonymous letters, written in the darkest and most menacing terms. Some of them she showed to me; I could not guess at their drift. Evidently they glanced at Maximilian, and bade her beware of a connexion with him; and dreadful things were insinuated about him. Could these letters be written by Ferdinand? Written they were not; but could they be dictated by him? Much I feared that they were; and the more so for one reason.

All at once, and most inexplicably, Margaret's grandfather showed a total change of opinion in his views as to her marriage: instead of favouring Harrelstein's pretensions, as he had hitherto done, he now threw the feeble weight of his encouragement into Maximilian's scale; though, from the situation of all the parties, nobody attached any *practical* importance to the change in Mr Liebenheim's way of thinking. Nobody? Is that true? No; one person *did* attach the great-est weight to the change; poor ruined Ferdinand;—he, so long as there was one person to take his part, so long as the grandfather of Margaret showed countenance to himself, had still felt his situation not utterly desperate.

Thus were things situated, when in November, all the leaves daily blowing off from the woods, and leaving bare the most secret haunts of the thickets, the body of the jailer was left exposed in the forest; but not, as I and my friend had conjectured, hanged; no; he had died, apparently, by a more horrid death—by that of crucifixion. The tree, a remarkable one, bore upon a part of its trunk this brief but savage inscription:—'T. H., jailer at ——; *Crucified, July* 1, 1816.'

A great deal of talk went on throughout the city upon this dis-covery; nobody uttered one word of regret on account of the wretched jailer; on the contrary, the voice of vengeance, rising up in many a cottage, reached my ears in every direction as I walked abroad. The hatred in itself seemed horrid and unchristian, and still more so after the man's death; but, though horrid and fiendish for itself, it was much more impressive, considered as the measure and exponent of the damnable oppression which must have existed to produce it.

At first, when the absence of the jailer was a recent occurrence, and the presence of the murderers amongst us was, in consequence, revived to our anxious thoughts, it was an event which few alluded to without fear. But matters were changed now; the jailer had been dead for months, and this interval, during which the murderer's hand had slept, encouraged every body to hope that the storm had passed over our city; that peace had returned to our hearths; and that, henceforth, weakness might sleep in safety, and innocence without anxiety. Once more we had peace within our walls, and tranquillity by our firesides. Again the child went to bed in cheerfulness, and the old man said his prayers in serenity. Confidence was restored; peace was re-established; and once again the sanctity of human life became the rule and the principle for all human hands amongst us. Great was the joy; the happiness was universal.

Oh, heavens! by what a thunderbolt were we awakened from our security!—On the night of the 27th of December, half an hour, it might be, after twelve o'clock, an alarm was given that all was not right in the house of Mr Liebenheim. Vast was the crowd which soon collected in breathless agitation. In two minutes a man who had gone round by the back of the house was heard unbarring Mr Liebenheim's door: he was incapable of uttering a word; but his gestures, as he threw the door open and beckoned to the crowd, were quite enough. In the hall, at the further extremity, and as if arrested in the act of making for the back, lay the bodies of old Mr Liebenheim and one of his sisters, an aged widow; on the stair lay another sister, younger, and unmarried, but upwards of sixty. The hall and lower flight of stairs were floating with blood. Where, then, was Miss Liebenheim, the grand-daughter? That was the universal cry; for she was beloved as generally as she was admired. Had the infernal murderers been devilish enough to break into that temple of innocent and happy life?—Every one asked the question, and every one held his breath to listen; but for a few moments no one dared to advance; for the silence of the house was ominous. At length some one cried out, that Miss Liebenheim had that day gone upon a visit to a friend, whose house was forty miles distant in the forest. 'Ay,' replied another, 'she had settled to go; but I heard that something had stopped her.' The suspense was now at its height, and the

crowd passed from room to room, but found no traces of Miss Liebenheim. At length they ascended the stair, and in the very first
room, a small closet or *boudoir*, lay Margaret, with her dress soiled
hideously with blood. The first impression was that she also had
been murdered; but, on a nearer approach, she appeared to be
unwounded, and was manifestly alive. Life had not departed, for her
breath sent a haze over a mirror, but it was suspended, and she was
labouring in some kind of fit. The first act of the crowd was to carry
her into the house of a friend on the opposite side of the street, by
which time medical assistance had crowded to the spot. Their attentions to Miss Liebenheim had naturally deranged the condition of
things in the little room, but not before many people found time to
remark that one of the murderers must have carried her with his
bloody hands to the sofa on which she lay, for water had been sprin-
kled profusely over her face and throat, and water was even placed
ready to her hand, when she might happen to recover, upon a low
footstool by the side of the sofa.

On the following morning, Maximilian, who had been upon a
hunting-party in the forest, returned to the city, and immediately
learned the news. I did not see him for some hours after, but he then
appeared to me thoroughly agitated, for the first time I had known
him to be so. In the evening another perplexing piece of intelligence
transpired with regard to Miss Liebenheim, which at first afflicted
every friend of that young lady. It was, that she had been seized with
the pains of childbirth, and delivered of a son, who, however, being
born prematurely, did not live many hours. Scandal, however, was
not allowed long to batten upon this imaginary triumph, for within
two hours after the circulation of this first rumour, followed a second, authenticated, announcing that Maximilian had appeared with
the confessor of the Liebenheim family, at the residence of the chief
magistrate, and there produced satisfactory proofs of his marriage
with Miss Liebenheim, which had been duly celebrated, though with
great secrecy, nearly eight months before. In our city, as in all the cities
of our country, clandestine marriages, witnessed, perhaps, by two
friends only of the parties, besides the officiating priest, are exceedingly common. In the mere fact, therefore, taken separately, there
was nothing to surprise us, but, taken in connexion with the general
position of the parties, it *did* surprise us all; nor could we conjecture
the reason for a step apparently so needless. For, that Maximilian

could have thought it any point of prudence or necessity to secure the hand of Margaret Liebenheim by a private marriage, against the final opposition of her grandfather, nobody who knew the parties, who knew the perfect love which possessed Miss Liebenbeim, the growing imbecility of her grandfather, or the utter contempt with which Maximilian regarded him, could for a moment believe. Altogether, the matter was one of profound mystery.

Mean-time, it rejoiced me that poor Margaret's name had been thus rescued from the fangs of the scandal-mongers: these harpies had their prey torn from them at the very moment when they were sitting down to the unhallowed banquet. For this I rejoiced, but else there was little subject for rejoicing in any thing which concerned poor Margaret. Long she lay in deep insensibility, taking no notice of any thing, rarely opening her eyes, and apparently unconscious of the revolutions, as they succeeded, of morning or evening, light or darkness, yesterday or to-day. Great was the agitation which convulsed the heart of Maximilian during this period; he walked up and down in the Cathedral nearly all day long, and the ravages which anxiety was working in his physical system might be read in his face. People felt it an intrusion upon the sanctity of his grief to look at him too narrowly, and the whole town sympathised with his situation.

At length a change took place in Margaret, but one which the medical men announced to Maximilian as boding ill for her recovery. The wanderings of her mind did not depart, but they altered their character. She became more agitated, she would start up suddenly, and strain her eyesight after some figure which she seemed to see; then she would apostrophise some person in the most piteous terms, beseeching him, with streaming tears, to spare her old grandfather. 'Look, look,' she would cry out, 'look at his grey hairs; oh, sir! he is but a child; he does not know what he says; and he will soon be out of the way and in his grave; and very soon, sir, he will give you no more trouble.' Then, again, she would mutter indistinctly for hours together; sometimes, she would cry out frantically, and say things which terrified the bystanders, and which the physicians would solemnly caution them how they repeated; then she would weep, and invoke Maximilian to come and aid her. But seldom, indeed, did that name pass her lips that she did not again begin to strain her eyeballs, and start up in bed to watch some phantom of her poor fevered heart, as if it seemed vanishing into some mighty distance.

After nearly seven weeks passed in this agitating state, suddenly, on one morning, the earliest and the loveliest of dawning spring, a change was announced to us all as having taken place in Margaret; but it was a change, alas! that ushered in the last great change of all. The conflict, which had for so long a period raged within her, and overthrown her reason, was at an end; the strife was over; and nature was settling into an everlasting rest. In the course of the night she had recovered her senses; when the morning light penetrated through her curtain, she recognised her attendants, made enquiries as to the month and the day of the month, and then, sensible that she could not outlive the day, she requested that her confessor might be summoned.

About an hour and a half the confessor remained alone with her. At the end of that time he came out, and hastily summoned the attendants, for Margaret, he said, was sinking into a fainting fit. The confessor, himself, might have passed through many a fit, so much was he changed by the results of this interview. I crossed him coming out of the house. I spoke to him—I called to him; but he heard me not—he saw me not.* He saw nobody. Onwards he strode to the Cathedral, where Maximilian was sure to be found, pacing about upon the graves. Him he seized by the arm, whispered something into his ear, and then both retired into one of the many sequestered chapels in which lights are continually burning. There they had some conversation, but not very long, for within five minutes Maximilian strode away to the house in which his young wife was dying. One step seemed to carry him up-stairs; the attendants, according to the directions they had received from the physicians, mustered at the head of the stairs to oppose him. But that was idle: before the rights which he held as a lover and a husband, before the still more sacred rights of grief, which he carried in his countenance, all opposition fled like a dream. There was, besides, a fury in his eye. A motion of his hand waved them off like summer flies; he entered the room, and once again, for the last time, he was in company with his beloved.

What passed, who could pretend to guess? Something more than two hours had elapsed, during which Margaret had been able to talk occasionally, which was known, because at times the attendants heard the sound of Maximilian's voice evidently in tones of reply to something which she had said. At the end of that time, a little bell, placed near the bedside, was rung hastily; a fainting fit had seized Margaret, but she recovered almost before her women applied the usual remedies. They lingered, however, a little, looking at the youthful couple with an interest which no restraints availed to check. Their hands were locked together, and in Margaret's eyes there gleamed a farewell light of love, which settled upon Maximilian, and seemed to indicate that she was becoming speechless. Just at this moment she made a feeble effort to draw Maximilian towards her; he bent forward and kissed her with an anguish that made the most callous weep, and then he whispered something into her ear, upon which the attendants retired, taking this as a proof that their presence was a hindrance to a free communication. But they heard no more talking, and in less than ten minutes they returned. Maximilian and Margaret still retained their former position. Their hands were fast locked together; the same parting ray of affection, the same farewell light of love, was in the eye of Margaret, and still it settled upon Maximilian. But her eyes were beginning to grow dim; mists were rapidly stealing over them. Maximilian, who sat stupefied and like one not in his right mind, now, at the gentle request of the women, resigned his seat, for the hand which had clasped his had already relaxed its hold; the farewell gleam of love had departed; one of the women closed her eyelids; and there fell asleep for ever the loveliest flower that our city had reared for generations.

The funeral took place on the fourth day after her death. In the morning of that day, from strong affection—having known her from an infant—I begged permission to see the corpse. She was in her coffin; snow-drops and crocuses were laid upon her innocent bosom, and roses of that sort which the season allowed, over her person. These and other lovely symbols of youth, of springtime, and of resurrection, caught my eye for the first moment; but in the next it fell upon her face. Mighty God! what a change! what a transfiguration! Still, indeed, there was the same innocent sweetness; still there was something of the same loveliness; the expression still remained; but for the features—all trace of flesh seemed to have vanished; mere outline of bony structure remained; mere pencillings and shadowings of what she once had been. This is indeed, I exclaimed, 'dust to dust—ashes to ashes!'*

Maximilian, to the astonishment of every body, attended the funeral. It was celebrated in the Cathedral. All made way for him, and at times he seemed collected; at times, he reeled like one who was drunk. He heard as one who hears not; he saw as one in a dream.

The whole ceremony went on by torch-light, and towards the close he stood like a pillar, motionless, torpid, frozen. But the great burst of the choir, and the mighty blare ascending from our vast organ at the closing of the grave, recalled him to himself, and he strode rapidly homewards. Half-an-hour after I returned, I was summoned to his bed-room. He was in bed, calm and collected. What he said to me I remember as if it had been yesterday, and the very tone with which he said it, although more than twenty years have passed since then. He began thus: 'I have not long to live;' and when he saw me start, suddenly awakened into a consciousness that perhaps he had taken poison, and meant to intimate as much, he continued,—'You fancy I have taken poison;—no matter whether I have or not; if I have, the poison is such that no antidotes will now avail; or, if they would, you well know that some griefs are of a kind which leave no opening to any hope. What difference, therefore, can it make whether I leave this earth to-day, to-morrow, or the next day? Be assured of this— that whatever I have determined to do is past all power of being affected by a human opposition. Occupy yourself not with any fruit- less attempts, but calmly listen to me, else I know what to do.' Seeing a suppressed fury in his eye, notwithstanding that I saw also some change stealing over his features as if from some subtle poison beginning to work upon his frame, awe-struck I consented to listen, and sate still. 'It is well that you do so, for my time is short. Here is my will, legally drawn up, and you will see that I have committed an immense property to your discretion. Here, again, is a paper still more important in my eyes; it is also testamentary, and binds you to duties which may not be so easy to execute as the disposal of my property. But now listen to something else which concerns neither of these papers. Promise me, in the first place, solemnly, that whenever I die you will see me buried in the same grave as my wife, from whose funeral we are just returned. Promise.' I promised. 'Swear.' I swore. 'Finally, promise me that, when you read this second paper which I have put into your hands, whatsoever you may think of it, you will say nothing—publish nothing to the world, until three years shall have passed.' I promised. 'And now farewell for three hours; come to me again about ten o'clock and take a glass of wine in memory of old times.' This he said laughingly; but even then a dark spasm crossed his face. Yet, thinking that this might be the mere working of mental anguish within him, I complied with his desire, and retired. Feeling, however, but little at ease, I devised an excuse for looking in upon him about one hour and a half after I had left him. I knocked gently at his door; there was no answer. I knocked louder; still no answer. I went in. The light of day was gone, and I could see nothing. But I was alarmed by the utter stillness of the room. I listened earnestly, but not a breath could be heard. I rushed back hastily into the hall for a lamp; I returned; I looked in upon this marvel of manly beauty, and the first glance informed me; that he and all his splendid endowments had departed for ever. He had died, probably, soon after I left him, and had dismissed me from some growing instinct which informed him that his last agonies were at hand.

I took up his two testamentary documents; both were addressed in the shape of letters to myself. The first was a rapid, though distinct, appropriation of his enormous property. General rules were laid down upon which the property was to be distributed, but the details were left to my discretion, and to the guidance of circumstances as they should happen to emerge from the various enquiries which it would become necessary to set on foot. This first document I soon laid aside, both because I found that its provisions were dependant for their meaning upon the second, and because to this second document I looked with confidence for a solution of many mysteries—of the profound sadness which had, from the first of my acquaintance with him, possessed a man so gorgeously endowed as the favourite of nature and fortune—of his motives for huddling up, in a clandestine manner, that connexion which formed the glory of his life—and possibly (but then I hesitated) of the late unintelligible murders, which still lay under as profound a cloud as ever. Much of this *would* be unveiled—all might be: and there and then, with the corpse lying beside me of the gifted and mysterious writer, I seated myself, and read the following statement:—

'March 26, 1817.

'My trial is finished;* my conscience, my duty, my honour, are liberated; my "warfare is accomplished."* Margaret, my innocent young wife, I have seen for the last time. Her, the crown that might have been of my earthly felicity—her, the one temptation to put aside the bitter cup which awaited me—her, sole seductress (oh, innocent seductress!) from the stern duties which my fate had imposed upon me—her, even her, I have sacrificed.

'Before I go, partly lest the innocent should be brought into question for acts almost exclusively mine, but still more lest the lesson and the warning which God, by my hand, has written in blood upon your guilty walls, should perish for want of its authentic exposition, hear my last dying avowal, that the murders which have desolated so many families within your walls, and made the household hearth no sanctuary, age no charter of protection, are all due originally to my head, if not always to my hand, as the minister of a dreadful retribution.

'That account of my history, and my prospects, which you received from the Russian diplomatist, amongst some errors of little importance, is essentially correct. My father was not so immediately connected with English blood as is there represented. However, it is true that he claimed descent from an English family of even higher distinction than that which is assigned in the Russian statement. He was proud of this English descent, and the more so, as the war with Revolutionary France brought out more prominently than ever the moral and civil grandeur of England. This pride was generous, but it was imprudent in his situation. His immediate progenitors had been settled in Italy—at Rome first, but latterly at Milan; and his whole property, large and scattered, came, by the progress of the Revolution, to stand under French domination. Many spoliations he suffered; but still he was too rich to be seriously injured. But he foresaw, in the progress of events, still greater perils menacing his most capital resources. Many of the states or princes in Italy were deeply in his debt; and in the great convulsions which threatened his country, he saw that both the contending parties would find a colourable excuse for absolving themselves from engagements which pressed unpleasantly upon their finances. In this embarrassment he formed an intimacy with a French officer of high rank and high principle. My father's friend saw his danger, and advised him to enter the French service. In his younger days, my father had served extensively under many princes, and had found in every other military service a spirit of honour governing the conduct of the officers; here only, and for the first time, he found ruffian manners and universal rapacity. He could not draw his sword in company with such men, nor in such a cause. But at length, under the pressure of necessity, he accepted (or rather bought with an immense bribe) the place of a commissary to the French forces in Italy. With this one resource, eventually he succeeded in making good the whole of his public claims upon the Italian States. These vast sums he remitted, through various channels, to England, where he became a proprietor in the funds* to an immense amount. Incautiously, however, something of this transpired,* and the result was doubly unfortunate; for, whilst his intentions were thus made known as finally pointing to England, which of itself made him an object of hatred and suspicion, it also diminished his means of bribery. These considerations, along with another, made some French officers of high rank and influence the bitter enemies of my father. My mother, whom he had married when holding a brigadier-general's commission in the Austrian service, was, by birth and by religion, a Jewess. She was of exquisite beauty, and had been sought in Morganatic marriage* by an archduke of the Austrian family; but she had relied upon this plea, that hers was the purest and noblest blood amongst all Jewish families; that her family traced themselves, by tradition and a vast series of attestations, under the hands of the Jewish high-priests, to the Maccabees,* and to the royal houses of Judea; and that for her it would be a degradation to accept even of a sovereign prince on the terms of such marriage. This was no vain pretension of ostentatious vanity. It was one which had been admitted as valid for time immemorial in Transylvania and adjacent countries, where my mother's family were rich and honoured, and took their seat amongst the dignitaries of the land. The French officers I have alluded to, without capacity for any thing so dignified as a deep passion, but merely in pursuit of a vagrant fancy that would, on the next day, have given place to another equally fleeting, had dared to insult my mother with proposals the most licentious—proposals as much below her rank and birth, as, at any rate, they would have been below her dignity of mind and her purity. These she had communicated to my father, who bitterly resented the chains of subordination which tied up his hands from avenging his injuries. Still his eye told a tale which his superiors could brook as little as they could the disdainful neglect of his wife. More than one had been concerned in the injuries to my father and mother; more than one were interested in obtaining revenge. Things could be done in German towns, and by favour of old German laws or usages, which even in France could not have been tolerated. This my father's enemies well knew, but this my father also knew; and he endeavoured to lay down his office of commissary.

That, however, was a favour which he could not obtain. He was compelled to serve on the German campaign then commencing, and on the subsequent one of Friedland and Eylau.* Here he was caught in some one of the snares laid for him; first trepanned* into an act which violated some rule of the service; and then provoked into a breach of discipline against the general officer who had thus trepanned him. Now was the long-sought opportunity gained, and in that very quarter of Germany best fitted for improving it. My father was thrown into prison in your city, subjected to the atrocious oppression of your jailer, and the more detestable oppression of your local laws. The charges against him were thought even to affect his life, and he was humbled into suing for permission to send for his wife and children. Already, to his proud spirit, it was punishment enough that he should be reduced to sue for favour to one of his bitterest foes. But it was no part of their plan to refuse *that*. By way of expediting my mother's arrival, a military courier, with every facility for the journey, was forwarded to her without delay. My mother, her two daughters, and myself, were then residing in Venice. I had, through the aid of my father's connexions in Austria, been appointed in the imperial service, and held a high commission for my age. But on my father's marching northwards with the French army, I had been recalled as an indispensable support to my mother. Not that my years could have made me such, for I had barely accomplished my twelfth year; but my premature growth, and my military station, had given me considerable knowledge of the world and presence of mind.

'Our journey I pass over; but as I approach your city, that sepulchre of honour and happiness to my poor family, my heart beats with frantic emotions. Never do I see that venerable dome of your minster from the forest, but I curse its form which reminds me of what we then surveyed for many a mile as we traversed the forest. For leagues before we approached the city, this object lay before us in relief upon the frosty blue sky; and still it seemed never to increase. Such was the complaint of my little sister Mariamne. Most innocent child! would that it never had increased for thy eyes, but remained for ever at a distance! That same hour began the series of monstrous indignities which terminated the career of my ill-fated family. As we drew up to the city gates, the officer who inspected the passports, finding my mother and sisters described as Jewesses, which in my mother's ears (reared in a region where Jews are not dishonoured) always sounded a title of distinction, summoned a subordinate agent, who in coarse terms demanded his toll. We presumed this to be a road-tax for the carriage and horses, but we were quickly undeceived; a small sum was demanded for each of my sisters and my mother, as for so many head of cattle. I, fancying some mistake, spoke to the man temperately, and, to do him justice, he did not seem desirous of insulting us; but he produced a printed board, on which, along with the vilest animals, Jews and Jewesses were rated at so much a head. Whilst we were debating the point, the officers of the gate wore a sneering smile upon their faces; the postilions were laughing together; and this, too, in the presence of three creatures whose exquisite beauty in different styles, agreeably to their different ages, would have caused noblemen to have fallen down and worshipped. My mother, who had never yet met with any flagrant insult on account of her national distinctions, was too much shocked to be capable of speaking. I whispered to her a few words, recalling her to her native dignity of mind, paid the money, and we drove to the prison. But the hour was past at which we could be admitted, and, as Jewesses, my mother and sisters could not be allowed to stay in the city; they were to go into the Jewish quarter, a part of the suburb set apart for Jews, in which it was scarcely possible to obtain a lodging tolerably clean. My father, on the next day, we found, to our horror, at the point of death. To my mother he did not tell the worst of what he had endured. To me he told, that, driven to madness by the insults offered to him, he had upbraided the court-martial with their corrupt propensities, and had even mentioned that overtures had been made to him for quashing the proceedings in return for a sum of two millions of francs; and that his sole reason for not entertaining the proposal was his distrust of those who made it. "They would have taken my money," said he, "and then found a pretext for putting me to death—that I might tell no secrets." This was too near the truth to be tolerated; in concert with the local authorities, the military enemies of my father conspired against him; witnesses were suborned; and, finally, under some antiquated law of the place, he was subjected, in secret, to a mode of torture which still lingers in the east of Europe.

'He sank under the torture and the degradation. I, too, thoughtlessly—but by a natural movement of filial indignation—suffered

the truth to escape me in conversing with my mother. And she ——;
but I will preserve the regular succession of things. My father died:
but he had taken such measures, in concert with me, that his enemies
should never benefit by his property. Mean-time my mother and
sisters had closed my father's eyes; had attended his remains to the
grave; and in every act connected with this last sad rite, had met with
insults and degradations too mighty for human patience. My
mother, now become incapable of self-command, in the fury of her
righteous grief, publicly and in court denounced the conduct of the
magistracy; taxed some of them with the vilest proposals to herself;
taxed them as a body with having used instruments of torture upon
my father; and finally, accused them of collusion with the French
military oppressors of the district. This last was a charge under
which they quailed, for by that time the French had made themselves odious to all who retained a spark of patriotic feeling. My
heart sank within me when I looked up at the bench, this tribunal of
tyrants, all purple or livid with rage; when I looked at them alternately and at my noble mother with her weeping daughters—these
so powerless, those so basely vindictive, and locally so omnipotent.
Willingly I would have sacrificed all my wealth for a simple permission to quit this infernal city with my poor female relations, safe and
undishonoured. But far other were the intentions of that incensed
magistracy. My mother was arrested, charged with some offence
equal to petty treason, or *scandalum magnatum*,* or the sowing of
sedition: and though what she said was true, where, alas! was she to
look for evidence? Here was seen the want of gentlemen. Gentlemen,
had they been even equally tyrannical, would have recoiled with
shame from taking vengeance on a woman. And what a vengeance!
Oh, heavenly powers! that I should live to mention such a thing!
Man that is born of woman, to inflict upon woman personal scour-
ging on the bare back, and through the streets at noonday! Even for
Christian women, the punishment was severe which the laws
assigned to the offence in question. But for Jewesses, by one of the
ancient laws against that persecuted people, far heavier and more
degrading punishments were annexed to almost every offence. What
else could be looked for in a city which welcomed its Jewish guests by
valuing them at its gates as brute beasts? Sentence was passed, and
the punishment was to be inflicted on two separate days, with an
interval between each; doubtless to prolong the tortures of mind, but

under a vile pretence of alleviating the physical torture. Three days after would come the first day of punishment. My mother spent the time in reading her native Scriptures; she spent it in prayer and in musing; whilst her daughters clung and wept around her day and night,—grovelling on the ground at the feet of any people in authority that entered their mother's cell. That same interval—how was it passed by me? Now mark, my friend. Every man in office, or that could be presumed to bear the slightest influence, every wife, mother, sister, daughter of such men, I besieged morning, noon, and night. I wearied them with my supplications. I humbled myself to the dust; I, the haughtiest of God's creatures, knelt and prayed to them for the sake of my mother. I besought them that I might undergo the punishment ten times over in her stead. And once or twice I *did* obtain the encouragement of a few natural tears—given more, however, as I was told, to my piety than to my mother's deserts. But rarely was I heard out with patience; and from some houses repelled with personal indignities. The day came: I saw my mother half undressed by the base officials: I heard the prison gates expand; I heard the trumpets of the magistracy sound. She had warned me what to do; I had warned myself. Would I sacrifice a retribution sacred and comprehensive, for the momentary triumph over an individual? If not, let me forbear to look out of doors: for I felt that in the self-same moment in which I saw the dog of an executioner raise his accursed hand against my mother, swifter than the lightning would my dagger search his heart. When I heard the roar of the cruel mob, I paused; endured; forbore. I stole out by by-lanes of the city from my poor exhausted sisters, whom I left sleeping in each other's innocent arms, into the forest. There I listened to the shouting populace: there even I fancied that I could trace my poor mother's route by the course of the triumphant cries. There, even then, even then, I made—oh! silent forest, thou heardst me when I made—a vow that I have kept too faithfully. Mother, thou art avenged: sleep, daughter of Jerusalem!* For at length the oppressor sleeps with thee. And thy poor son has paid, in discharge of his vow, the forfeit of his own happiness, of a Paradise opening upon earth, of a heart as innocent as thine, and a face as fair.

'I returned, and found my mother returned: she slept by starts, but she was feverish and agitated; and when she awoke and first saw me, she blushed as if I could think that real degradation had settled upon her. Then it was that I told her of my vow. Her eyes were lambent with fierce light for a moment; but, when I went on more eagerly to speak of my hopes and projects, she called me to her, kissed me, and whispered—"Oh, not so, my son! think not of me: think not of vengeance, think only of poor Berenice and Mariamne."

Ay, that thought *was* startling. Yet this magnanimous and forbearing mother, as I knew by the report of our one faithful female servant, had, in the morning, during her bitter trial, behaved as might have become a daughter of Judas Maccabaeus: she had looked serenely upon the vile mob, and awed even them by her serenity; she had disdained to utter a shriek when the cruel lash fell upon her fair skin. There is a point that makes the triumph over natural feelings of pain easy or not easy—the degree in which we count upon the sympathy of the by-standers. My mother had it not in the beginning; but long before the end her celestial beauty, the divinity of injured innocence, the pleading of common womanhood in the minds of the lowest class, and the reaction of manly feeling in the men, had worked a great change in the mob. Some began now to threaten those who had been active in insulting her: the silence of awe and respect succeeded to noise and uproar; and feelings which they scarcely understood mastered the rude rabble as they witnessed more and more the patient fortitude of the sufferer. Menaces began to rise towards the executioner. Things wore such an aspect that the magistrates put a sudden end to the scene.

'That day we received permission to go home to our poor house in the Jewish quarter. I know not whether you are learned enough in Jewish usages to be aware, that in every Jewish house, where old traditions are kept up, there is one room consecrated to confusion; a room always locked up and sequestered from vulgar use, except on occasions of memorable affliction, where every thing is purposely in disorder—broken—shattered—mutilated,—to typify, by symbols appalling to the eye, that desolation which has so long trampled on Jerusalem, and the ravages of the boar within the vineyards of Judea. My mother, as a Hebrew princess, maintained all traditional customs. Even in this wretched suburb she had her "chamber of desolation."* There it was that I and my sisters heard her last words. The rest of her sentence was to be carried into effect within a week. She, mean-time, had disdained to utter any word of fear; but that energy of self-control had made the suffering but the more bitter. Fever and dreadful agitation had succeeded. Her dreams showed sufficiently to us, who watched her couch, that terror for the future mingled with the sense of degradation for the past. Nature asserted her rights. But the more she shrank from the suffering, the more did she proclaim how severe it had been, and consequently how noble the selfconquest. Yet, as her weakness increased, so did her terror; until I besought her to take comfort, assuring her that, in case any attempt should be made to force her out again to public exposure, I would kill the man who came to execute the order—that we would all die together—and there would be a common end to her injuries and her fears. She was reassured by what I told her of my belief that no future attempt would be made upon her. She slept more tranquilly; but her fever increased; and slowly she slept away into the everlasting sleep which knows of no to-morrow.

'Here came a crisis in my fate. Should I stay and attempt to protect my sisters? But, alas! what power had I to do so amongst our enemies? Rachael and I consulted; and many a scheme we planned. Even whilst we consulted, and the very night after my mother had been committed to the Jewish burying-ground, came an officer, bearing an order for me to repair to Vienna. Some officer in the French army having watched the transaction respecting my parents, was filled with shame and grief. He wrote a statement of the whole to an Austrian officer of rank, my father's friend, who obtained from the Emperor an order, claiming me as a page of his own, and an officer in the household service. Oh, Heavens! what a neglect that it did not include my sisters! However, the next best thing was that I should use my influence at the imperial court to get them passed to Vienna. This I did, to the utmost of my power. But seven months elapsed before I saw the Emperor. If my applications ever met his eye he might readily suppose that your city, my friend, was as safe a place as another for my sisters. Nor did I myself know all its dangers. At length, with the Emperor's leave of absence, I returned. And what did I find? Eight months had passed, and the faithful Rachael had died. The poor sisters, clinging together, but now utterly bereft of friends, knew not which way to turn. In this abandonment they fell into the insidious hands of the ruffian jailer. My eldest sister, Berenice, the stateliest and noblest of beauties, had attracted this ruffian's admiration whilst she was in the prison with her mother. And when I returned to your city, armed with the imperial passports for all,

I found that Berenice had died in the villain's custody: nor could I obtain any thing beyond a legal certificate of her death. And finally, the blooming laughing Mariamne, she also had died—and of affliction for the loss of her sister. You, my friend, had been absent upon your travels during the calamitous history I have recited. You had seen neither my father nor my mother. But you came in time to take under your protection, from the abhorred wretch the jailer, my little broken-hearted Mariamne. And when sometimes you fancied that you had seen me under other circumstances, in her it was, my dear friend, and in her features that you saw mine.

'Now was the world a desert to me. I cared little, in the way of love, which way I turned. But in the way of hatred I cared every thing. I transferred myself to the Russian service, with the view of gaining some appointment on the Polish frontier which might put it in my power to execute my vow of destroying all the magistrates of your city. War, however, raged, and carried me into far other regions. It ceased, and there was little prospect that another generation would see it relighted; for the disturber of peace was a prisoner for ever, and all nations were exhausted. Now, then, it became necessary that I should adopt some new mode for executing my vengeance; and the more so, because annually some were dying of those whom it was my mission to punish. A voice ascended to me, day and night, from the graves of my father and mother, calling for vengeance before it should be too late. I took my measures thus:—Many Jews were present at Waterloo. From amongst these, all irritated against Napoleon for the expectations he had raised, only to disappoint, by his great assembly of Jews at Paris,* I selected eight, whom I knew familiarly as men hardened by military experience against the movements of pity. With these as my beagles, I hunted for some time in your forest before opening my regular campaign; and I am surprised that you did not hear of the death which met the executioner, him I mean who dared to lift his hand against my mother. This man I met by accident in the forest; and I slew him. I talked with the wretch as a stranger at first upon the memorable case of the Jewish lady. Had he relented, had he expressed compunction, *I* might have relented. But far otherwise: the dog, not dreaming to whom he spoke, exulted; he —— But why repeat the villain's words? I cut him to pieces. Next I did this: my agents I caused to matriculate separately at the college. They assumed the college dress. And now mark the solution of that mystery which caused such perplexity. Simply as students we all had an unsuspected admission at any house. Just then there was a common practice, as you will remember, amongst the younger students, of going out a-masking,—that is, of entering houses in the academic dress and with the face masked. This practice subsisted even during the most intense alarm from the murderers; for the dress of the students was supposed to bring protection along with it. But even after suspicion had connected itself with this dress, it was sufficient that I should appear unmasked at the head of the maskers, to insure them a friendly reception. Hence the facility with which death was inflicted, and that unaccountable absence of any motion towards an alarm. I took hold of my victim, and he looked at me with smiling security. Our weapons were hid under our academic robes; and even when we drew them out, and at the moment of applying them to the throat, they still supposed our gestures to be part of the pantomime we were performing. Did I relish this abuse of personal confidence in myself? No—I loathed it, and I grieved for its necessity; but my mother, a phantom not seen with bodily eyes, but ever present to my mind, continually ascended before me; and still I shouted aloud to my astounded victim, "This comes from the Jewess! Hound of hounds! Do you remember the Jewess whom you dishonoured, and the oaths which you broke in order that you might dishonour her, and the righteous law which you violated, and the cry of anguish from her son, which you scoffed at?" Who I was, what I avenged, and whom, I made every man aware, and every woman, before I punished them. The details of the cases I need not repeat. One or two I was obliged, at the beginning, to commit to my Jews. The suspicion was thus, from the first, turned aside by the notoriety of my presence elsewhere; but I took care that none suffered who had not either been upon the guilty list of magistrates who condemned the mother, or of those who turned away with mockery from the supplication of the son.

'It pleased God, however, to place a mighty temptation in my path, which might have persuaded me to forego all thoughts of vengeance, to forget my vow, to forget the voices which invoked me from the grave. This was Margaret Liebenheim. Ah! how terrific appeared my duty of bloody retribution, after her angel's face and angel's voice had calmed me. With respect to her grandfather, strange it is to mention, that never did my innocent wife appear so lovely as precisely in the relation of grand-daughter. So beautiful was her goodness to the old man, and so divine was the childlike innocence on her part, contrasted with the guilty recollections associated with him—for he was amongst the guiltiest towards my mother—still I delayed *his* punishment to the last; and, for his child's sake, I would have pardoned him—nay, I had resolved to do so, when a fierce Jew, who had a deep malignity towards this man, swore that he would accomplish *his* vengeance at all events, and perhaps might be obliged to include Margaret in the ruin, unless I adhered to the original scheme. Then I yielded; for circumstances armed this man with momentary power. But the night fixed on was one in which I had reason to know that my wife would be absent; for so I had myself arranged with her, and the unhappy counter-arrangement I do not yet understand. Let me add, that the sole purpose of my clandestine marriage was to sting her grandfather's mind with the belief that *his* family had been dishonoured, even as he had dishonoured mine. He learned, as I took care that he should, that his grand-daughter carried about with her the promises of a mother, and did not know that she had the sanction of a wife. This discovery made him, in one day, become eager for the marriage he had previously opposed; and this discovery also embittered the misery of his death. At that moment I attempted to think only of my mother's wrongs; but in spite of all I could do, this old man appeared to me in the light of Margaret's grandfather; and, had I been left to myself, he would have been saved. As it was, never was horror equal to mine when I met her flying to his succour. I had relied upon her absence; and the misery of that moment, when her eye fell upon me in the very act of seizing her grandfather, far transcended all else that I have suffered in these terrific scenes. She fainted in my arms, and I and another carried her up-stairs and procured water; mean-time her grandfather had been murdered even whilst Margaret fainted. I had, however, under the fear of discovery, though never anticipating a rencontre with herself, forestalled the explanation requisite in such a case, to make my conduct intelligible. I had told her, under feigned names, the story of my mother and my sisters. She knew their wrongs; she had heard me contend for the right of vengeance. Consequently, in our parting interview, one word only was required to place myself in a new position to her thoughts. I needed only to say I was that son; that unhappy mother, so miserably degraded and outraged, was mine.

'As to the jailer, he was met by a party of us. Not suspecting that any of us could be connected with the family, he was led to talk of the most hideous details with regard to my poor Berenice. The child had not, as had been insinuated, aided her own degradation, but had nobly sustained the dignity of her sex and her family. Such advantages as the monster pretended to have gained over her—sick, desolate, and latterly delirious—were, by his own confession, not obtained without violence. This was too much. Forty thousand lives,* had he possessed them, could not have gratified my thirst for revenge. Yet, had he but showed courage, he should have died the death of a soldier. But the wretch showed cowardice the most abject, and —— but you know his fate.

'Now, then, all is finished, and human nature is avenged. Yet, if you complain of the bloodshed and the terror, think of the wrongs which created my rights; think of the sacrifice by which I gave a tenfold strength to those rights; think of the necessity for a dreadful concussion, and shock to society, in order to carry my lesson into the councils of princes.

'This will now have been effected. And ye, victims of dishonour, will be glorified in your deaths; ye will not have suffered in vain, nor died without a monument. Sleep, therefore, sister Berenice,—sleep, gentle Mariamne, in peace. And thou, noble mother, let the outrages sown in thy dishonour rise again and blossom in wide harvests of honour for the women of thy afflicted race. Sleep, daughters of Jerusalem, in the sanctity of your sufferings. And thou, if it be possible, even more beloved daughter of a Christian fold, whose company was too soon denied to him in life, open thy grave to receive *him*, who, in the hour of death, wishes to remember no title which he wore on earth but that of thy chosen and adoring lover,

'MAXIMILIAN.'

SECOND PAPER ON MURDER CONSIDERED AS ONE OF THE FINE ARTS

DOCTOR NORTH,*

YOU are a liberal man: liberal in the true classical sense, not in the slang sense of modern politicians and education-mongers. Being so, I am sure that you will sympathize with my case. I am an ill-used man, Dr North—particularly ill used; and, with your permission, I will briefly explain how. A black scene of calumny will be laid open; but you, Doctor, will make all things square again. One frown from you, directed to the proper quarter, or a warning shake of the crutch,* will set me right in public opinion, which at present, I am sorry to say, is rather hostile to me and mine—all owing to the wicked arts of slanderers. But you shall hear.

A good many years ago you may remember that I came forward in the character of a *dilettante* in murder.* Perhaps *dilettante* may be too strong a word. *Connoisseur* is better suited to the scruples and infirmity of public taste. I suppose there is no harm in *that* at least. A man is not bound to put his eyes, ears, and understanding into his breeches pocket when he meets with a murder. If he is not in a downright comatose state, I suppose he must see that one murder is better or worse than another in point of good taste. Murders have their little differences and shades of merit as well as statues, pictures, oratorios, cameos, intaglios, or what not. You may be angry with the man for talking too much, or too publicly, (as to the too much, that I deny—a man can never cultivate his taste too highly;) but you must allow him to think, at any rate; and you, Doctor—you think, I am sure, both deeply and correctly on the subject. Well, would you believe it? all my neighbours came to hear of that little aesthetic essay which you had published; and, unfortunately, hearing at the very same time of a Club that I was connected with, and a Dinner at which I presided—both tending to the same little object as the essay, viz., the diffusion of a just taste among her Majesty's subjects, they got up the most barbarous calumnies against me. In particular, they said that I, or that the Club, which comes to the same thing, had offered bounties on well-conducted homicides—with a scale of drawbacks, in case of any one defect or flaw, according to a table issued to private friends.

Now, Doctor, I'll tell you the whole truth about the Dinner and the Club, and you'll see how malicious the world is. But first let me tell you, confidentially, what my real principles are upon the matters in question.

As to murder, I never committed one in my life. It's a well-known thing amongst all my friends. I can get a paper to certify as much, signed by lots of people. Indeed, if you come to that, I doubt whether many people could produce as strong a certificate. Mine would be as big as a table-cloth. There is indeed one member of the Club, who pretends to say that he caught me once making too free with his throat on a club night, after every body else had retired. But, observe, he shuffles in his story according to his state of civilation.* When not far gone, he contents himself with saying that he caught me ogling his throat; and that I was melancholy for some weeks after, and that my voice sounded in a way expressing, to the nice ear of a connoisseur, *the sense of opportunities lost*—but the Club all know that he's a disappointed man himself, and that he speaks querulously at times about the fatal neglect of a man's coming abroad without his tools. Besides, all this is an affair between two amateurs, and every body makes allowances for little asperities and sorenesses in such a case. 'But,' say you, 'if no murderer, my correspondent may have encouraged, or even have bespoke a murder.' No, upon my honour— nothing of the kind. And that was the very point I wished to argue for your satisfaction. The truth is, I am a very particular man in every thing relating to murder; and perhaps I carry my delicacy too far. The Stagyrite most justly, and possibly with a view to my case, placed virtue in the τὸ μέσον or middle point between two extremes.* A golden mean is certainly what every man should aim at. But it is easier talking than doing: and, my infirmity being notoriously too much milkiness of heart, I find it difficult to maintain that steady equatorial line between the two poles of too much murder on the one hand, and too little on the other. I am too soft—Doctor, too soft; and people get excused through me—nay go through life without an attempt made upon them, that ought not to be excused. I believe if I had the management of things there would hardly be a murder from year's end to year's end. In fact I'm for virtue, and goodness, and all that sort of thing. And two instances I'll give you to what an extremity I carry my virtue. The first may seem a trifle; but not if you knew my nephew, who was certainly born to be hanged,* and would have been so long ago, but for my restraining voice. He is horribly ambitious, and thinks himself a man of cultivated taste in most branches of murder, whereas, in fact, he has not one idea on the subject, but such as he has stolen from me. This is so well known, that the Club has twice blackballed him, though every indulgence was shown to him as my relative. People came to me and said—'Now really, President, we would do much to serve a relative of yours. But still, what can be said? You know yourself that he'll disgrace us. If we were to elect him, why, the next thing we should hear of would be some vile butcherly murder, by way of justifying our choice. And what sort of a concern would it be? You know, as well as we do, that it would be a disgraceful affair, more worthy of the shambles than of an artist's *attelier*.* He would fall upon some great big man, some huge farmer returning drunk from a fair. There would be plenty of blood, and *that* he would expect us to take in lieu of taste, finish, scenical grouping. Then, again, how would he tool? Why, most probably with a cleaver and a couple of paving stones: so that the whole *coup d'oeil*.* would remind you rather of some hidious Ogre or Cyclops,* than of the delicate operator of the 19th century.' The picture was drawn with the hand of truth; *that* I could not but allow, and, as to personal feelings in the matter, I dismissed them from the first. The next morning I spoke to my nephew—I was delicately situated, as you see, but I determined that no consideration should induce me to flinch from my duty. 'John,' said I, 'you seem to me to have taken an erroneous view of life and its duties. Pushed on by ambition, you are dreaming rather of what it might be glorious to attempt than what it would be possible for you to accomplish. Believe me, it is not necessary to a man's respectability that he should commit a murder. Many a man has passed through life most respectably, without attempting any species of homicide—good, bad, or indifferent. It is your first duty to ask yourself, *quid valeant humeri, quid ferre recusent*?* We cannot all be brilliant men in this life. And it is for your interest to be contented rather with a humble station well filled, than to shock everybody with failures, the more conspicuous by contrast with the ostentation of their promises.' John made no answer; he looked very sulky at the moment, and I am in high hopes that I have saved a near relation from making a fool of himself by attempting what is as much beyond his capacity as an epic poem. Others, however, tell me that he is meditating a revenge upon me and the whole Club. But let this be as

it may, *liberavi animam meam;** and, as you see, have run some risk
with a wish to diminish the amount of homicide. But the other case
still more forcibly illustrates my virtue. A man came to me as a
candidate for the place of my servant, just then vacant. He had the
reputation of having dabbled a little in our art; some said not without
merit. What startled me, however, was, that he supposed this art to
be part of his regular duties in my service. Now that was a thing I
would not allow; so I said at once, 'Richard, (or James, as the case
might be,) you misunderstand my character. If a man will and must
practise this difficult (and allow me to add, dangerous) branch of
art—if he has an overruling genius for it, why, he might as well
pursue his studies whilst living in my service as in another's. And
also, I may observe, that it can do no harm either to himself or to the
subject on whom he operates, that he should be guided by men of
more taste than himself. Genius may do much, but long study of
the art must always entitle a man to offer advice. So far I will go—
general principles I will suggest. But, as to any particular case, once
for all I will have nothing to do with it. Never tell me of any special
work of art you are meditating—I set my face against it *in toto*.* For if
once a man indulges himself in murder, very soon he comes to think
little of robbing; and from robbing he comes next to drinking and
Sabbath-breaking, and from that to incivility and procrastination.
Once begin upon this downward path, you never know where you
are to stop. Many a man has dated his ruin from some murder or
other that perhaps he thought little of at the time. *Principiis obsta**—
that's my rule.' Such was my speech, and I have always acted up to it;
so if that is not being virtuous, I should be glad to know what is. But
now about the Dinner and the Club. The Club was not particularly
of my creation; it arose pretty much as other similar associations, for
the propagation of truth and the communication of new ideas, rather
from the necessities of things than upon any one man's suggestion.
As to the Dinner, if any man more than another could be held
responsible for that, it was a member known amongst us by the name
of *Toad-in-the-hole*. He was so called from his gloomy misanthrop-
ical disposition, which led him into constant disparagements of all
modern murders as vicious abortions, belonging to no authentic
school of art. The finest performances of our own age he snarled at
cynically; and at length this querulous humour grew upon him so
much, and he became so notorious as a *laudator temporis acti*,* that

few people cared to seek his society. This made him still more fierce and truculent. He went about muttering and growling; wherever you met him he was soliloquizing and saying, 'despicable pretender— without grouping—without two ideas upon handling—without'— and there you lost him. At length existence seemed to be painful to him; he rarely spoke, he seemed conversing with phantoms in the air, his housekeeper informed us that his reading was nearly confined to *God's Revenge upon Murder*, by Reynolds,* and a more ancient book of the same title, noticed by Sir Walter Scott in his *Fortunes of Nigel.** Sometimes, perhaps, he might read in the Newgate Calendar* down to the year 1788, but he never looked into a book more recent. In fact, he had a theory with regard to the French Revolution, as having been the great cause of degeneration in murder. 'Very soon, sir,' he used to say, 'men will have lost the art of killing poultry: the very rudiments of the art will have perished!' In the year 1811 he retired from general society. Toad-in-the-hole was no more seen in any public resort. We missed him from his wonted haunts—nor up the lawn, nor at the wood was he. By the side of the main conduit his listless length at noontide he would stretch, and pore upon the filth that muddled by.* 'Even dogs are not what they were, sir—not what they should be. I remember in my grandfather's time that some dogs had an idea of murder. I have known a mastiff lie in ambush for a rival, sir, and murder him with pleasing circumstances of good taste. Yes, sir, I knew a tom-cat that was an assassin. But now'—and then, the subject growing too painful, he dashed his hand to his forehead, and went off abruptly in a homeward direction towards his favourite conduit, where he was seen by an amateur in such a state that he thought it dangerous to address him. Soon after he shut himself entirely up; it was understood that he had resigned himself to melancholy; and at length the prevailing notion was—that Toad-in-the-hole had hanged himself.

The world was wrong *there*, as it has been on some other questions. Toad-in-the-hole might be sleeping, but dead he was not; and of that we soon had ocular proof. One morning in 1812* an amateur surprised us with the news that he had seen Toad-in-the-hole brushing with hasty steps the dews away to meet the postman by the conduit side.* Even that was something: how much more, to hear that he had shaved his beard—had laid aside his sad-coloured clothes, and was adorned like a bridegroom of ancient days. What could be the meaning of all this? Was Toad-in-the-hole mad? or how? Soon after the secret was explained—in more than a figurative sense 'the murder was out.' For in came the London morning papers, by which it appeared that but three days before a murder, the most superb of the century by many degrees, had occurred in the heart of London. I need hardly say, that this was the great exterminating *chef-d'oeuvre** of Williams at Mr Marr's, No. 29, Ratcliffe Highway. That was the *début* of the artist; at least for anything the public knew. What occurred at Mr Williamson's,* twelve nights afterwards—the second work turned out from the same chisel—some people pronounced even superior. But Toad-in-the-hole always 'reclaimed'*—he was even angry at comparisons. 'This vulgar *gout de comparaison*, as La Bruyère calls it,'* he would often remark, 'will be our ruin; each work has its own separate characteristics—each in and for itself is incomparable. One, perhaps, might suggest the *Iliad*—the other the *Odyssey*:* what do you get by such comparisons? Neither ever was, or will be surpassed; and when you've talked for hours, you must still come back to that.' Vain, however, as all criticism might be, he often said that volumes might be written on each case for itself; and he even proposed to publish in quarto on the subject.

Meantime, how had Toad-in-the-hole happened to hear of this great work of art so early in the morning? He had received an account by express, dispatched by a correspondent in London, who watched the progress of art on *Toady's* behalf, with a general commission to send off a special express, at whatever cost, in the event of any estimable works appearing—how much more upon occasion of a *ne plus ultra** in art! The express arrived in the night time; Toad-in-the-hole was then gone to bed; he had been muttering and grumbling for hours, but of course he was called up. On reading the account, he threw his arms round the express, called him his brother and his preserver; settled a pension upon him for three lives, and expressed his regret at not having it in his power to knight him. We, on our part—we amateurs, I mean—having heard that he was abroad, and therefore had *not* hanged himself, made sure of soon seeing him amongst us. Accordingly he soon arrived, knocked over the porter on his road to the reading-room; he seized every man's hand as he passed him—wrung it almost frantically, and kept ejaculating, 'Why, now, here's something like a murder!—this is the real thing—this is genuine—this is what you can approve, can recommend to a friend:

this—says every man, on reflection—this is the thing that ought to be!' Then, looking at particular friends, he said—'Why, Jack, how are you? Why, Tom, how are you?—bless me, you look ten years younger than when I last saw you.' 'No, sir,' I replied, 'it is you who look ten years younger.' 'Do I?—well, I shouldn't wonder if I did; such works are enough to make us all young.' And in fact the general opinion is, that Toad-in-the-hole would have died but for this regeneration of art, which he called a second age of Leo the Tenth;* and it was our duty, he said solemnly, to commemorate it. At present, and *en attendant**—rather as an occasion for a public participation in public sympathy, than as in itself any commensurate testimony of our interest—he proposed that the Club should meet and dine together. A splendid public Dinner, therefore, was given by the Club; to which all amateurs were invited from a distance of 100 miles.

Of this Dinner there are ample short-hand notes amongst the archives of the Club. But they are not 'extended,' to speak diplomatically; and the reporter is missing—I believe, murdered. Meantime, in years long after that day, and on an occasion perhaps equally interesting, viz., the turning up of Thugs and Thuggism,* another Dinner was given. Of this I myself kept notes, for fear of another accident to the short-hand reporter. And I here subjoin them. Toad-in-the-hole, I must mention, was present at this Dinner. In fact, it was one of its sentimental incidents. Being as old as the valleys at the Dinner of 1812; naturally, he was as old as the hills at the Thug Dinner of 1838. He had taken to wearing his beard again; why, or with what view, it passes my persimmon* to tell you. But so it was. And his appearance was most benign and venerable. Nothing could equal the angelic radiance of his smile as he enquired after the unfortunate reporter, (whom, as a piece of private scandal, I should tell you that he was himself supposed to have murdered, in a rapture of creative art:) the answer was, with roars of laughter, from the under-sheriff of our county—'non est inventus.'* Toad-in-the-hole laughed outrageously at this: in fact, we all thought he was choking; and, at the earnest request of the company, a musical composer furnished a most beautiful glee upon the occasion, which was sung five times after dinner, with universal applause and inextinguishable laughter, the words being these, (and the chorus so contrived, as most beautifully to mimic the peculiar laughter of Toad-in-the-hole:)—

Et interrogatum est à Toad-in-the-hole—Ubi est ille reporter?
Et responsum est cum cachinno—Non est inventus.

CHORUS

Deinde iteratum est ab omnibus, cum cachinnatione undulante—
Non est inventus.*

Toad-in-the-hole, I ought to mention, about nine years before,
when an express from Edinburgh brought him the earliest intelligence of the Burke-and-Hare* revolution in the art, went mad upon
the spot; and, instead of a pension to the express for even one life, or
a knighthood, endeavoured to burke him; in consequence of which
he was put into a strait waistcoat. And that was the reason we had
no dinner then. But now all of us were alive and kicking, strait-
waistcoaters and others; in fact, not one absentee was reported upon
the entire roll. There were also many foreign amateurs present.

Dinner being over, and the cloth drawn, there was a general call
made for the new glee of *Non est inventus*; but, as this would have
interfered with the requisite gravity of the company during the earlier toasts, I overruled the call. After the national toasts had been
given, the first official toast of the day was—*The Old Man of the
Mountains**—drunk in solemn silence.

Toad-in-the-hole returned thanks in a neat speech. He likened
himself to the Old Man of the Mountains, in a few brief allusions,
that made the company absolutely yell with laughter; and he concluded with giving the health of *Mr Von Hammer*,* with many thanks
to him for his learned History of the Old Man and his subjects the
Assassins.

Upon this I rose and said, that doubtless most of the company
were aware of the distinguished place assigned by orientalists to the
very learned Turkish scholar Von Hammer the Austrian; that he had
made the profoundest researches into our art as connected with
those early and eminent artists the Syrian assassins in the period of
the Crusaders; that his work had been for several years deposited, as
a rare treasure of art, in the library of the Club. Even the author's
name, gentlemen, pointed him out as the historian of our art—Von
Hammer—

'Yes, yes,' interrupted Toad-in-the-hole, who never can sit still—
'Yes, yes, Von Hammer—he's the man for a *malleus haereticorum*:*
think rightly of our art, or he's the man to tickle your catastrophes.*

You all know what consideration Williams bestowed on the hammer, or the ship carpenter's mallet,* which is the same thing. Gentlemen, I give you another great hammer—Charles the Hammer, the Marteau, or, in old French, the Martel*—he hammered the Saracens till they were all as dead as door-nails:—he did, believe me.'

'*Charles Martel*, with all the honours.'

But the explosion of Toad-in-the-hole, together with the uproarious cheers for the grandpapa of Charlemagne,* had now made the company unmanageable. The orchestra was again challenged with shouts the stormiest for the new glee. I made again a powerful effort to overrule the challenge. I might as well have talked to the winds. I foresaw a tempestuous evening; and I ordered myself to be strengthened with three waiters on each side; the vice-president with as many. Symptoms of unruly enthusiasm were beginning to show out; and I own that I myself was considerably excited as the orchestra opened with its storm of music, and the impassioned glee began— '*Et interrogatum est à Toad-in-the-hole—Ubi est ille Reporter?*' And the frenzy of the passion became absolutely convulsing, as the full chorus fell in—'*Et iteratum est ab omnibus—Non est inventus.*'

By this time I saw how things were going: wine and music were making most of the amateurs wild. Particularly Toad-in-the-hole, though considerably above a hundred years old, was getting as vicious as a young leopard. It was a fixed impression with the company that he had murdered the reporter in the year 1812; since which time (viz. twenty-six years) 'ille reporter' had been constantly reported 'non est inventus.' Consequently, the glee about himself, which of itself was most tumultuous and jubilant, carried him off his feet. Like the famous choral songs amongst the citizens of Abdera,* nobody could hear it without a contagious desire for falling back into the agitating music of 'Et interrogatum est à Toad-in-the-hole,' &c. I enjoined vigilance upon my assessors, and the business of the evening proceeded.

The next toast was—*The Jewish Sicarii.**

Upon which I made the following explanation to the company:— 'Gentlemen, I am sure it will interest you all to hear that the assassins, ancient as they were, had a race of predecessors in the very same country. All over Syria, but particularly in Palestine, during the early years of the Emperor Nero,* there was a band of murderers, who prosecuted their studies in a very novel manner. They did not practise in the night-time, or in lonely places; but justly considering that great crowds are in themselves a sort of darkness by means of the dense pressure and the impossibility of finding out who it was that gave the blow, they mingled with mobs everywhere; particularly at the great paschal feast in Jerusalem; where they actually had the audacity, as Josephus* assures us, to press into the temple,—and whom should they choose for operating upon but Jonathan himself, the Pontifex Maximus?* They murdered him, gentlemen, as beautifully as if they had had him alone on a moonless night in a dark lane. And when it was asked, who was the murderer, and where he was'—

'Why, then, it was answered,' interrupted Toad-in-the-hole, '*non est inventus*.' And then, in spite of all I could do or say, the orchestra opened, and the whole company began—'Et interrogatum est à Toad-in-the-hole—Ubi est ille Sicarius? Et responsum est ab omnibus—*Non est inventus*.'*

When the tempestuous chorus had subsided, I began again:— 'Gentlemen, you will find a very circumstantial account of the Sicarii in at least three different parts of Josephus; once in Book XX. sect. v. c. 8, of his *Antiquities*;* once in Book I. of his *Wars*:* but in sect. 10 of the chapter first cited you will find a particular description of their tooling. This is what he says—"They tooled with small scymetars not much different from the Persian *acinacae*, but more curved, and for all the world most like the Roman sickles or *sicae*."* It is perfectly magnificent, gentlemen, to hear the sequel of their history. Perhaps the only case on record where a regular army of murderers was assembled, a *justus exercitus*,* was in the case of these *Sicarii*. They mustered in such strength in the wilderness, that Festus* himself was obliged to march against them with the Roman legionary force.'

Upon which Toad-in-the-hole, that cursed interrupter, broke out a-singing—'Et interrogatum est à Toad-in-the-hole—Ubi est ille exercitus? Et responsum est ab omnibus—Non est inventus.'*

'No, no, Toad—you are wrong for once: that army *was* found, and was all cut to pieces in the desert. Heavens, gentlemen, what a sublime picture! The Roman legions—the wilderness—Jerusalem in the distance—an army of murderers in the foreground!'

Mr R., a member, now gave the next toast.—'To the further improvement of Tooling, and thanks to the Committee for their services.'

Mr L., on behalf of the Committee who had reported on that

subject, returned thanks. He made an interesting extract from the Report, by which it appeared how very much stress had been laid formerly on the mode of Tooling by the Fathers, both Greek and Latin. In confirmation of this pleasing fact, he made a very striking statement in reference to the earliest work of antediluvian art. Father Mersenne, that learned Roman Catholic, in page one thousand four hundred and thirty-one[1] of his operose Commentary on Genesis,* mentions, on the authority of several Rabbis, that the quarrel of Cain with Abel was about a young woman; that, by various accounts, Cain had tooled with his teeth, (Abelem fuisse *morsibus* dilaceratum à Cain;*) by many others, with the jaw-bone of an ass; which is the tooling adopted by most painters. But it is pleasing to the mind of sensibility to know that, as science expanded, sounder views were adopted. One author contends for a pitchfork, St Chrysostom* for a sword, Irenaeus* for a scythe, and Prudentius* for a hedging-bill. This last writer delivers his opinion thus:—

> Frater, probatae sanctitatis aemulus,
> Germana curvo colla frangit sarculo:

i.e. his brother, jealous of his attested sanctity, fractures his brotherly throat with a curved hedging-bill.* 'All which is respectfully submitted by your Committee, not so much as decisive of the question, (for it is not,) but in order to impress upon the youthful mind the importance which has ever been attached to the quality of the tooling by such men as Chrysostom and Irenaeus.'

'Dang Irenaeus!' said Toad-in-the-hole, who now rose impatiently to give the next toast:—'Our Irish friends—and a speedy revolution in their mode of Tooling, as well as every thing else connected with the art!'

'Gentlemen, I'll tell you the plain truth. Every day of the year we take up a paper, we read the opening of a murder. We say, this is good—this is charming—this is excellent! But, behold you! scarcely have we read a little farther before the word Tipperary or Ballina-something betrays the Irish manufacture. Instantly we loathe it: we call to the waiter; we say, "Waiter, take away this paper; send it out of the house; it is absolutely offensive to all just taste." I appeal to every man whether, on finding a murder (otherwise perhaps promising

---

[1] 'Page one thousand four hundred and thirty-one'—*literally*, good reader, and no joke at all.

enough) to be Irish, he does not feel himself as much insulted as when Madeira being ordered he finds it to be Cape;* or when, taking up what he believes to be a mushroom, it turns out what children call a toadstool. Tithes, politics, or something wrong in principle, vitiate every Irish murder. Gentlemen, this must be reformed, or Ireland will not be a land to live in; at least, if we do live there, we must import all our murders, that's clear.' Toad-in-the-hole sat down growling with suppressed wrath, and the universal 'Hear, hear!' sufficiently showed that he spoke the general feeling.

The next toast was—'The sublime epoch of Burkism and Harism!'

This was drunk with enthusiasm; and one of the members, who spoke to the question, made a very curious communication to the company:—'Gentlemen, we fancy Burkism to be a pure invention of our own times: and in fact no Pancirollus has ever enumerated this branch of art when writing *de rebus deperditis*.* Still I have ascertained that the essential principle of the art *was* known to the ancients, although, like the art of painting upon glass, of making the myrrhine cups, &c., it was lost in the dark ages for want of encouragement. In the famous collection of Greek epigrams made by Planudes* is one upon a very charming little case of Burkism: it is a perfect little gem of art. The epigram itself I cannot lay my hand upon at this moment:* but the following is an abstract of it by Salmasius,* as I find it in his notes on Vopiscus:* "Est et elegans epigramma Lucilii, (well he might call it "elegans!") ubi medicus et pollinctor de compacto sic egerunt, ut medicus aegros omnes curae suae commissos occideret"*—this was the basis of the contract, you see, that on the one part the doctor for himself and his assigns doth undertake and contract duly and truly to murder all the patients committed to his charge: but why? There lies the beauty of the case—"Et ut pollinctori amico suo traderet pollingendos."* The *pollinctor*, you are aware, was a person whose business it was to dress and prepare dead bodies for burial. The original ground of the transaction appears to have been sentimental: "he was my friend," says the murderous doctor—"he was dear to me," in speaking of the pollinctor. But the law, gentlemen, is stern and harsh: the law will not hear of these tender motives: to sustain a contract of this nature in law, it is essential that a "consideration" should be given. Now, what *was* the consideration? For thus far all is on the side of the pollinctor: he will be well paid for his services; but meantime, the generous, the noble-minded doctor, gets nothing. What *was* the little consideration, again, I ask, which the law would insist on the doctor's taking? You shall hear: "Et ut pollinctor vicissim τελαμῶνας quos furabatur de pollinctione mortuorum medico mitteret doni ad alliganda vulnera eorum quos curabat."* Now, the case is clear: the whole went on a principle of reciprocity which would have kept up the trade for ever. The doctor was also a surgeon: he could not murder *all* his patients: some of the surgical patients must be retained intact; *re infectâ.** For these he wanted linen bandages. But unhappily the Romans wore woollen, on which account they bathed so often. Meantime, there *was* linen to be had in Rome: but it was monstrously dear: and the τελαμῶνες or linen swathing bandages in which superstition obliged them to bind up corpses, would answer capitally for the surgeon. The doctor, therefore, contracts to furnish his friend with a constant succession of corpses, provided, and be it understood always, that his said friend in return should supply him with one-half of the articles he would receive from the friends of the parties murdered or to be murdered. The doctor invariably recommended his invaluable friend the pollinctor, (whom let us call the undertaker;) the undertaker, with equal regard to the sacred rights of friendship, uniformly recommended the doctor. Like Pylades and Orestes,* they were models of a perfect friendship: in their lives they were lovely; and on the gallows, it is to be hoped, they were not divided.

'Gentlemen, it makes me laugh horribly when I think of those two friends drawing and redrawing on each other: "Pollinctor in account with Doctor, debtor by sixteen corpses; creditor by forty-five bandages, two of which damaged." Their names unfortunately are lost; but I conceive they must have been Quintus Burkius and Publius Harius. By the way, gentlemen, has anybody heard lately of Hare? I understand he is comfortably settled in Ireland, considerably to the west, and does a little business now and then; but, as he observes with a sigh, only as a retailer—nothing like the fine thriving wholesale concern so carelessly blown up at Edinburgh. "You see what comes of neglecting business,"—is the chief moral, the ἐπιμύθιον, as Aesop* would say, which he draws from his past experience.'

At length came the toast of the day—*Thugdom in all its branches*.

The speeches *attempted* at this crisis of the Dinner were past all counting. But the applause was so furious, the music so stormy, and the crashing of glasses so incessant, from the general resolution never again to drink an inferior toast from the same glass, that my power is not equal to the task of reporting. Besides which, Toad-in-the-hole now became quite ungovernable. He kept firing pistols in every direction; sent his servant for a blunderbuss, and talked of loading with ball-cartridge. We conceived that his former madness had returned at the mention of Burke and Hare; or, that being again weary of life, he had resolved to go off in a general massacre. This we could not think of allowing: it became indispensable, therefore, to kick him out, which we did with universal consent, the whole company lending their toes *uno pede,** as I may say, though pitying his grey hairs and his angelic smile. During the operation the orchestra poured in their old chorus. The universal company sang, and (what surprised us most of all) Toad-in-the-hole joined us furiously in singing—

Et interrogatum est ab omnibus—Ubi est ille Toad-in-the-hole?
Et responsum est ab omnibus—Non est inventus.

POSTSCRIPT [TO ON MURDER CONSIDERED AS ONE OF THE FINE ARTS]

IT IS impossible to conciliate readers of so saturnine and gloomy a class, that they cannot enter with genial sympathy into any gaiety whatever, but, least of all, when the gaiety trespasses a little into the province of the extravagant. In such a case, not to sympathise is not to understand; and the playfulness, which is not relished, becomes flat and insipid, or absolutely without meaning. Fortunately, after all such churls have withdrawn from my audience in high displeasure, there remains a large majority who are loud in acknowledging the amusement which they have derived from this little paper; at the same time proving the sincerity of their praise by one hesitating expression of censure. Repeatedly they have suggested to me, that perhaps the extravagance, though clearly intentional, and forming one element in the general gaiety of the conception, went too far. I am not myself of that opinion; and I beg to remind these friendly censors, that it is amongst the direct purposes and efforts of this *bagatelle** to graze the brink of horror, and of all that would in actual realisation be most repulsive. The very excess of the extravagance, in fact, by suggesting to the reader continually the mere aeriality of the entire speculation, furnishes the surest means of disenchanting him from the horror which might else gather upon his feelings. Let me remind such objectors, once for all, of Dean Swift's proposal for turning to account the supernumerary infants of the three kingdoms, which, in those days, both at Dublin and at London, were provided for in foundling hospitals, by cooking and eating them.* This was an extravaganza, though really bolder and more coarsely practical than mine, which did not provoke any reproaches even to a dignitary of the supreme Irish church; its own monstrosity was its excuse; mere extravagance was felt to license and accredit the little *jeu d'esprit,** precisely as the blank impossibilities of Lilliput, of Laputa, of the Yahoos,* &c., had licensed those. If, therefore, any man thinks it worth his while to tilt against so mere a foam-bubble of gaiety as this lecture on the aesthetics of murder, I shelter myself for the moment under the Telamonian shield* of the Dean. But, in reality, which (to say the truth) formed one motive for detaining the reader by this

Postscript, my own little paper may plead a privileged excuse for its extravagance, such as is altogether wanting to the Dean's. Nobody can pretend, for a moment, on behalf of the Dean, that there is any ordinary and natural tendency in human thoughts, which could ever turn to infants as articles of diet; under any conceivable circumstances, this would be felt as the most aggravated form of cannibalism—cannibalism applying itself to the most defenceless part of the species. But, on the other hand, the tendency to a critical or aesthetic valuation of fires and murders is universal. If you are summoned to the spectacle of a great fire,* undoubtedly the first impulse is—to assist in putting it out. But that field of exertion is very limited, and is soon filled by regular professional people, trained and equipped for the service. In the case of a fire which is operating upon *private* property, pity for a neighbour's calamity checks us at first in treating the affair as a scenic spectacle. But perhaps the fire may be confined to public buildings. And in any case, after we have paid our tribute of regret to the affair, considered as a calamity, inevitably, and without restraint, we go on to consider it as a stage spectacle. Exclamations of—How grand! how magnificent! arise in a sort of rapture from the crowd. For instance, when Drury Lane* was burned down in the first decennium of this century, the falling in of the roof was signalised by a mimic suicide of the protecting Apollo* that surmounted and crested the centre of this roof. The god was stationary with his lyre, and seemed looking down upon the fiery ruins that were so rapidly approaching him. Suddenly the supporting timbers below him gave way; a convulsive heave of the billowing flames seemed for a moment to raise the statue; and then, as if on some impulse of despair, the presiding deity appeared not to fall, but to throw himself into the fiery deluge, for he went down head foremost; and in all respects, the descent had the air of a voluntary act. What followed? From every one of the bridges over the river, and from other open areas which commanded the spectacle, there arose a sustained uproar of admiration and sympathy. Some few years before this event, a prodigious fire occurred at Liverpool; the *Goree*,* a vast pile of warehouses close to one of the docks, was burned to the ground. The huge edifice, eight or nine storeys high, and laden with most combustible goods, many thousand bales of cotton, wheat and oats in thousands of quarters, tar, turpentine, rum, gunpowder, &c., continued through many hours of darkness to feed this tremendous fire. To aggravate the calamity, it blew a regular gale of wind; luckily for the shipping, it blew inland, that is, to the east; and all the way down to Warrington, eighteen miles distant to the eastward, the whole air was illuminated by flakes of cotton, often saturated with rum, and by what seemed absolute worlds of blazing sparks, that lighted up all the upper chambers of the air. All the cattle lying abroad in the fields through a breadth of eighteen miles, were thrown into terror and agitation. Men, of course, read in this hurrying overhead of scintillating and blazing vortices, the annunciation of some gigantic calamity going on in Liverpool; and the lamentation on that account was universal. But that mood of public sympathy did not at all interfere to suppress or even to check the momentary bursts of rapturous admiration, as this arrowy sleet* of many-coloured fire rode on the wings of hurricane, alternately through open depths of air, or through dark clouds overhead.

Precisely the same treatment is applied to murders. After the first tribute of sorrow to those who have perished, but, at all events, after the personal interests have been tranquillised by time, inevitably the scenical features (what aesthetically may be called the comparative *advantages*) of the several murders are reviewed and valued. One murder is compared with another; and the circumstances of superiority, as, for example, in the incidence and effects of surprise, of mystery, &c., are collated and appraised. I, therefore, for *my* extravagance, claim an inevitable and perpetual ground in the spontaneous tendencies of the human mind when left to itself. But no one will pretend that any corresponding plea can be advanced on behalf of Swift.

In this important distinction between myself and the Dean, lies one reason which prompted the present Postscript. A second purpose of the Postscript is, to make the reader acquainted circumstantially with three memorable cases of murder, which long ago the voice of amateurs has crowned with laurel, but especially with the two earliest of the three, viz., the immortal Williams' murders of 1812.* The act and the actor are each separately in the highest degree interesting; and, as forty-two years have elapsed since 1812, it cannot be supposed that either is known circumstantially to the men of the current generation.

Never, throughout the annals of universal Christendom, has there indeed been any act of one solitary insulated individual, armed with power so appalling over the hearts of men, as that exterminating murder, by which, during the winter of 1812, John Williams, in one hour, smote two houses with emptiness, exterminated all but two entire households, and asserted his own supremacy above all the children of Cain.* It would be absolutely impossible adequately to describe the frenzy of feelings which, throughout the next fortnight, mastered the popular heart; the mere delirium of indignant horror in some, the mere delirium of panic in others. For twelve succeeding days, under some groundless notion that the unknown murderer had quitted London, the panic which had convulsed the mighty metropolis diffused itself all over the island. I was myself at that time nearly three hundred miles from London;* but there, and everywhere, the panic was indescribable. One lady, my next neighbour, whom personally I knew, living at the moment, during the absence of her husband, with a few servants in a very solitary house, never rested until she had placed eighteen doors (so she told me, and, indeed, satisfied me by ocular proof), each secured by ponderous bolts, and bars, and chains, between her own bedroom and any intruder of human build. To reach her, even in her drawing-room, was like going, as a flag of truce, into a beleaguered fortress; at every sixth step one was stopped by a sort of portcullis. The panic was not confined to the rich; women in the humblest ranks more than once died upon the spot, from the shock attending some suspicious attempts at intrusion upon the part of vagrants, meditating probably nothing worse than a robbery, but whom the poor women, misled by the London newspapers, had fancied to be the dreadful London murderer. Meantime, this solitary artist, that rested in the centre of London, self-supported by his own conscious grandeur, as a domestic Attila, or 'scourge of God;'* this man, that walked in darkness, and relied upon murder (as afterwards transpired) for bread, for clothes, for promotion in life, was silently preparing an effectual answer to the public journals; and on the twelfth day after his inaugural murder, he advertised his presence in London, and published to all men the absurdity of ascribing to *him* any ruralising propensities, by striking a second blow, and accomplishing a second family extermination. Somewhat lightened was the *provincial* panic by this proof that the murderer had not condescended to sneak into the country, or to abandon for a moment, under any motive of caution or fear, the great metropolitan *castra stativa** of gigantic crime, seated for ever on the Thames. In fact, the great artist disdained a provincial reputation; and he must have felt, as a case of ludicrous disproportion, the contrast between a country town or village, on the one hand, and, on the other, a work more lasting than brass—a χλημα ὲς αει*—a murder such in quality as any murder that *he* would condescend to own for a work turned out from his own *studio*.

Coleridge, whom I saw some months after these terrific murders, told me, that, for *his* part, though at the time resident in London, he had not shared in the prevailing panic;* *him* they affected only as a philosopher, and threw him into a profound reverie upon the tremendous power which is laid open in a moment to any man who can reconcile himself to the abjuration of all conscientious restraints, if, at the same time, thoroughly without fear. Not sharing in the public panic, however, Coleridge did not consider that panic at all unreasonable; for, as he said most truly in that vast metropolis there are many thousands of households, composed exclusively of women and children; many other thousands there are who necessarily confide their safety, in the long evenings, to the discretion of a young servant girl; and if she suffers herself to be beguiled by the pretence of a message from her mother, sister, or sweetheart, into opening the door, there, in one second of time, goes to wreck the security of the house. However, at that time, and for many months afterwards, the practice of steadily putting the chain upon the door before it was opened prevailed generally, and for a long time served as a record of that deep impression left upon London by Mr Williams. Southey,* I may add, entered deeply into the public feeling on this occasion, and said to me, within a week or two of the first murder, that it was a private event of that order which rose to the dignity of a national event.[1] But now, having prepared the reader to appreciate on its true scale this dreadful tissue of murder (which, as a record belonging to an era that is now left forty-two years behind us, not one person in four of this generation can be expected to know correctly), let me pass to the circumstantial details of the affair.

Yet, first of all, one word as to the local scene of the murders. Ratcliffe Highway is a public thoroughfare in a most chaotic quarter

---

[1] I am not sure whether Southey held at this time his appointment to the editorship of the 'Edinburgh Annual Register.' If he did, no doubt in the domestic section of that chronicle will be found an excellent account of the whole.*

of eastern or nautical London; and at this time (viz., in 1812), when no adequate police existed except the *detective* police of Bow Street,* admirable for its own peculiar purposes, but utterly incommensurate to the general service of the capital, it was a most dangerous quarter. Every third man at the least might be set down as a foreigner. Lascars, Chinese, Moors, Negroes,* were met at every step. And apart from the manifold ruffianism, shrouded impenetrably under the mixed hats and turbans of men whose past was untraceable to any European eye, it is well known that the navy (especially, in time of war, the commercial navy) of Christendom is the sure receptacle of all the murderers and ruffians whose crimes have given them a motive for withdrawing themselves for a season from the public eye. It is true, that few of this class are qualified to act as 'able' seamen: but at all times, and especially during war, only a small proportion (or *nucleus*) of each ship's company consists of such men: the large majority being mere untutored landsmen. John Williams, however, who had been occasionally rated as a seaman on board of various Indiamen, &c., was probably a very accomplished seaman. Pretty generally, in fact, he was a ready and adroit man, fertile in resources under all sudden difficulties, and most flexibly adapting himself to all varieties of social life. Williams was a man of middle stature (five feet seven and a-half, to five feet eight inches high), slenderly built, rather thin, but wiry, tolerably muscular, and clear of all superfluous flesh.* A lady, who saw him under examination (I think at the Thames Police Office), assured me that his hair was of the most extraordinary and vivid colour, viz., bright yellow, something between an orange and a lemon colour. Williams had been in India; chiefly in Bengal and Madras; but he had also been upon the Indus.* Now, it is notorious that, in the Punjaub, horses of a high caste are often painted—crimson, blue, green, purple; and it struck me that Williams might, for some casual purpose of disguise, have taken a hint from this practice of Scinde and Lahore,* so that the colour might not have been natural. In other respects, his appearance was natural enough; and, judging by a plaster cast of him, which I purchased in London, I should say mean, as regarded his facial structure. One fact, however, was striking, and fell in with the impression of his natural tiger character, that his face wore at all times a bloodless ghastly pallor. 'You might imagine,' said my informant, 'that in his veins circulated not red life-blood, such as could kindle into the blush of shame, of wrath, of pity—but a green sap that welled from no human heart.' His eyes seemed frozen and glazed, as if their light were all converged upon some victim lurking in the far background. So far his appearance might have repelled; but, on the other hand, the concurrent testimony of many witnesses, and also the silent testimony of facts, showed that the oiliness and snaky insinuation of his demeanour counteracted the repulsiveness of his ghastly face, and amongst inexperienced young women won for him a very favourable reception.* In particular, one gentle-mannered girl, whom Williams had undoubtedly designed to mur-der, gave in evidence—that once, when sitting alone with her, he had said, 'Now, Miss R., supposing that I should appear about midnight at your bedside, armed with a carving knife, what would you say?' To which the confiding girl had replied, 'Oh, Mr Williams, if it was anybody else, I should be frightened. But, as soon as I heard *your* voice, I should be tranquil.'* Poor girl! had this outline sketch of Mr Williams been filled in and realised, she would have seen some-thing in the corpse-like face, and heard something in the sinister voice, that would have unsettled her tranquillity for ever. But nothing short of such dreadful experiences could avail to unmask Mr John Williams.

Into this perilous region it was that, on a Saturday night in December, Mr Williams, whom we must suppose to have long since made his *coup d'essai*,* forced his way through the crowded streets, bound on business. To say, was to do. And this night he had said to himself secretly, that he would execute a design which he had already sketched, and which, when finished, was destined on the following day to strike consternation into 'all that mighty heart'* of London, from centre to circumference. It was afterwards remembered that he had quitted his lodgings on this dark errand about eleven o'clock P.M.; not that he meant to begin so soon: but he needed to recon-noitre. He carried his tools closely buttoned up under his loose roomy coat. It was in harmony with the general subtlety of his character, and his polished hatred of brutality, that by universal agreement his manners were distinguished for exquisite suavity: the tiger's heart was masked by the most insinuating and snaky refinement. All his acquaintances afterwards described his dissimulation as so ready and so perfect, that if, in making his way through the streets, always so crowded on a Saturday night in neighbourhoods so poor, he had accidentally jostled any person, he would (as they were all satisfied) have stopped to offer the most gentlemanly apologies: with his devilish heart brooding over the most hellish of purposes, he would yet have paused to express a benign hope that the huge mallet, buttoned up under his elegant surtout,* with a view to the little business that awaited him about ninety minutes further on, had not inflicted any pain on the stranger with whom he had come into collision. Titian, I believe, but certainly Rubens, and perhaps Vandyke, made it a rule never to practise his art but in full dress*— point ruffles, bag wig, and diamond-hilted sword: and Mr Williams, there is reason to believe, when he went out for a grand compound massacre (in another sense, one might have applied to it the Oxford phrase of *going out as Grand Compounder**), always assumed black silk stockings and pumps; nor would he on any account have degraded his position as an artist by wearing a morning gown. In his second great performance, it was particularly noticed and recorded by the one sole trembling man, who under killing agonies of fear was compelled (as the reader will find) from a secret stand to become the solitary spectator of his atrocities, that Mr Williams wore a long blue frock, of the very finest cloth, and richly lined with silk.* Amongst the anecdotes which circulated about him, it was also said at the time, that Mr Williams employed the first of dentists, and also the first of chiropodists. On no account would he patronise any second-rate skill. And beyond a doubt, in that perilous little branch of business which was practised by himself, he might be regarded as the most aristocratic and fastidious of artists.

But who meantime was the victim, to whose abode he was hurrying? For surely he never could be so indiscreet as to be sailing about on a roving cruise in search of some chance person to murder? Oh, no: he had suited himself with a victim some time before, viz., an old and very intimate friend. For he seems to have laid it down as a maxim—that the best person to murder was a friend; and, in default of a friend, which is an article one cannot always command, an acquaintance: because, in either case, on first approaching his subject, suspicion would be disarmed: whereas a stranger might take alarm, and find in the very countenance of his murderer elect a warning summons to place himself on guard. However, in the present case, his destined victim was supposed to unite both characters: originally he had been a friend; but subsequently, on good cause arising, he had become an enemy. Or more probably, as others said, the feelings had long since languished which gave life to either relation of friendship or of enmity. Marr* was the name of that unhappy man, who (whether in the character of friend or enemy) had been selected for the subject of this present Saturday night's performance. And the story current at that time about the connection between Williams and Marr, having (whether true, or not true) never been contradicted upon authority, was, that they sailed in the same Indiaman to Calcutta; that they had quarrelled when at sea; but another version of the story said—no: they had quarrelled after returning from sea; and the subject of their quarrel was Mrs Marr, a very pretty young woman, for whose favour they had been rival candidates, and at one time with most bitter enmity towards each other.* Some circumstances give a colour of probability to this story. Otherwise it has sometimes happened, on occasion of a murder not sufficiently accounted for, that, from pure goodness of heart intolerant of a mere sordid motive for a striking murder, some person has forged, and the public has accredited, a story representing the murderer as having moved under some loftier excitement: and in this case the public, too much shocked at the idea of Williams having on the single motive of gain consummated so complex a tragedy, welcomed the tale which represented him as governed by deadly malice, growing out of the more impassioned and noble rivalry for the favour of a woman. The case remains in some degree doubtful; but, certainly, the probability is, that Mrs Marr had been the true cause, the *causa teterrima*,* of the feud between the men. Meantime, the minutes are numbered, the sands of the hour-glass are running out, that measure the duration of this feud upon earth. This night it shall cease. To-morrow is the day which in England they call Sunday, which in Scotland they call by the Judaic name of 'Sabbath.' To both nations, under different names, the day has the same functions; to both it is a day of rest. For thee also, Marr, it shall be a day of rest; so is it written; thou, too, young Marr, shalt find rest—thou, and thy household, and the stranger that is within thy gates. But that rest must be in the world which lies beyond the grave. On this side the grave ye have all slept your final sleep.

The night was one of exceeding darkness; and in this humble quarter of London, whatever the night happened to be, light or dark, quiet or stormy, all shops were kept open on Saturday nights until twelve o'clock, at the least, and many for half an hour longer. There was no rigorous and pedantic Jewish superstition about the exact limits of Sunday.* At the very worst, the Sunday stretched over from one o'clock A.M. of one day, up to eight o'clock A.M. of the next, making a clear circuit of thirty-one hours. This, surely, was long enough. Marr, on this particular Saturday night, would be content if it were even shorter, provided it would come more quickly, for he has been toiling through sixteen hours behind his counter. Marr's position in life was this: he kept a little hosier's shop, and had invested in his stock and the fittings of his shop about £180. Like all men engaged in trade, he suffered some anxieties. He was a new beginner; but, already, bad debts had alarmed him; and bills were coming to maturity that were not likely to be met by commensurate sales. Yet, constitutionally, he was a sanguine hoper. At this time he was a stout, fresh-coloured young man of twenty-seven;* in some slight degree uneasy from his commercial prospects; but still cheerful, and anticipating—(how vainly!)—that for this night, and the next night, at least, he will rest his wearied head and his cares upon the faithful bosom of his sweet lovely young wife. The household of Marr, consisting of five persons, is as follows: First, there is himself, who, if he should happen to be ruined, in a limited commercial sense, has energy enough to jump up again, like a pyramid of fire, and soar high above ruin many times repeated. Yes, poor Marr, so it might be, if thou wert left to thy native energies unmolested; but even now there stands on the other side of the street one born of hell, who puts his peremptory negative on all these flattering prospects. Second in the list of this household, stands his pretty and amiable wife, who is happy after the fashion of youthful wives, for she is only twenty-two, and anxious (if at all) only on account of her darling infant. For, thirdly, there is in a cradle, not quite nine feet below the street, viz., in a warm, cosy kitchen, and rocked at intervals by the young mother, a baby eight months old. Nineteen months have Marr and herself been married; and this is their first-born child. Grieve not for this child, that it must keep the deep rest of Sunday in some other world; for wherefore should an orphan, steeped to the lips in poverty, when once bereaved of father and mother, linger upon an alien and a murderous earth? Fourthly, there is a stoutish boy, an apprentice, say thirteen years old; a Devonshire boy, with handsome features, such as most Devonshire youths have;[2] satisfied with his place; not overworked; treated kindly, and aware that he was treated kindly, by his master and mistress. Fifthly, and lastly, bringing up the rear of this quiet household, is a servant girl; a grown-up young woman; and she, being particularly kind-hearted, occupied (as often happens in families of humble pretensions as to rank) a sort of sisterly place in her relation to her mistress. A great democratic change is at this very time (1854), and has been for twenty years, passing over British society. Multitudes of persons are becoming ashamed of saying, 'my master,' or 'my mistress:' the term now in the slow process of superseding it is, 'my employer.' Now, in the United States, such an expression of democratic hauteur, though disagreeable as a needless proclamation of independence which nobody is disputing, leaves, however, no lasting bad effect. For the domestic 'helps' are pretty generally in a state of transition so sure and so rapid to the headship of domestic establishments belonging to themselves, that in effect they are but ignoring, for the present moment, a relation which would at any rate dissolve itself in a year or two. But in England, where no such resources exist of everlasting surplus lands, the tendency of the change is painful. It carries with it a sullen and a coarse expression of immunity from a yoke which was in any case a light one, and often a benign one. In some other place, I will illustrate my meaning. Here, apparently, in Mrs Marr's service, the principle concerned illustrated itself practically. Mary, the female servant, felt a sincere and unaffected respect for a mistress whom she saw so steadily occupied with her domestic duties, and who, though so young, and invested with some slight authority, never exerted it capriciously, or even showed it at all conspicuously. According to the testimony of all the neighbours, she treated her mistress with a shade of unobtrusive respect on the one hand, and yet was eager to relieve her, whenever that was possible, from the weight of her maternal duties, with the cheerful voluntary service of a sister.

To this young woman it was, that, suddenly, within three or four minutes of midnight, Marr called aloud from the head of the stairs— directing her to go out and purchase some oysters for the family

---

[2] An artist told me in this year, 1812, that having accidentally seen a native Devonshire regiment (either volunteers or militia), nine hundred strong, marching past a station at which he had posted himself, he did not observe a dozen men that would not have been described in common parlance as 'good-looking.'

supper. Upon what slender accidents hang oftentimes solemn lifelong results! Marr occupied in the concerns of his shop, Mrs Marr occupied with some little ailment and restlessness of her baby, had both forgotten the affair of supper; the time was now narrowing every moment, as regarded any variety of choice; and oysters were perhaps ordered as the likeliest article to be had at all, after twelve o'clock should have struck. And yet, upon this trivial circumstance depended Mary's life. Had she been sent abroad for supper at the ordinary time of ten or eleven o'clock, it is almost certain that she, the solitary member of the household who escaped from the exterminating tragedy, would *not* have escaped; too surely she would have shared the general fate. It had now become necessary to be quick. Hastily, therefore, receiving money from Marr, with a basket in her hand, but unbonneted, Mary tripped out of the shop. It became afterwards, on recollection, a heart-chilling remembrance to herself—that, precisely as she emerged from the shop-door, she noticed, on the opposite side of the street, by the light of the lamps, a man's figure; stationary at the instant, but in the next instant slowly moving. This was Williams; as a little incident, either just before or just after (at present it is impossible to say which), sufficiently proved. Now, when one considers the inevitable hurry and trepidation of Mary under the circumstances stated, time barely sufficing for any chance of executing her errand, it becomes evident that she must have connected some deep feeling of mysterious uneasiness with the movements of this unknown man; else, assuredly, she would not have found her attention disposable for such a case. Thus far, she herself threw some little light upon what it might be that, semi-consciously, was then passing through her mind; she said, that, notwithstanding the darkness, which would not permit her to trace the man's features, or to ascertain the exact direction of his eyes, it yet struck her, that from his carriage when in motion, and from the apparent inclination of his person, he must be looking at No. 29. The little incident which I have alluded to as confirming Mary's belief was, that, at some period not very far from midnight, the watchman had specially noticed this stranger; he had observed him continually peeping into the window of Marr's shop; and had thought this act, connected with the man's appearance, so suspicious, that he stepped into Marr's shop, and communicated what he had seen. This fact he afterwards stated before the magistrates; and he added, that subsequently, viz., a few minutes after twelve (eight or ten minutes, probably, after the departure of Mary), he (the watchman), when re-entering upon his ordinary half-hourly beat, was requested by Marr to assist him in closing the shutters. Here they had a final communication with each other; and the watchman mentioned to Marr that the mysterious stranger had now apparently taken himself off: for that he had not been visible since the first communication made to Marr by the watchman. There is little doubt that Williams had observed the watchman's visit to Marr, and had thus had his attention seasonably drawn to the indiscretion of his own demeanour; so that the warning, given unavailingly to Marr, had been turned to account by Williams. There can be still less doubt, that the bloodhound had commenced his work within one minute of the watchman's assisting Marr to put up his shutters. And on the following consideration:—that which prevented Williams from commencing even earlier, was the exposure of the shop's whole interior to the gaze of street passengers. It was indispensable that the shutters should be accurately closed before Williams could safely get to work. But, as soon as ever this preliminary precaution had been completed, once having secured that concealment from the public eye, it then became of still greater importance not to lose a moment by delay, than previously it had been not to hazard anything by precipitance. For all depended upon going in before Marr should have locked the door. On any other mode of effecting an entrance (as, for instance, by waiting for the return of Mary, and making his entrance simultaneously with her), it will be seen that Williams must have forfeited that particular advantage which mute facts, when read into their true construction, will soon show the reader that he must have employed. Williams waited, of necessity, for the sound of the watchman's retreating steps; waited, perhaps, for thirty seconds; but when that danger was past, the next danger was, lest Marr should lock the door; one turn of the key, and the murderer would have been locked out. In, therefore, he bolted, and by a dexterous movement of his left hand, no doubt, turned the key, without letting Marr perceive this fatal stratagem. It is really wonderful and most interesting to pursue the successive steps of this monster, and to notice the absolute certainty with which the silent hieroglyphics of the case betray to us the whole process and movements of the bloody drama, not less surely and fully than if we had been ourselves hidden in Marr's shop, or had looked down from the heavens of mercy upon this hell-kite,* that knew not what mercy meant. That he had concealed from Marr his trick, secret and rapid, upon the lock, is evident; because else, Marr would instantly have taken the alarm, especially after what the watchman had communicated. But it will soon be seen that Marr had *not* been alarmed. In reality, towards the full success of Williams, it was important, in the last degree, to intercept and forestall any yell or shout of agony from Marr. Such an outcry, and in a situation so slenderly fenced off from the street, viz., by walls the very thinnest, makes itself heard outside pretty nearly as well as if it were uttered in the street. Such an outcry it was indispensable to stifle. It *was* stifled; and the reader will soon understand *how*. Meantime, at this point, let us leave the murderer alone with his victims. For fifty minutes* let him work his pleasure. The front-door, as we know, is now fastened against all help. Help there is none.* Let us, therefore, in vision, attach ourselves to Mary; and, when all is over, let us come back with *her*, again raise the curtain, and read the dreadful record of all that has passed in her absence.

The poor girl, uneasy in her mind to an extent that she could but half understand, roamed up and down in search of an oyster shop; and finding none that was still open, within any circuit that her ordinary experience had made her acquainted with, she fancied it best to try the chances of some remoter district.* Lights she saw gleaming or twinkling at a distance, that still tempted her onwards; and thus, amongst unknown streets poorly lighted,[3] and on a night of peculiar darkness, and in a region of London where ferocious tumults were continually turning her out of what seemed to be the direct course, naturally she got bewildered. The purpose with which she started, had by this time become hopeless. Nothing remained for her now but to retrace her steps. But this was difficult; for she was afraid to ask directions from chance passengers, whose appearance the darkness prevented her from reconnoitring. At length by his lantern she recognised a watchman; through him she was guided into the right road; and in ten minutes more, she found herself back at the

---

[3] I do not remember, chronologically, the history of gas-lights. But in London, long after Mr Winsor* had shown the value of gas-lighting, and its applicability to street purposes, various districts were prevented, for many years, from resorting to the new system, in consequence of old contracts with oil dealers, subsisting through long terms of years.

door of No. 29, in Ratcliffe Highway. But by this time she felt satisfied that she must have been absent for fifty or sixty minutes; indeed, she had heard, at a distance, the cry of *past one o'clock*,* which, commencing a few seconds after one, lasted intermittingly for ten or thirteen minutes.

In the tumult of agonising thoughts that very soon surprised her, naturally it became hard for her to recall distinctly the whole succession of doubts, and jealousies, and shadowy misgivings that soon opened upon her. But, so far as could be collected, she had not in the first moment of reaching home noticed anything decisively alarming. In very many cities bells are the main instruments for communicating between the street and the interior of houses: but in London knockers prevail. At Marr's there was both a knocker and a bell. Mary rang, and at the same time very gently knocked.* She had no fear of disturbing her master or mistress; *them* she made sure of finding still up. Her anxiety was for the baby, who being disturbed might again rob her mistress of a night's rest. And she well knew that, with three people all anxiously awaiting her return, and by this time, perhaps, seriously uneasy at her delay, the least audible whisper from herself would in a moment bring one of them to the door. Yet how is this? To her astonishment, but with the astonishment came creeping over her an icy horror, no stir nor murmur was heard ascending from the kitchen. At this moment came back upon her, with shuddering anguish, the indistinct image of the stranger in the loose dark coat, whom she had seen stealing along under the shadowy lamp-light, and too certainly watching her master's motions: keenly she now reproached herself that, under whatever stress of hurry, she had not acquainted Mr Marr with the suspicious appearances. Poor girl! she did not then know that, if this communication could have availed to put Marr upon his guard, it had reached him from another quarter; so that her own omission, which had in reality arisen under her hurry to execute her master's commission, could not be charged with any bad consequences. But all such reflections this way or that* were swallowed up at this point in overmastering panic. That her double summons *could* have been unnoticed—this solitary fact in one moment made a revelation of horror. One person might have fallen asleep, but two—but three—*that* was a mere impossibility. And even supposing all three together with the baby locked in sleep, still how unaccountable was this utter—utter silence!

Most naturally at this moment something like hysterical horror over-shadowed the poor girl, and now at last she rang the bell with the violence that belongs to sickening terror. This done, she paused: self-command enough she still retained, though fast and fast it was slipping away from her, to bethink herself—that, if any overwhelming accident *had* compelled both Marr and his apprentice-boy to leave the house in order to summon surgical aid from opposite quarters—a thing barely supposable—still, even in that case Mrs Marr and her infant would be left; and some murmuring reply, under any extremity, would be elicited from the poor mother. To pause, therefore, to impose stern silence upon herself, so as to leave room for the possible answer to this final appeal, became a duty of spasmodic effort. Listen, therefore, poor trembling heart; listen, and for twenty seconds be still as death. Still as death she was: and during that dreadful stillness, when she hushed her breath that she might listen, occurred an incident of killing fear, that to her dying day would never cease to renew its echoes in her ear. She, Mary, the poor trembling girl, checking and overruling herself by a final effort, that she might leave full opening for her dear young mistress's answer to her own last frantic appeal, heard at last and most distinctly a sound within the house. Yes, now beyond a doubt there is coming an answer to her summons. What was it? On the stairs, not the stairs that led downwards to the kitchen, but the stairs that led upwards to the single storey of bedchambers above, was heard a creaking sound. Next was heard most distinctly a footfall: one, two, three, four, five stairs were slowly and distinctly descended. Then the dreadful footsteps were heard advancing along the little narrow passage to the door. The steps—oh heavens! *whose* steps?—have paused at the door. The very breathing can be heard of that dreadful being, who has silenced all breathing except his own in the house. There is but a door between him and Mary. What is he doing on the other side of the door? A cautious step, a stealthy step it was that came down the stairs, then paced along the little narrow passage—narrow as a coffin—till at last the step pauses at the door. How hard the fellow breathes! He, the solitary murderer, is on one side the door; Mary is on the other side. Now, suppose that he should suddenly open the door, and that incautiously in the dark Mary should rush in, and find herself in the arms of the murderer. Thus far the case is a possible one—that to a certainty, had this little trick been tried immediately upon Mary's return, it would have succeeded; had the door been opened suddenly upon her first tingle-tingle, headlong she would have tumbled in, and perished. But now Mary is upon her guard. The unknown murderer and she have both their lips upon the door, listening, breathing hard; but luckily they are on different sides of the door; and upon the least indication of unlocking or unlatching, she would have recoiled into the asylum of general darkness.

What was the murderer's meaning in coming along the passage to the front door? The meaning was this: separately, as an individual, Mary was worth nothing at all to him. But, considered as a member of a household, she had this value, viz., that she, if caught and murdered, perfected and rounded the desolation of the house. The case being reported, as reported it would be all over Christendom, led the imagination captive. The whole covey of victims was thus netted; the household ruin was thus full and orbicular; and in that proportion the tendency of men and women, flutter as they might, would be helplessly and hopelessly to sink into the all-conquering hands of the mighty murderer. He had but to say—my testimonials are dated from No. 29 Ratcliffe Highway, and the poor vanquished imagination sank powerless before the fascinating rattlesnake eye of the murderer. There is not a doubt that the motive of the murderer for standing on the inner side of Marr's front-door, whilst Mary stood on the outside, was—a hope that, if he quietly opened the door, whisperingly counterfeiting Marr's voice, and saying, What made you stay so long? possibly she might have been inveigled. He was wrong; the time was past for that; Mary was now maniacally awake; she began now to ring the bell and to ply the knocker with unintermitting violence. And the natural consequence was, that the next door neighbour, who had recently gone to bed and instantly fallen asleep, was roused; and by the incessant violence of the ringing and the knocking, which now obeyed a delirious and uncontrollable impulse in Mary, he became sensible that some very dreadful event must be at the root of so clamorous an uproar. To rise, to throw up the sash, to demand angrily the cause of this unseasonable tumult, was the work of a moment. The poor girl remained sufficiently mistress of herself rapidly to explain the circumstance of her own absence for an hour; her belief that Mr and Mrs Marr's family had all been murdered in the interval; and that at this very moment the murderer was in the house.

The person to whom she addressed this statement was a pawn-broker;* and a thoroughly brave man he must have been; for it was a perilous undertaking, merely as a trial of physical strength, singly to face a mysterious assassin, who had apparently signalised his prowess by a triumph so comprehensive. But, again, for the imagination it required an effort of self-conquest to rush headlong into the presence of one invested with a cloud of mystery, whose nation, age, motives, were all alike unknown. Rarely on any field of battle has a soldier been called upon to face so complex a danger. For if the entire family of his neighbour Marr had been exterminated, were this indeed true, such a scale of bloodshed would seem to argue that there must have been two persons as the perpetrators; or if one singly had accomplished such a ruin, in that case how colossal must have been his audacity! probably, also, his skill and animal power! Moreover, the unknown enemy (whether single or double) would, doubtless, be elaborately armed. Yet, under all these disadvantages, did this fear-less man rush at once to the field of butchery in his neighbour's house. Waiting only to draw on his trousers, and to arm himself with the kitchen poker, he went down into his own little back-yard. On this mode of approach, he would have a chance of intercepting the murderer; whereas from the front there would be no such chance; and there would also be considerable delay in the process of breaking open the door. A brick wall, 9 or 10 feet high, divided his own back premises from those of Marr. Over this he vaulted; and at the moment when he was recalling himself to the necessity of going back for a candle, he suddenly perceived a feeble ray of light already glimmering on some part of Marr's premises. Marr's back-door stood wide open. Probably the murderer had passed through it one half minute before. Rapidly the brave man passed onwards to the shop, and there beheld the carnage of the night stretched out on the floor, and the narrow premises so floated with gore, that it was hardly possible to escape the pollution of blood in picking out a path to the front-door. In the lock of the door still remained the key which had given to the unknown murderer so fatal an advantage over his vic-tims. By this time, the heart-shaking news involved in the outcries of Mary (to whom it occurred that by possibility some one out of so many victims might still be within the reach of medical aid, but that all would depend upon speed) had availed, even at that late hour, to gather a small mob about the house. The pawnbroker threw open the door. One or two watchmen headed the crowd; but the soul-harrowing spectacle checked them and impressed sudden silence upon their voices, previously so loud. The tragic drama read aloud its own history, and the succession of its several steps—few and summary. The murderer was as yet altogether unknown; not even suspected. But there were reasons for thinking that he must have been a person familiarly known to Marr. He had entered the shop by opening the door after it had been closed by Marr. But it was justly argued—that, after the caution conveyed to Marr by the watchman, the appearance of any stranger in the shop at that hour, and in so dangerous a neighbourhood, and entering by so irregular and suspicious a course (*i.e.*, walking in after the door had been closed, and after the closing of the shutters had cut off all open communication with the street), would naturally have roused Marr to an attitude of vigilance and self-defence. Any indication, therefore, that Marr had *not* been so roused, would argue to a certainty that *something* had occurred to neutralise this alarm, and fatally to disarm the prudent jealousies of Marr. But this 'something' could only have lain in one simple fact, viz., that the person of the murderer was familiarly known to Marr as that of an ordinary and unsuspected acquaintance. This being presupposed as the key to all the rest, the whole course and evolution of the subsequent drama becomes clear as daylight. The murderer, it is evident, had opened gently, and again closed behind him with equal gentleness, the street-door. He had then advanced to the little counter, all the while exchanging the ordinary salutation of an old acquaintance with the unsuspecting Marr. Having reached the counter, he would then ask Marr for a pair of unbleached cotton socks. In a shop so small as Marr's, there could be no great latitude of choice for disposing of the different commodities. The arrangement of these had no doubt become familiar to the murderer; and he had already ascertained that, in order to reach down the particular parcel wanted at present, Marr would find it requisite to face round to the rear, and, at the same moment, to raise his eyes and his hands to a level eighteen inches above his own head. This movement placed him in the most disadvantageous possible position with regard to the murderer, who now, at the instant when Marr's hands and eyes were embarrassed, and the back of his head fully exposed, suddenly from below his large surtout, had unslung a heavy ship carpenter's mallet, and, with one solitary blow, had so thoroughly stunned his victim, as to leave him incapable of resistance. The whole position of Marr told its own tale. He had collapsed naturally behind the counter, with his hands so occupied as to confirm the whole outline of the affair as I have here suggested it. Probable enough it is that the very first blow, the first indication of treachery that reached Marr, would also be the last blow as regarded the abolition of consciousness. The murderer's plan and *rationale* of murder started systematically from this infliction of apoplexy, or at least of a stunning sufficient to insure a long loss of consciousness. This opening step placed the murderer at his ease. But still, as returning sense might constantly have led to the fullest exposures, it was his settled practice, by way of consummation, to cut the throat. To one invariable type all the murders on this occasion conformed: the skull was first shattered; this step secured the murderer from instant retaliation; and then, by way of locking up all into eternal silence, uniformly the throat was cut. The rest of the circumstances, as self-revealed, were these. The fall of Marr might, probably enough, cause a dull confused sound of a scuffle, and the more so, as it could not now be confounded with any street uproar—the shop-door being shut. It is more probable, however, that the signal for the alarm passing down to the kitchen, would arise when the murderer proceeded to cut Marr's throat. The very confined situation behind the counter would render it impossible, under the critical hurry of the case, to expose the throat broadly; the horrid scene would proceed by partial and interrupted cuts; deep groans would arise; and then would come the rush up-stairs. Against this, as the only dangerous stage in the transaction, the murderer would have specially prepared. Mrs Marr and the apprentice-boy, both young and active, would make, of course, for the street-door; had Mary been at home, and three persons at once had combined to distract the purposes of the murderer, it is barely possible that one of them would have succeeded in reaching the street. But the dreadful swing of the heavy mallet intercepted both the boy and his mistress before they could reach the door. Each of them lay stretched out on the centre of the shop floor; and the very moment that this disabling was accomplished, the accursed hound was down upon their throats with his razor. The fact is, that, in the mere blindness of pity for poor Marr, on hearing his groans, Mrs Marr had lost sight of her obvious policy; she and the boy ought to have made for the back door; the alarm would thus have been given in the open air; which, of itself, was a great point; and several means of distracting the murderer's attention offered upon that course, which the extreme limitation of the shop denied to them upon the other.

Vain would be all attempts to convey the horror which thrilled the gathering spectators of this piteous tragedy. It was known to the crowd that one person had, by some accident, escaped the general massacre; but she was now speechless, and probably delirious; so that, in compassion for her pitiable situation, one female neighbour had carried her away, and put her to bed. Hence it had happened, for a longer space of time than could else have been possible, that no person present was sufficiently acquainted with the Marrs to be aware of the little infant; for the bold pawnbroker had gone off to make a communication to the coroner; and another neighbour, to lodge some evidence which he thought urgent at a neighbouring police-office. Suddenly some person appeared amongst the crowd who was aware that the murdered parents had a young infant; this would be found either below-stairs, or in one of the bedrooms above. Immediately a stream of people poured down into the kitchen, where at once they saw the cradle—but with the bedclothes in a state of indescribable confusion. On disentangling these, pools of blood became visible; and the next ominous sign was, that the hood of the cradle had been smashed to pieces. It became evident that the wretch had found himself doubly embarrassed—first, by the arched hood at the head of the cradle, which accordingly he had beat into a ruin with his mallet, and secondly, by the gathering of the blankets and pillows about the baby's head. The free play of his blows had thus been baffled. And he had therefore finished the scene by applying his razor to the throat of the little innocent; after which, with no apparent purpose, as though he had become confused by the spectacle of his own atrocities, he had busied himself in piling the clothes elaborately over the child's corpse. This incident undeniably gave the character of a vindictive proceeding to the whole affair, and so far confirmed the current rumour that the quarrel between Williams and Marr had originated in rivalship. One writer, indeed, alleged that the murderer might have found it necessary for his own safety to extinguish the crying of the child; but it was justly replied, that a child only eight months old could not have cried under any sense of the tragedy proceeding, but simply in its ordinary way for the absence of its mother; and such a cry, even if audible at all out of the house, must have been precisely what the neighbours were hearing constantly, so that it could have drawn no special attention, nor suggested any reasonable alarm to the murderer. No one incident, indeed, throughout the whole tissue of atrocities, so much envenomed the popular fury against the unknown ruffian, as this useless butchery of the infant.

Naturally, on the Sunday morning that dawned four or five hours later, the case was too full of horror not to diffuse itself in all directions; but I have no reason to think that it crept into any one of the numerous Sunday papers. In the regular course, any ordinary occurrence, not occurring, or not transpiring until 15 minutes after 1 A.M. on a Sunday morning, would first reach the public ear through the Monday editions of the Sunday papers, and the regular morning papers of the Monday. But, if such were the course pursued on this occasion, never can there have been a more signal oversight. For it is certain, that to have met the public demand for details on the Sunday, which might so easily have been done by cancelling a couple of dull columns, and substituting a circumstantial narrative, for which the pawnbroker and the watchman could have furnished the materials, would have made a small fortune. By proper handbills dispersed through all quarters of the infinite metropolis, 250,000 extra copies might have been sold; that is, by any journal that should have collected *exclusive* materials, meeting the public excitement, everywhere stirred to the centre by flying rumours, and everywhere burning for ampler information. On the Sunday se'ennight (Sunday the *octave** from the event), took place the funeral of the Marrs; in the first coffin was placed Marr; in the second Mrs Marr, and the baby in her arms; in the third the apprentice boy. They were buried side by side; and 30,000 labouring people followed the funeral procession, with horror and grief written in their countenances.

As yet no whisper was astir that indicated, even conjecturally, the hideous author of these ruins—this patron of gravediggers. Had as much been known on this Sunday of the funeral concerning that person as became known universally six days later, the people would have gone right from the churchyard to the murderer's lodgings, and (brooking no delay) would have torn him limb from limb. As yet, however, in mere default of any object on whom reasonable suspicion could settle, the public wrath was compelled to suspend itself. Else, far indeed from showing any tendency to subside, the public emotion strengthened every day conspicuously, as the reverberation of the shock began to travel back from the provinces to the capital. On every great road in the kingdom, continual arrests were made of vagrants and 'trampers,' who could give no satisfactory account of themselves, or whose appearance in any respect answered to the imperfect description of Williams furnished by the watchman.

With this mighty tide of pity and indignation pointing backwards to the dreadful past, there mingled also in the thoughts of reflecting persons an under-current of fearful expectation for the immediate future. 'The earthquake,' to quote a fragment from a striking passage in Wordsworth—

> The earthquake is not satisfied at once.*

All perils, specially malignant, are recurrent. A murderer, who is such by passion and by a wolfish craving for bloodshed as a mode of unnatural luxury, cannot relapse into *inertia*. Such a man, even more than the Alpine chamois hunter, comes to crave the dangers and the hairbreadth escapes of his trade, as a condiment for seasoning the insipid monotonies of daily life. But, apart from the hellish instincts that might too surely be relied on for renewed atrocities, it was clear that the murderer of the Marrs, wheresoever lurking, must be a needy man; and a needy man of that class least likely to seek or to find resources in honourable modes of industry; for which, equally by haughty disgust and by disuse of the appropriate habits, men of violence are specially disqualified. Were it, therefore, merely for a livelihood, the murderer, whom all hearts were yearning to decipher, might be expected to make his resurrection on some stage of horror, after a reasonable interval. Even in the Marr murder, granting that it had been governed chiefly by cruel and vindictive impulses, it was still clear that the desire of booty had co-operated with such feelings. Equally clear it was that this desire must have been disappointed: excepting the trivial sum reserved by Marr for the week's expenditure, the murderer found, doubtless, little or nothing that he could turn to account. Two guineas, perhaps, would be the outside of what he had obtained in the way of booty. A week or so would see the end of that. The conviction, therefore, of all people was, that in a month or two, when the fever of excitement might a little have cooled down, or have been superseded by other topics of fresher interest, so that the newborn vigilance of household life would have had time to relax, some new murder, equally appalling, might be counted upon.

Such was the public expectation. Let the reader then figure to himself the pure frenzy of horror when in this hush of expectation, looking, indeed, and waiting for the unknown arm to strike once more, but not believing that any audacity could be equal to such an attempt as yet, whilst all eyes were watching, suddenly, on the twelfth night from the Marr murder, a second case of the same mysterious nature, a murder on the same exterminating plan, was perpetrated in the very same neighbourhood. It was on the Thursday next but one succeeding to the Marr murder that this second atrocity took place;* and many people thought at the time, that in its dramatic features of thrilling interest this second case even went beyond the first. The family which suffered in this instance was that of a Mr Williamson;* and the house was situated, if not absolutely *in* Ratcliffe Highway, at any rate immediately round the corner of some secondary street, running at right angles to this public thoroughfare. Mr Williamson was a well-known and respectable man, long settled in that district; he was supposed to be rich; and more with a view to the employment furnished by such a calling, than with much anxiety for further accumulations, he kept a sort of tavern; which, in this respect, might be considered on an old patriarchal footing—that, although people of considerable property resorted to the house in the evenings, no kind of anxious separation was maintained between them and the other visiters from the class of artisans or common labourers. Anybody who conducted himself with propriety was free to take a seat, and call for any liquor that he might prefer. And thus the society was pretty miscellaneous; in part stationary, but in some proportion fluctuating. The household consisted of the following five persons:*—1. Mr Williamson, its head, who was an old man above seventy, and was well fitted for his situation, being civil, and not at all morose, but, at the same time, firm in maintaining order; 2. Mrs Williamson, his wife, about ten years younger than himself; 3. a little granddaughter, about nine years old; 4. a housemaid, who was nearly forty years old; 5. a young journeyman, aged about twenty-six, belonging to some manufacturing establishment (of what class I have forgotten); neither do I remember of what nation he was. It was the established rule at Mr Williamson's, that, exactly as the clock struck eleven, all the company, without favour or exception, moved off. That was one of the customs by which, in so stormy a district, Mr Williamson had found it possible to keep his house free from brawls. On the present Thursday night everything had gone on as usual, except for one slight shadow of suspicion, which had caught the attention of more persons than one. Perhaps at a less agitating time it would hardly have been noticed; but now, when the first question and the last in all social meetings turned upon the Marrs, and their unknown murderer, it was a circumstance naturally fitted to cause some uneasiness, that a stranger, of sinister appearance, in a wide surtout, had flitted in and out of the room at intervals during the evening; had sometimes retired from the light into obscure corners; and, by more than one person, had been observed stealing into the private passages of the house. It was presumed in general that the man must be known to Williamson. And, in some slight degree, as an occasional customer of the house, it is not impossible that he *was*. But afterwards, this repulsive stranger, with his cadaverous ghastliness, extraordinary hair, and glazed eyes, showing himself intermittingly through the hours from 8 to 11 P.M., revolved upon the memory of all who had steadily observed him with something of the same freezing effect as belongs to the two assassins in 'Macbeth,' who present themselves reeking from the murder of Banquo, and gleaming dimly, with dreadful faces, from the misty background, athwart the pomps of the regal banquet.*

Meantime the clock struck eleven; the company broke up; the door of entrance was nearly closed; and at this moment of general dispersion the situation of the five inmates left upon the premises was precisely this: the three elders, viz., Williamson, his wife, and his female servant, were all occupied on the ground-floor—Williamson himself was drawing ale, porter, &c., for those neighbours in whose favour the house-door had been left ajar, until the hour of twelve should strike; Mrs Williamson and her servant were moving to and fro between the back-kitchen and a little parlour; the little grand-daughter, whose sleeping-room was on the *first* floor (which term in London means always the floor raised by one flight of stairs above the level of the street), had been fast asleep since nine o'clock; lastly, the journeyman artisan had retired to rest for some time. He was a regular lodger in the house; and his bedroom was on the second floor. For some time he had been undressed, and had lain down in bed. Being, as a working man, bound to habits of early rising, he was naturally anxious to fall asleep as soon as possible. But, on this particular night, his uneasiness, arising from the recent murders at No. 29, rose to a paroxysm of nervous excitement which kept him awake. It is possible, that from somebody he had heard of the suspicious-looking stranger, or might even personally have observed him slinking about. But, were it otherwise, he was aware of several circumstances dangerously affecting this house; for instance, the ruffianism of this whole neighbourhood, and the disagreeable fact that the Marrs had lived within a few doors of this very house, which again argued that the murderer also lived at no great distance. These were matters of *general* alarm. But there were others peculiar to this house; in particular, the notoriety of Williamson's opulence; the belief, whether well or ill founded, that he accumulated, in desks and drawers, the money continually flowing into his hands; and lastly, the danger so ostentatiously courted by that habit of leaving the house-door ajar through one entire hour—and that hour loaded with extra danger, by the well-advertised assurance that no collision need be feared with chance convivial visiters, since all such people were banished at eleven. A regulation, which had hitherto operated beneficially for the character and comfort of the house, now, on the contrary, under altered circumstances, became a positive proclamation of exposure and defencelessness, through one entire period of an hour. Williamson himself, it was said generally, being a large unwieldy man, past seventy, and signally inactive, ought, in prudence, to make the locking of his door coincident with the dismissal of his evening party.

Upon these and other grounds of alarm (particularly this, that Mrs Williamson was reported to possess a considerable quantity of plate), the journeyman was musing painfully, and the time might be within twenty-eight or twenty-five minutes of twelve, when all at once, with a crash, proclaiming some hand of hideous violence, the house-door was suddenly shut and locked. Here, then, beyond all doubt, was the diabolic man, clothed in mystery, from No. 29 Ratcliffe Highway. Yes, that dreadful being, who for twelve days had employed all thoughts and all tongues, was now, too certainly, in this defenceless house, and would, in a few minutes, be face to face with every one of its inmates. A question still lingered in the public mind—whether at Marr's there might not have been *two* men at work. If so, there would be two at present; and one of the two would be immediately disposable for the up-stairs work; since no danger could obviously be more immediately fatal to such an attack than any alarm given from an upper window to the passengers in the street. Through one half-minute the poor panicstricken man sat up motionless in bed. But then he rose, his first movement being towards the door of his room. Not for any purpose of securing it against intrusion—too well he knew that there was no fastening of any sort—neither lock, nor bolt; nor was there any such moveable furniture in the room as might have availed to barricade the door, even if time could be counted on for such an attempt. It was no effect of prudence, merely the fascination of killing fear it was, that drove him to open the door. One step brought him to the head of the stairs; he lowered his head over the balustrade in order to listen; and at that moment ascended, from the little parlour, this agonising cry from the woman-servant, 'Lord Jesus Christ! we shall all be murdered!'* What a Medusa's head* must have lurked in those dreadful bloodless features, and those glazed rigid eyes, that seemed rightfully belonging to a corpse, when one glance at them sufficed to proclaim a death-warrant.

Three separate death-struggles were by this time over; and the poor petrified journeyman, quite unconscious of what he was doing, in blind, passive, self-surrender to panic, absolutely descended both flights of stairs. Infinite terror inspired him with the same impulse as might have been inspired by headlong courage. In his shirt, and upon old decaying stairs, that at times creaked under his feet, he continued to descend, until he had reached the lowest step but four. The situation was tremendous beyond any that is on record. A sneeze, a cough, almost a breathing, and the young man would be a corpse, without a chance or a struggle for his life. The murderer was at that time in the little parlour—the door of which parlour faced you in descending the stairs; and this door stood ajar; indeed, much more considerably open than what is understood by the term 'ajar.' Of that quadrant, or 90 degrees, which the door would describe in swinging so far open as to stand at right angles to the lobby, or to itself, in a closed position, 55 degrees at the least were exposed. Consequently, two out of three corpses were exposed to the young man's gaze. Where was the third? And the murderer—where was he? As to the murderer, he was walking rapidly backwards and forwards in the parlour, audible but not visible at first, being engaged with something or other in that part of the room which the door still concealed. What the something might be, the sound soon explained; he was applying keys tentatively to a cupboard, a closet, and a scrutoire,* in the hidden part of the room. Very soon, however, he came into view; but, fortunately for the young man, at this critical moment, the murderer's purpose too entirely absorbed him to allow of his throwing a glance to the staircase, on which else the white figure of the journeyman, standing in motionless horror, would have been detected in one instant, and seasoned for the grave in the second. As to the third corpse, the missing corpse, viz., Mr Williamson's, *that* is in the cellar; and how its local position can be accounted for, remains as a separate question much discussed at the time, but never satisfactorily cleared up. Meantime, that Williamson was dead, became evident to the young man; since else he would have been heard stirring or groaning. Three friends, therefore, out of four, whom the young man had parted with forty minutes ago, were now extinguished; remained, therefore, 40 per cent. (a large per centage for Williams to leave); remained, in fact, himself and his pretty young friend, the little grand-daughter, whose childish innocence was still slumbering without fear for herself, or grief for her aged grandparents. If *they* are gone for ever, happily one friend (for such he will prove himself, indeed, if from such a danger he can save this child) is pretty near to her. But alas! he is still nearer to a murderer. At this moment he is unnerved for any exertion whatever; he has changed into a pillar of ice; for the objects before him, separated by just thirteen feet, are these:—The housemaid had been caught by the murderer on her knees; she was kneeling before the fire-grate, which she had been polishing with black lead. That part of her task was finished; and she had passed on to another task, viz., the filling of the grate with wood and coals, not for kindling at this moment, but so as to have it ready for kindling on the next day. The appearances all showed that she must have been engaged in this labour at the very moment when the murderer entered; and perhaps the succession of the incidents arranged itself as follows:—From the awful ejaculation and loud outcry to Christ, as overheard by the journeyman, it was clear that then first she had been alarmed; yet this was at least one and a-half or even two minutes after the door-slamming. Consequently the alarm which had so fearfully and seasonably alarmed the young man, must, in some unaccountable way, have been misinterpreted by the two women. It was said, at the time, that Mrs Williamson laboured under some dulness of hearing; and it was conjectured that the servant, having her ears filled with the noise of her own scrubbing, and her head half under the grate, might have confounded it with the street noises, or else might have imputed this violent closure to some mischievous boys. But, howsoever explained, the fact was evident, that, until the words of appeal to Christ, the servant had noticed nothing suspicious, nothing which interrupted her labours. If so, it followed that neither had Mrs Williamson noticed anything; for, in that case, she would have communicated her own alarm to the servant, since both were in the same small room. Apparently the course of things after the murderer had entered the room was this:—Mrs Williamson had probably not seen him, from the accident of standing with her back to the door. Her, therefore, before he was himself observed at all, he had stunned and prostrated by a shattering blow on the back of her head; this blow, inflicted by a crow-bar, had smashed in the hinder part of the skull. She fell; and by the noise of her fall (for all was the work of a moment) had first roused the attention of the servant; who then uttered the cry which had reached the young man; but before she could repeat it, the murderer had descended with his uplifted instrument upon *her* head, crushing the skull inwards upon the brain. Both the women were irrecoverably destroyed, so that further outrages were needless; and, moreover, the murderer was conscious of the imminent danger from delay; and yet, in spite of his hurry, so fully did he appreciate the fatal consequences to himself, if any of his victims should so far revive into consciousness as to make circumstantial depositions, that, by way of making this impossible, he had proceeded instantly to cut the throats of each. All this tallied with the appearances as now presenting themselves. Mrs Williamson had fallen backwards with her head to the door; the servant, from her kneeling posture, had been incapable of rising, and had presented her head passively to blows; after which, the miscreant had but to bend her head backwards so as to expose her throat, and the murder was finished. It is remarkable that the young artisan, paralysed as he had been by fear, and evidently fascinated for a time so as to walk right towards the lion's mouth, yet found himself able to notice everything important. The reader must suppose him at this point watching the murderer whilst hanging over the body of Mrs Williamson, and whilst renewing his search for certain important keys. Doubtless it was an anxious situation for the murderer; for, unless he speedily found the keys wanted, all this hideous tragedy would end in nothing but a prodigious increase of the public horror, in tenfold precautions therefore, and redoubled obstacles interposed between himself and his future game. Nay, there was even a nearer interest at stake; his own immediate safety might, by a probable accident, be compromised. Most of those who came to the house for liquor were giddy girls or children, who, on finding this house closed, would go off carelessly to some other; but, let any thoughtful woman or man come to the door now, a full quarter of an hour before the established time of closing, in that case suspicion would arise too powerful to be checked. There would be a sudden alarm given; after which, mere luck would decide the event. For it is a remarkable fact, and one that illustrates the singular inconsistency of this villain, who, being often so superfluously subtle, was in other directions so reckless and improvident, that at this very moment, standing amongst corpses that had deluged the little parlour with blood, Williams must have been in considerable doubt whether he had any sure means of egress. There were windows, he knew, to the back; but upon what ground they opened, he seems to have had no certain information; and in a neighbourhood so dangerous, the windows of the lower storey would not improbably be nailed down; those in the upper might be free, but then came the necessity of a leap too formidable. From all this, however, the sole practical inference was to hurry forward with the trial of further keys, and to detect the hidden treasure. This it was, this intense absorption in one overmastering pursuit, that dulled the murderer's perceptions as to all around him; otherwise, he must have heard the breathing of the young man, which to himself at times became fearfully audible. As the murderer stood once more over the body of Mrs Williamson, and searched her pockets more narrowly, he pulled out various clusters of keys, one of which dropping, gave a harsh jingling sound upon the floor. At this time it was that the secret witness, from his secret stand, noticed the fact of Williams's surtout being lined with silk of the finest quality. One other fact he noticed, which eventually became more immediately important than many stronger circumstances of incrimination; this was, that the shoes of the murderer, apparently new, and bought, probably, with poor Marr's money, creaked as he walked, harshly and frequently. With the new clusters of keys, the murderer walked off to the hidden section of the parlour. And here, at last, was suggested to the journeyman the sudden opening for an escape. Some minutes would be lost to a certainty in trying all these keys; and subsequently in searching the drawers, supposing that the keys answered—or in violently forcing them, supposing that they did *not*. He might thus count upon a brief interval of leisure, whilst the rattling of the keys might obscure to the murderer the creaking of the stairs under the re-ascending journeyman. His plan was now formed: on regaining his bedroom, he placed the bed against the door by way of a transient retardation to the enemy, that might give him a short warning, and in the worst extremity, might give him a chance for life by means of a desperate leap. This change made as quietly as was possible, he tore the sheets, pillow-cases, and blankets into broad ribbons; and after plaiting them into ropes, spliced the different lengths together. But at the very first he descries this ugly addition to his labours. Where shall he look for any staple, hook, bar, or other fixture, from which his rope, when twisted, may safely depend? Measured from the window-*sill*—*i. e.*, the lowest part of the window architrave—there count but twenty-two or twenty-three feet to the ground. Of this length ten or twelve feet may be looked upon as cancelled, because to that extent he might drop without danger. So much being deducted, there would remain, say, a dozen feet of rope to prepare. But, unhappily, there is no stout iron fixture anywhere about his window. The nearest, indeed the sole fixture of that sort, is not near to the window at all; it is a spike fixed (for no reason at all that is apparent) in the bed-tester;* now, the bed being shifted, the spike is shifted; and its distance from the window, having always been four feet, is now seven. Seven entire feet, therefore, must be added to that which would have sufficed if measured from the window. But courage! God, by the proverb of all nations in Christendom, helps those that help themselves. This our young man thankfully acknowledges; he reads already, in the very fact of any spike at all being found where hitherto it has been useless, an earnest of providential aid. Were it only for himself that he worked, he could not feel himself meritoriously employed; but this is not so; in deep sincerity, he is now agitated for the poor child, whom he knows and loves; every minute, he feels, brings ruin nearer to *her*; and, as he passed her door, his first thought had been to take her out of bed in his arms, and to carry her where she might share his chances.* But, on consideration, he felt that this sudden awaking of her, and the impossibility of even whispering any explanation, would cause her to cry audibly; and the inevitable indiscretion of one would be fatal to the two. As the Alpine avalanches, when suspended above the traveller's head, oftentimes (we are told) come down through the stirring of the air by a simple whisper, precisely on such a tenure of a whisper was now suspended the murderous malice of the man below. No; there is but one way to save the child; towards *her* deliverance, the first step is through his own. And he has made an excellent beginning; for the spike, which too fearfully he had expected to see torn away by any strain upon it from the half-carious* wood, stands firmly when tried against the pressure of his own weight. He has rapidly fastened on to it three lengths of his new rope, measuring eleven feet. He plaits it roughly; so that only three feet have been lost in the intertwisting; he has spliced on a second length equal to the first; so that, already, sixteen feet are ready to throw out of the window; and thus, let the worst come to the worst, it will not be absolute ruin to swarm down the rope so far as it will reach, and then to drop boldly. All this has been accomplished in about six minutes; and the hot contest between above and below is still steadily but fervently proceeding. Murderer is working hard in the parlour; journeyman is working hard in the bedroom. Miscreant is getting on famously down-stairs; one batch of bank-notes he has already bagged; and is hard upon the scent of a second. He has also sprung a covey of golden coins. Sovereigns as yet were not;* but guineas at this period fetched thirty shillings a-piece; and he has worked his way into a little quarry of these. Murderer is almost joyous; and if any creature is still living in this house, as shrewdly he suspects, and very soon means to know, with that creature he would be happy, before cutting the creature's throat, to drink a glass of something. Instead of the glass, might he not make a present to the poor creature of its throat? Oh no! impossible! Throats are a sort of thing that he never makes presents of; business— business must be attended to. Really the two men, considered simply as men of business, are both meritorious. Like chorus and semi-chorus, strophe and antistrophe,* they work each against the other. Pull journeyman, pull murderer! Pull baker, pull devil!* As regards the journeyman, he is now safe. To his sixteen feet, of which seven are neutralised by the distance of the bed, he has at last added six feet more, which will be short of reaching the ground by perhaps ten feet—a trifle which man or boy may drop without injury. All is safe, therefore, for him: which is more than one can be sure of for miscreant in the parlour. Miscreant, however, takes it coolly enough: the reason being, that, with all his cleverness, for once in his life miscreant has been over-reached. The reader and I know, but miscreant does not in the least suspect, a little fact of some importance, viz., that just now through a space of full three minutes he has been overlooked and studied by one, who (though reading in a dreadful book, and suffering under mortal panic) took accurate notes of so much as his limited opportunities allowed him to see, and will assuredly report the creaking shoes* and the silk-mounted surtout in quarters where such little facts will tell very little to his advantage. But, although it is true that Mr Williams, unaware of the journeyman's having 'assisted' at the examination of Mrs Williamson's pockets, could not connect any anxiety with that person's subsequent proceedings, nor specially, therefore, with his having embarked in the rope-weaving line, assuredly he knew of reasons enough for not loitering. And yet he *did* loiter. Reading his acts by the light of such mute traces as he left behind him, the police became aware that latterly he must have loitered. And the reason which governed him is striking; because at once it records—that murder was not pursued by him simply as a means to an end, but also as an end for itself. Mr Williams had now been upon the premises for perhaps fifteen or twenty minutes; and in that space of time he had despatched, in a style satisfactory to himself, a considerable amount of business. He had done, in commercial language, 'a good stroke of business.' Upon two floors, viz., the cellar-floor and the ground-floor, he has 'accounted for' all the population. But there remained at least two floors more; and it now occurred to Mr Williams that, although the landlord's somewhat chilling manner had shut him out from any familiar knowledge of the household arrangements, too probably on one or other of those floors there must be some throats. As to plunder, he has already bagged the whole. And it was next to impossible that any arrear the most trivial should still remain for a gleaner. But the throats—the throats—there it was that arrears and gleanings might perhaps be counted on. And thus it appeared that, in his wolfish thirst for blood, Mr Williams put to hazard the whole fruits of his night's work, and his life into the bargain. At this moment, if the murderer knew all, could he see the open window above stairs ready for the descent of the journeyman, could he witness the life-and-death rapidity with which that journeyman is working, could he guess at the almighty uproar which within ninety seconds will be maddening the population of this populous district—no picture of a maniac in flight of panic or in pursuit of vengeance would adequately represent the agony of haste with which he would himself be hurrying to the street-door for final evasion. That mode of escape was still free. Even at this moment, there yet remained time sufficient for a successful flight, and, therefore, for the following revolution in the romance of his own abominable life. He had in his pockets above a hundred pounds of booty; means, therefore, for a full disguise. This very night, if he will shave off his yellow hair, and blacken his eyebrows, buying, when morning light returns, a dark-coloured wig, and clothes such as may co-operate in personating the character of a grave professional man, he may elude all suspicions of impertinent policemen—may sail by any one of a hundred vessels bound for any port along the huge line of sea-board (stretching through 2400 miles) of the American United States; may enjoy fifty years for leisurely repentance; and may even die in the odour of sanctity.* On the other hand, if he prefer active life, it is not impossible that, with *his* subtlety, hardihood, and unscrupulousness, in a land where the simple process of naturalisation converts the alien at once into a child of the family, he might rise to the president's chair; might have a statue at his death; and afterwards a life in three volumes quarto, with no hint glancing towards No. 29 Ratcliffe Highway. But all depends on the next ninety seconds. Within that time there is a sharp turn to be taken; there is a wrong turn, and a right turn. Should his better angel guide him to the right one, all may yet go well as regards this world's prosperity. But behold! in two minutes from this point we shall see him take the wrong one: and then Nemesis will be at his heels with ruin perfect and sudden.

Meantime, if the murderer allows himself to loiter, the ropemaker overhead does *not*. Well he knows that the poor child's fate is on the edge of a razor: for all turns upon the alarm being raised before the murderer reaches her bedside. And at this very moment, whilst desperate agitation is nearly paralysing his fingers, he hears the sullen stealthy step of the murderer creeping up through the darkness. It had been the expectation of the journeyman (founded on the clamorous uproar with which the street-door was slammed) that Williams, when disposable for his up-stairs work, would come racing at a long jubilant gallop, and with a tiger roar; and perhaps, on his natural instincts, he would have done so. But this mode of approach, which was of dreadful effect when applied to a case of surprise, became dangerous in the case of people who might by this time have been placed fully upon their guard. The step which he had heard was on the staircase—but upon which stair? He fancied upon the lowest: and in a movement so slow and cautious, even this might make all the difference; yet might it not have been the tenth, twelfth, or fourteenth stair? Never, perhaps, in this world did any man feel his own responsibility so cruelly loaded and strained, as at this moment did the poor journeyman on behalf of the slumbering child. Lose but two seconds, through awkwardness or through the self-counteractions of panic, and for *her* the total difference arose between life and death. Still there is a hope: and nothing can so frightfully expound the hellish nature of him whose baleful shadow, to speak astrologically, at this moment darkens the house of life, than the simple expression of the ground on which this hope rested. The journeyman felt sure that the murderer would not be satisfied to kill the poor child whilst unconscious. This would be to defeat his whole purpose in murdering her at all. To an epicure in murder such as Williams, it would be taking away the very sting of the enjoyment, if the poor child should be suffered to drink off the bitter cup of death without fully apprehending the misery of the situation. But this luckily would require time: the double confusion of mind, first, from being roused up at so unusual an hour, and, secondly, from the horror of the occasion when explained to her, would at first produce fainting, or some mode of insensibility or distraction, such as must occupy a considerable time. The logic of the case, in short, all rested upon the *ultra* fiendishness of Williams. Were he likely to be content with the mere fact of the child's death, apart from the process and leisurely expansion of its mental agony—in that case there would be no hope. But, because our present murderer is fastidiously finical in his exactions—a sort of martinet in the scenical grouping and draping of the circumstances in his murders—therefore it is that hope becomes reasonable, since all such refinements of preparation demand time. Murders of mere necessity Williams was obliged to hurry; but, in a murder of pure voluptuousness, entirely disinterested, where no hostile witness was to be removed, no extra booty to be gained, and no revenge to be gratified, it is clear that to hurry would be altogether to ruin. If this child, therefore, is to be saved, it will be on pure aesthetical considerations.[4]

But all considerations whatever are at this moment suddenly cut short. A second step is heard on the stairs, but still stealthy and cautious; a third—and then the child's doom seems fixed. But just at that moment all is ready. The window is wide open; the rope is swinging free; the journeyman has launched himself; and already he is in the first stage of his descent. Simply by the weight of his person he descended, and by the resistance of his hands he retarded the descent. The danger was, that the rope should run too smoothly through his hands, and that by too rapid an acceleration of pace he should come violently to the ground. Happily he was able to resist the descending impetus: the knots of the splicings furnished a succession of retardations. But the rope proved shorter by four or five feet than he had calculated: ten or eleven feet from the ground he hung suspended in the air; speechless for the present, through long-continued agitation; and not daring to drop boldly on the rough carriage pavement, lest he should fracture his legs. But the night was not dark, as it had been on occasion of the Marr murders. And yet, for purposes of criminal police, it was by accident worse than the darkest night that ever hid a murder or baffled a pursuit. London, from east to west, was covered with a deep pall (rising from the river) of universal fog. Hence it happened, that for twenty or thirty seconds the young man hanging in the air was not observed. His white shirt at length attracted notice. Three or four people ran up,* and received him in their arms, all anticipating some dreadful annunciation. To what house did he belong? Even *that* was not instantly apparent; but he pointed with his finger to Williamson's door, and said in a half-choking whisper—'*Marr's murderer, now at work!*'

---

[4] Let the reader, who is disposed to regard as exaggerated or romantic the pure fiendishness imputed to Williams, recollect that, except for the luxurious purpose of basking and revelling in the anguish of dying despair, he had no motive at all, small or great, for attempting the murder of this young girl. She had seen nothing, heard nothing—was fast asleep, and her door was closed; so that, as a witness against him, he knew that she was as useless as any one of the three corpses. And yet he *was* making preparations for her murder, when the alarm in the street interrupted him.

All explained itself in a moment: the silent language of the fact made its own eloquent revelation. The mysterious exterminator of No. 29 Ratcliffe Highway had visited another house; and, behold! one man only had escaped through the air, and in his night-dress, to tell the tale. Superstitiously, there was something to check the pursuit of this unintelligible criminal. Morally, and in the interests of vindictive justice, there was everything to rouse, quicken, and sustain it.

Yes, Marr's murderer—the man of mystery—was again at work; at this moment perhaps extinguishing some lamp of life, and not at any remote place, but here—in the very house which the listeners to this dreadful announcement were actually touching. The chaos and blind uproar of the scene which followed, measured by the crowded reports in the journals of many subsequent days, and in one feature of that case, has never to my knowledge had its parallel; or, if a parallel, only in one case—what followed, I mean, on the acquittal of the seven bishops at Westminster in 1688.* At present there was more than passionate enthusiasm. The frenzied movement of mixed horror and exultation—the ululation of vengeance which ascended instantaneously from the individual street, and then by a sublime sort of magnetic contagion from all the adjacent streets, can be adequately expressed only by a rapturous passage in Shelley:—

> The transport of a fierce and monstrous gladness
> > Spread through the multitudinous streets, fast flying
> Upon the wings of fear:—From his dull madness
> > The starveling waked, and died in joy: the dying,
> Among the corpses in stark agony lying,
> > Just heard the happy tidings, and in hope
> Closed their faint eyes: from house to house replying
> > With loud acclaim the living shook heaven's cope,
> And fill'd the startled earth with echoes.[5]

There was something, indeed, half inexplicable in the instantaneous interpretation of the gathering shout according to its true meaning. In fact, the deadly roar of vengeance, and its sublime unity, *could* point in this district only to the one demon whose idea had brooded and tyrannised, for twelve days, over the general heart: every door, every window in the neighbourhood, flew open as if at a word of command; multitudes, without waiting for the regular means of

[5] 'Revolt of Islam,' canto xii.*

egress, leaped down at once from the windows on the lower storey; sick men rose from their beds; in one instance, as if expressly to verify the image of Shelley (in v. 4, 5, 6, 7), a man whose death had been looked for through some days, and who actually *did* die on the following day, rose, armed himself with a sword, and descended in his shirt into the street.* The chance was a good one, and the mob were made aware of it, for catching the wolfish dog in the high noon and carnival of his bloody revels—in the very centre of his own shambles. For a moment the mob was self-baffled by its own numbers and its own fury. But even that fury felt the call for self-control. It was evident that the massy street-door must be driven in, since there was no longer any living person to co-operate with their efforts from within, excepting only a female child. Crowbars dexterously applied in one minute threw the door out of hangings, and the people entered like a torrent. It may be guessed with what fret and irritation to their consuming fury, a signal of pause and absolute silence was made by a person of local importance. In the hope of receiving some useful communication, the mob became silent. 'Now listen,' said the man of authority, 'and we shall learn whether he is above-stairs or below.' Immediately a noise was heard as if of some one forcing windows, and clearly the sound came from a bedroom above. Yes, the fact was apparent that the murderer was even yet in the house: he had been caught in a trap. Not having made himself familiar with the details of Williamson's house, to all appearance he had suddenly become a prisoner in one of the upper rooms. Towards this the crowd now rushed impetuously. The door, however, was found to be slightly fastened; and, at the moment when this was forced, a loud crash of the window, both glass and frame, announced that the wretch had made his escape. He had leaped down; and several persons in the crowd, who burned with the general fury, leaped after him. These persons had not troubled themselves about the nature of the ground; but now, on making an examination of it with torches, they reported it to be an inclined plane, or embankment of clay, very wet and adhesive. The prints of the man's footsteps were deeply impressed upon the clay, and therefore easily traced up to the summit of the embankment; but it was perceived at once that pursuit would be useless, from the density of the mist. Two feet ahead of you, a man was entirely withdrawn from your power of identification; and, on overtaking him, you could not venture to challenge him as the same whom you had lost sight of. Never, through the course of a whole century, could there be a night expected more propitious to an escaping criminal: means of disguise Williams now had in excess; and the dens were innumerable in the neighbourhood of the river that could have sheltered him for years from troublesome inquiries. But favours are thrown away upon the reckless and the thankless. That night, when the turning-point offered itself for his whole future career, Williams took the wrong turn; for, out of mere indolence, he took the turn to his old lodgings—that place which, in all England, he had just now the most reason to shun.

Meantime the crowd had thoroughly searched the premises of Williamson. The first inquiry was for the young grand-daughter. Williams, it was evident, had gone into her room: but in this room apparently it was that the sudden uproar in the streets had surprised him; after which his undivided attention had been directed to the windows, since through these only any retreat had been left open to him. Even this retreat he owed only to the fog and to the hurry of the moment, and to the difficulty of approaching the premises by the rear. The little girl was naturally agitated by the influx of strangers at that hour; but otherwise, through the humane precautions of the neighbours, she was preserved from all knowledge of the dreadful events that had occurred whilst she herself was sleeping. Her poor old grandfather was still missing, until the crowd descended into the cellar; he was then found lying prostrate on the cellar floor: apparently he had been thrown down from the top of the cellar stairs, and with so much violence, that one leg was broken. After he had been thus disabled, Williams had gone down to him, and cut his throat. There was much discussion at the time, in some of the public journals, upon the possibility of reconciling these incidents with other circumstantialities of the case, supposing that only one man had been concerned in the affair.* That there *was* only one man concerned, seems to be certain. One only was seen or heard at Marr's: one only, and beyond all doubt the same man, was seen by the young journeyman in Mrs Williamson's parlour; and one only was traced by his footmarks on the clay embankment. Apparently the course which he had pursued was this: he had introduced himself to Williamson by ordering some beer. This order would oblige the old man to go down into the cellar; Williams would wait until he had reached it, and would then 'slam' and lock the street-door in the violent way described. Williamson would come up in agitation upon hearing this violence. The murderer, aware that he would do so, met him, no doubt, at the head of the cellar stairs, and threw him down; after which he would go down to consummate the murder in his ordinary way. All this would occupy a minute, or a minute and a-half; and in that way the interval would be accounted for that elapsed between the alarming sound of the street-door as heard by the journeyman, and the lamentable outcry of the female servant. It is evident also, that the reason why no cry whatsoever had been heard from the lips of Mrs Williamson, is due to the positions of the parties as I have sketched them. Coming behind Mrs Williamson, unseen therefore, and from her deafness unheard, the murderer would inflict entire abolition of consciousness while she was yet unaware of his presence. But with the servant, who had unavoidably witnessed the attack upon her mistress, the murderer could not obtain the same fulness of advantage; and *she* therefore had time for making an agonising ejaculation.

It has been mentioned, that the murderer of the Marrs was not for nearly a fortnight so much as suspected; meaning that, previously to the Williamson murder, no vestige of any ground for suspicion in any direction whatever had occurred either to the general public or to the police. But there were two very limited exceptions to this state of absolute ignorance. Some of the magistrates had in their possession something which, when closely examined, offered a very probable means for tracing the criminal. But as yet they had *not* traced him. Until the Friday morning next after the destruction of the Williamsons, they had not published the important fact, that upon the ship-carpenter's mallet (with which, as regarded the stunning or disabling process, the murders had been achieved) were inscribed the letters 'J. P.'* This mallet had, by a strange oversight on the part of the murderer, been left behind in Marr's shop; and it is an interesting fact, therefore, that, had the villain been intercepted by the brave pawnbroker, he would have been met virtually disarmed. This public notification was made officially on the Friday, viz., on the thirteenth day after the first murder. And it was instantly followed (as will be seen) by a most important result. Meantime, within the secrecy of one single bedroom in all London, it is a fact that Williams had been whisperingly the object of very deep suspicion from the very first— that is, within that same hour which witnessed the Marr tragedy.

And singular it is, that the suspicion was due entirely to his own folly. Williams lodged, in company with other men of various nations, at a public-house.* In a large dormitory there were arranged five or six beds; these were occupied by artisans, generally of respectable character. One or two Englishmen there were, one or two Scotchmen, three or four Germans, and Williams, whose birth-place was not certainly known. On the fatal Saturday night, about half-past one o'clock, when Williams returned from his dreadful labours, he found the English and Scotch party asleep, but the Germans awake: one of them was sitting up with a lighted candle in his hands, and reading aloud to the other two. Upon this, Williams said, in an angry and very peremptory tone, 'Oh, put that candle out; put it out directly: we shall all be burned in our beds.' Had the British party in the room been awake, Mr Williams would have roused a mutinous protest against this arrogant mandate. But Germans are generally mild and facile in their tempers; so the light was complaisantly extinguished. Yet, as there were no curtains, it struck the Germans that the danger was really none at all; for bed-clothes, massed upon each other, will no more burn than the leaves of a closed book. Privately, therefore, the Germans drew an inference, that Mr Williams must have had some urgent motive for withdrawing his own person and dress from observation. What this motive might be, the next day's news diffused all over London, and of course at this house, not two furlongs from Marr's shop, made awfully evident; and, as may well be supposed, the suspicion was communicated to the other members of the dormitory. All of them, however, were aware of the legal danger attaching, under English law, to insinuations against a man, even if true, which might not admit of proof. In reality, had Williams used the most obvious precautions, had he simply walked down to the Thames (not a stone's-throw distant), and flung two of his implements into the river, no conclusive proof could have been adduced against him. And he might have realised the scheme of Courvoisier (the murderer of Lord William Russell)*—viz., have sought each separate month's support in a separate well-concerted murder. The party in the dormitory, meantime, were satisfied themselves, but waited for evidences that might satisfy others. No sooner, therefore, had the official notice been published as to the initials J. P. on the mallet, than every man in the house recognised at once the well-known initials of an honest Norwegian ship-carpenter, John

Petersen, who had worked in the English dockyards until the present year; but, having occasion to revisit his native land, had left his box of tools in the garrets of this inn. These garrets were now searched. Petersen's tool-chest was found, but wanting the mallet; and, on further examination, another overwhelming discovery was made. The surgeon, who examined the corpses at Williamson's, had given it as his opinion that the throats were not cut by means of a razor, but of some implement differently shaped. It was now remembered that Williams had recently borrowed a large French knife of peculiar construction; and accordingly, from a heap of old lumber and rags, there was soon extricated a waistcoat, which the whole house could swear to as recently worn by Williams. In this waistcoat, and glued by gore to the lining of its pockets, was found the French knife. Next, it was matter of notoriety to everybody in the inn, that Williams ordinarily wore at present a pair of creaking shoes, and a brown surtout lined with silk. Many other presumptions seemed scarcely called for. Williams was immediately apprehended, and briefly examined. This was on the Friday. On the Saturday morning (viz., fourteen days from the Marr murders) he was again brought up. The circumstantial evidence was overwhelming; Williams watched its course, but said very little. At the close, he was fully committed for trial at the next sessions; and it is needless to say, that, on his road to prison, he was pursued by mobs so fierce, that, under ordinary circumstances, there would have been small hope of escaping summary vengeance. But upon this occasion a powerful escort had been provided; so that he was safely lodged in jail. In this particular jail at this time, the regulation was, that at five o'clock P.M. all the prisoners on the criminal side should be finally locked up for the night, and without candles. For fourteen hours (that is, until seven o'clock on the next morning) they were left unvisited, and in total darkness. Time, therefore, Williams had for committing suicide. The means in other respects were small. One iron bar there was, meant (if I remember) for the suspension of a lamp; upon this he had hanged himself by his braces.* At what hour was uncertain: some people fancied at midnight. And in that case, precisely at the hour when, fourteen days before, he had been spreading horror and desolation through the quiet family of poor Marr, now was he forced into drinking of the same cup, presented to his lips by the same accursed hands.

The case of the M'Keans, which has been specially alluded to, merits also a slight rehearsal for the dreadful picturesqueness of some two or three amongst its circumstances. The scene of this murder was at a rustic inn, some few miles (I think) from Manchester; and the advantageous situation of this inn it was, out of which arose the twofold temptations of the case. Generally speaking, an inn argues, of course, a close cincture of neighbours—as the original motive for opening such an establishment. But, in this case, the house individually was solitary, so that no interruption was to be looked for from any persons living within reach of screams; and yet, on the other hand, the circumjacent vicinity was eminently populous; as one consequence of which, a benefit club had established its weekly rendezvous in this inn, and left the pecuniary accumulations in their club-room, under the custody of the landlord. This fund arose often to a considerable amount, fifty or seventy pounds, before it was transferred to the hands of a banker. Here, therefore, was a treasure worth some little risk, and a situation that promised next to none. These attractive circumstances had, by accident, become accurately known to one or both of the two M'Keans; and, unfortunately, at a moment of overwhelming misfortune to themselves. They were hawkers; and, until lately, had borne most respectable characters: but some mercantile crash had overtaken them with utter ruin, in which their joint capital had been swallowed up to the last shilling. This sudden prostration had made them desperate: their own little property had been swallowed up in a large *social* catastrophe, and society at large they looked upon as accountable to them for a robbery. In preying, therefore, upon society, they considered themselves as pursuing a wild natural justice* of retaliation. The money aimed at did certainly assume the character of public money, being the product of many separate subscriptions. They forgot, however, that in the murderous acts, which too certainly they meditated as preliminaries to the robbery, they could plead no such imaginary social precedent. In dealing with a family that seemed almost helpless, if all went smoothly, they relied entirely upon their own bodily strength. They were stout young men, twenty-eight to thirty-two years old; somewhat undersized as to height; but squarely built, deep-chested, broad-shouldered, and so beautifully formed, as regarded the symmetry of their limbs and their articulations, that, after their execution, the bodies were privately exhibited by the sur-

geons of the Manchester Infirmary, as objects of statuesque interest.*
On the other hand, the household which they proposed to attack
consisted of the following four persons:—1. the landlord, a stoutish
farmer—but *him* they intended to disable by a trick then newly
introduced amongst robbers, and termed *hocussing, i. e.*, clandestinely
drugging the liquor of the victim with laudanum;* 2. the landlord's
wife; 3. a young servant-woman; 4. a boy, twelve or fourteen years
old. The danger was, that out of four persons, scattered by possibility over a house which had two separate exits, one at least might
escape, and by better acquaintance with the adjacent paths, might
succeed in giving an alarm to some of the houses a furlong distant.
Their final resolution was, to be guided by circumstances as to the
mode of conducting the affair; and yet, as it seemed essential to
success that they should assume the air of strangers to each other, it
was necessary that they should preconcert some general outline of
their plan; since it would on this scheme be impossible, without
awaking violent suspicions, to make any communications under the
eyes of the family. This outline included, at the least, one murder: so
much was settled; but, otherwise, their subsequent proceedings
make it evident that they wished to have as little bloodshed as was
consistent with their final object. On the appointed day, they presented themselves separately at the rustic inn, and at different hours.
One came as early as four o'clock in the afternoon; the other not
until half-past seven. They saluted each other distantly and shyly;
and, though occasionally exchanging a few words in the character
of strangers, did not seem disposed to any familiar intercourse. With
the landlord, however, on his return about eight o'clock from
Manchester, one of the brothers entered into a lively conversation:
invited him to take a tumbler of punch; and, at a moment when the
landlord's absence from the room allowed it, poured into the punch a
spoonful of laudanum. Some time after this, the clock struck ten;
upon which the elder M'Kean, professing to be weary, asked to be
shown up to his bedroom: for each brother, immediately on arriving,
had engaged a bed. On this, the poor servant-girl presented herself
with a bed-candle to light him upstairs. At this critical moment the
family were distributed thus:—the landlord, stupified with the horrid
narcotic which he had drunk, had retired to a private room adjoining
the public room, for the purpose of reclining upon a sofa: and he,
luckily for his own safety, was looked upon as entirely incapacitated

for action. The landlady was occupied with her husband. And thus the younger M'Kean was left alone in the public room. He rose, therefore, softly, and placed himself at the foot of the stairs which his brother had just ascended, so as to be sure of intercepting any fugitive from the bedroom above. Into that room the elder M'Kean was ushered by the servant, who pointed to two beds—one of which was already half occupied by the boy, and the other empty: in these, she intimated that the two strangers must dispose of themselves for the night, according to any arrangement that they might agree upon. Saying this, she presented him with the candle, which he in a moment placed upon the table; and, intercepting her retreat from the room, threw his arms around her neck with a gesture as though he meant to kiss her. This was evidently what she herself anticipated, and endeavoured to prevent. Her horror may be imagined, when she felt the perfidious hand that clasped her neck armed with a razor, and violently cutting her throat. She was hardly able to utter one scream, before she sank powerless upon the floor. This dreadful spectacle was witnessed by the boy, who was not asleep, but had presence of mind enough instantly to close his eyes. The murderer advanced hastily to the bed, and anxiously examined the expression of the boy's features: satisfied he was not, and he then placed his hand upon the boy's heart, in order to judge by its beatings whether he were agitated or not. This was a dreadful trial: and no doubt the counterfeit sleep would immediately have been detected, when suddenly a dreadful spectacle drew off the attention of the murderer. Solemnly, and in ghostly silence, uprose in her dying delirium the murdered girl; she stood upright, she walked steadily for a moment or two, she bent her steps towards the door. The murderer turned away to pursue her; and at that moment the boy, feeling that his one solitary chance was to fly whilst this scene was in progress, bounded out of bed. On the landing at the head of the stairs was one murderer, at the foot of the stairs was the other: who could believe that the boy had the shadow of a chance for escaping? And yet, in the most natural way, he surmounted all hindrances. In the boy's horror, he laid his left hand on the balustrade, and took a flying leap over it, which landed him at the bottom of the stairs, without having touched a single stair. He had thus effectually passed one of the murderers: the other, it is true, was still to be passed; and this would have been impossible but for a sudden accident. The landlady had

been alarmed by the faint scream of the young woman; had hurried
from her private room to the girl's assistance; but at the foot of the
stairs had been intercepted by the younger brother, and was at this
moment struggling with *him*. The confusion of this life-and-death
conflict had allowed the boy to whirl past them. Luckily he took a
turn into a kitchen, out of which was a back-door, fastened by a
single bolt, that ran freely at a touch; and through this door he
rushed into the open fields. But at this moment the elder brother
was set free for pursuit by the death of the poor girl. There is no
doubt, that in her delirium the image moving through her thoughts
was that of the club, which met once a-week. She fancied it no
doubt sitting; and to this room, for help and for safety, she staggered
along; she entered it, and within the doorway once more she
dropped down, and instantly expired. Her murderer, who had followed her closely, now saw himself set at liberty for the pursuit of
the boy. At this critical moment, all was at stake; unless the boy were
caught, the enterprise was ruined. He passed his brother, therefore,
and the landlady without pausing, and rushed through the open
door into the fields. By a single second, perhaps, he was too late.
The boy was keenly aware, that if he continued in sight, he would
have no chance of escaping from a powerful young man. He made,
therefore, at once for a ditch, into which he tumbled headlong. Had
the murderer ventured to make a leisurely examination of the nearest ditch, he would easily have found the boy—made so conspicuous
by his white shirt. But he lost all heart, upon failing at once to arrest
the boy's flight. And every succeeding second made his despair the
greater. If the boy had really effected his escape to the neighbouring
farm-houses, a party of men might be gathered within five minutes;
and already it might have become difficult for himself and his
brother, unacquainted with the field paths, to evade being intercepted. Nothing remained, therefore, but to summon his brother
away. Thus it happened that the landlady, though mangled, escaped
with life, and eventually recovered. The landlord owed his safety to
the stupifying potion. And the baffled murderers had the misery of
knowing that their dreadful crime had been altogether profitless.
The road, indeed, was now open to the club-room; and, probably,
forty seconds would have sufficed to carry off the box of treasure,
which afterwards might have been burst open and pillaged at leisure. But the fear of intercepting enemies was too strongly upon

them; and they fled rapidly by a road which carried them actually within six feet of the lurking boy. That night they passed through Manchester. When daylight returned, they slept in a thicket twenty miles distant from the scene of their guilty attempt. On the second and third nights, they pursued their march on foot, resting again during the day. About sunrise on the fourth morning, they were entering some village near Kirby Lonsdale, in Westmoreland. They must have designedly quitted the direct line of route; for their object was Ayrshire, of which county they were natives; and the regular road would have led them through Shap, Penrith, Carlisle. Probably they were seeking to elude the persecution of the stage-coaches, which, for the last thirty hours, had been scattering at all the inns and road-side *cabarets** hand-bills describing their persons and dress. It happened (perhaps through design) that on this fourth morning they had separated, so as to enter the village ten minutes apart from each other. They were exhausted and footsore. In this condition it was easy to stop them. A blacksmith had silently reconnoitred them, and compared their appearance with the descriptions of the hand-bills. They were then easily overtaken, and separately arrested. Their trial and condemnation speedily followed at Lancaster; and in those days it followed, of course, that they were executed. Otherwise, their case fell so far within the sheltering limits of what would *now* be regarded as extenuating circumstances—that, whilst a murder more or less was not to repel them from their object, very evidently they were anxious to economise the bloodshed as much as possible. Immeasurable, therefore, was the interval which divided them from the monster Williams. They perished on the scaffold: Williams, as I have said, by his own hand; and, in obedience to the law as it then stood, he was buried in the centre of a *quadrivium,** or conflux of four roads (in this case four streets), with a stake driven through his heart.* And over him drives for ever the uproar of unresting London!

APPENDIXES

MANUSCRIPT WRITINGS

A. Peter Anthony Fonk

[This untitled manuscript fragment is in the National Library of Scotland, MS 4789, fos. 56–62. The date of the manuscript is conjectural, but 1825 seems the most plausible, as the paper is watermarked 1824 and 1825, and in the essay itself De Quincey describes Peter Fonk's father as 'still living in 1825'. The present transcription does not record De Quincey's deletions, except in one instance where the meaning requires that the deleted word 'distraction' be retained. It is given in angle brackets (< >). Superscript letters appear in regular type ('M' appears as 'Mr', for example; '22nd' as '22nd'). Underlined words are italicized. De Quincey wrote two footnotes for this essay but did not indicate where in the manuscript they were to appear. They are given below where he seems most likely to have intended their insertion. In the manuscript, the paragraph ending 'but to that inn he never more returned' is followed by the paragraph beginning 'On the 19th of December' (pp. 145–6). Between the two paragraphs, however, De Quincey inserted a request that the compositor move the paragraph beginning 'On the 19th of December' to a position immediately following the paragraph ending 'suspicions as to the guilty author of the catastrophe'. In the present transcription, De Quincey's instructions have been followed. For details of the manuscript, and a complete transcription, see *The Works of Thomas De Quincey: Volume Six*, ed. David Groves and Grevel Lindop (London, 2000), 279–93. Peter Anthony Fonk was a German businessman sentenced to death in 1822 for the murder of William Coenen, though at the time of writing the judgment had not yet received the Royal ratification and 'may be considered as still in suspense' (p. 150). Frederick Burwick identifies the source of De Quincey's narrative as the *Conversations-Lexicon*, published by Brockhaus of Leipzig, in 1824 ('De Quincey and the Aesthetics of Violence', *Wordsworth Circle*, 27 (1996), 77–82).]

PETER ANTHONY FONK was a merchant at Cologne;* and has become the object in some measure of an historical interest, in consequence of the long criminal process depending against him for the murder of William Coenen of Enfeld.* This process began as early as the year 1816, and was not finally closed until the 9th of June 1822, on which day Mr Fonk received sentence of death. The whole affair may be regarded as amongst the most remarkable events of our times, both for the extensive and profound interest which it excited on the continent, an interest fully justified by the inextricable perplexity of the circumstances, and also by the relation it bore to a question much agitated in modern Germany on the comparative merits of the French and German systems of criminal judicature: whether in short the French mode by public pleadings and oral examinations, wound up by a sentence grounded upon the individual opinions of the Jury, or the German mode by secret investigations terminating in a sentence of professional judges under predetermined rules of law, may be considered upon the whole as most favorable to the purposes of justice. A single case would seem to determine little either way: but, from the immense body of pamphlets which this particular case occasioned, it is perhaps justly regarded as having fixed an epoch in the history of that question.

Mr Fonk, the son of a rich merchant who was still living in 1825, and very respectably connected, was born in 1781; and originally was a partner in a firm at Amsterdam; but in 1809 he came to Cologne, and there married the daughter of a considerable tobacconist, Mr Foveaux, of a family well-known at that place. In 1815, conjointly with Schröder an apothecary at Enfeld Mr Fonk established a manufacture of brandy and liqueurs. The manufacturing part of the concern was superintended by Schröder; and the capital for this purpose, about 6000 dollars, was furnished by him. But the whole mercantile management, the sale of the brandy (in part by smuggling), the current disbursements and receipts &c. were conducted by Fonk. Spite of the great profits however, (which, in less than 18 months, by Fonk's own admission amounted to 20,000 dollars) misunderstandings and jealousies arose between the two partners. Schröder was represented by Fonk as having appropriated too large a share of the profits; but on the other hand it seems that Schröder suspected Fonk of having deceived him with regard to the real amount of the profits. At length, with the consent of Fonk, Schröder dispatched to Cologne a young merchant of the name of William Coenen, with a commission to compare the account delivered by Fonk with Fonk's books and papers. It was Schröder's intention that in this examination Coenen should have the assistance of one Elfes, a former servant of Fonk's. This Elfes in fact it was that had first raised Schröder's suspicions, by making known that Fonk had instructed him to report a lower price for the superior brandies than had actually been obtained, and also that he had been made acquainted with other dishonest practices of his by Hahnenbein Fonk's book-keeper. It was not extraordinary therefore that Elfes, on first presenting himself at Fonk's door (Nov. 1, 1816), was dismissed with indignation: but Coenen, though ungraciously received, was permitted to enter upon his duties. This person went to work in a spirit of determined mistrust, in which he was strengthened by the disclosures of Hahnenbein; and in various letters to his own friends and to Schröder he expressed himself in the most contemptuous terms possible of Fonk's behaviour — which he described as very unequal, at one time smooth and fawning, at another cold and repulsive. He began his examination by comparing the entries of Fonk with the acquittances; and found, to his great astonishment, that they tallied exactly with his report to Schröder. This part of his task he had closed on the 6th of November; and next he proceeded to demand from Fonk the inspection of his ledger and his day-book, in which (by Hahnenbein's account) there was evidence to a fraud of not less than 8000 dollars. Fonk replied to this demand with great violence, peremptorily refusing to comply; and that same day he set off for Neuss*— with the view of making some compromise with Schröder apart from Coenen's interferences. Schröder however, instructed and put on his guard by Coenen, declined his proposals; and on the 8th of November came himself to Cologne, whither Fonk also returned on Saturday the 9th between 11 and 12 in the forenoon. Immediately after his arrival, Coenen laid before him a proposal to this effect—that he (Fonk) should allow 18 thousand dollars more for the profit on the brandies, but on the other hand should appropriate the entire profit of that part of the stock not yet sold, and should have a considerable proportion of the utensils and machinery ceded in full property to himself. Upon this proposal a conference ensued between the parties; and this was held in Fonk's house as no room could be procured in either of the two inns to which they applied: and here it must be mentioned that, on the road thither, Hahnenbein pretends to have observed some signs of a secret understanding between Fonk and Coenen. In this conference Fonk agreed to make an allowance of 8 thousand dollars more on account of the profits: but this agreement was not finally concluded, because Schröder wished previously to consult Coenen in private. About 8 o'clock the party separated, and a second conference was fixed for the next morning (Sunday Nov. 10) as early as 9 o'clock. Coenen and Schröder went home to their inn, and, were there joined by Hahnenbein. At 10 o'clock the party broke up; and, upon Hahnenbein's preparing to move homewards, Coenen took his hat to accompany him—and to meet his unhappy and still mysterious end. He parted with Hahnenbein in the middle of the old market place, and turned back to the street in which his inn was situated not more than 30 paces off: but to that inn he never more returned.

Immediately upon the disappearance of Coenen, Schröder, in conjunction with the friends and relatives of the unfortunate man, set on foot a rigorous investigation: nobody could assign any reason for his disappearance; and the suspicion arose powerfully that he had been put out of the way on purpose to get rid of an obstruction to some guilty design; in which case no person stood open to the charge of having any interest of that nature, excepting only Fonk. Whilst these thoughts were gathering strength in the public mind, three friends of Coenen from Enfeld on the 21st of November paid a visit to Fonk: and his behaviour on that occasion was powerfully adapted to corroborate the existing suspicion. He read to these persons a letter which he had written upon this melancholy event; wept upon reading it; and formally solicited their attention to the tears which he was shedding. He displayed a note before them, exclaiming at the time—*See here the hand-writing of poor Coenen*: and upon examination it turned out *not* to be Coenen's hand-writing! He called his book-keeper, assuring the visitors that they would hear from him such things as would set their hair on end; and—after all it appeared that the book-keeper had nothing to tell!

As yet however the body had not been found; and as yet therefore no legal measures could be adopted against Fonk. Meantime the police exerted themselves greatly to find some traces for guiding their inquiries. A brothel, which Coenen had occasionally visited and where he was known to have made assignations with a Florentine girl, was searched; but no grounds of suspicion were discovered there. Coenen, it was affirmed, had not been there at all on that evening; and all the neighbours as well as the inmates of the brothel bore testimony that, on the 9th of November, no noise had been heard; a circumstance of considerable weight; because, from the situation and the construction of the house, no uproar could possibly have escaped notice, had any happened. A reward of 3 thousand francs was offered, but to no purpose. Fonk and Hahnenbein were vigilantly observed by the police; and with respect to the latter it should be here mentioned—that, on the same day on which he had received the visit of Coenen's three friends, he called on the police-officer Guisez, and begged his advice as to the most eligible course under these difficult circumstances: that advice had been to throw himself into the arms of justice; which however Fonk had not thought proper to comply with. The public anxiety had now reached it's height: curiosity, terror, and pity, divided the minds of men: nothing was talked of—nothing thought of but the too probable fate of poor Coenen; when at length a discovery was made which put an end to all further doubts on that subject, and greatly strengthened the suspicions as to the guilty author of the catastrophe.

On the 19th of December, that is just 40 days after the disappearance of Coenen, his body was found in the Rhine below Cologne. It's condition and appearance were as follows: the dress was perfect, only that the two uppermost buttons of his coat, which he usually wore closely buttoned, were torn off. A breast pocket, in which it was his custom to carry his pocket-book, was empty; and the pocket-book itself has never been discovered. On the other hand his gold watch was safe in his fob. Severe injuries had been inflicted on the head; a contused wound above the left eye, a violent contusion on the back of the head, an open wound upon the crown of the scull (which however had probably been occasioned by some accident in the water), and upon the throat marks of strangulation. The finding of the examiners was—that these injuries had been inflicted during life-time, and had been sufficient to produce death; and that the wound on the forehead had been inflicted by some sharp-edged instrument, such for instance as the back of a cooper's knife.* Some doubts thrown out by Dr Walther a celebrated anatomist at Bonn, and a consequent hypothesis that all these injuries might have been received in the water, were of no force to mislead any unprejudiced person, or in the least degree to unsettle the conviction of the public that Coenen had received his death from the hands of a murderer. How impossible it was for him either designedly or by accident to have met his death in the Rhine—appears from this, that he could not have reached the river without going through the city gates; but on that night no person whatever had applied to have the gates opened.

The wound upon the forehead had been thought to point pretty clearly to the instrument by which it had been inflicted—viz. a cooper's knife, such as was constantly lying in Fonk's counting-house, and hence, by a very natural following out of the suggestion, pointed to an accomplice in the person of one Christian Hamacher, a cooper in the service of Fonk, who was always at hand and bound to his interests by the closest ties. Against this man some circumstances of suspicion had already arisen; such as particular conversations which he was alleged to have held, and unusual habits of expense: but unfortunately these and other allegations had not been inquired into at the time. Enough however was now established to warrant the police in stronger measures against both Hamacher and his master: accordingly, on the 22nd of December, Fonk was confined to his house by a military guard; and, on the 31st of January 1817, Hamacher was taken into custody at a tavern. From the very first this man was openly reproached by the police as an accomplice in the murder of Coenen: endeavours were made to draw him into declarations which might argue a guilty knowledge of that transaction: a fellow prisoner was instructed to steal into his confidence; persons were set to overhear him: and finally he was confined in a dark and damp dungeon. Under this system of treatment on the 10th of March Christian Hamacher began to confess. His confession was made to the Procurator General von Sandt, and amounted to this—that on the night of the 9th of November William

Coenen had been murdered by Fonk in Fonk's house and with his assistance. It was not however until the 16th of April that this confession was reduced to legal form; and the circumstances of it were in substance these. As early as the 4th of November Fonk had tampered with him to murder Coenen; but at that time he had lent no ear to Fonk's proposals. On the 9th of November he was again working at Fonk's, and received orders to attend at 9 o'clock in the evening. He did so, was conducted by Fonk into the counting-house, and wine was there set before him. Coenen, he was informed by Fonk, had gone from the house at 8 o'clock; but (having left something behind him) was sure to return; and, upon his ringing the bell, Hamacher was to let him in. Rather more than a quarter after 10, or it might be as much as half after, there came a ring at the doorbell; upon which Hamacher went to the door, and found Coenen there, who inquired for Mr Fonk. Fonk immediately came forward: the two gentlemen exchanged salutations; and Coenen said that he had left something behind; to which Fonk replied—*Aye, so I thought.* (Here it should be explained that some people have thought it very unnatural that Fonk should know beforehand that Coenen would return, and return too at a particular hour, to fetch something which he had left behind: but, in answer to this, it may be said that, if (as Hahnenbein represented) some clandestine appointment had been arranged between Coenen and Fonk, this pretence about leaving something behind was the very best mode which they could concert for masquing the real purpose of the interview: for Hamacher, it must be recollected, was in Fonk's confidence, but not in Coenen's.) Fonk and Coenen then went up together to the room in which Schröder and the rest had conducted the business of that evening's conference; and, upon coming down, Fonk was talking of a particular brandy of Schröder's and comparing it with some very old French brandy which he proposed to Coenen that he should taste. Coenen at first declined; but upon that Fonk pressed him, and said—*Now, pray do me the favor to try it; do, I beg of you; I am confident you will say, upon trial, that you never tasted any thing like it before*; and at the same time he desired Hamacher to bring a glass, himself taking the cooper's knife which lay upon the table, and hiding it under his coat. All three then went into the packing room, which lay directly under the maid-servants' bed-room; and immediately upon arriving there the tragedy began.

The circumstances were these:—Fonk drew out the cooper's tool, and adjusted his hand as if going to strike the cask open; but all at once, whirling round, he struck Coenen upon the head, exclaiming '*There, fellow, take that for your sample!*'; thereupon Coenen began to bleed; and, upon receiving another blow from Fonk upon the breast, fell backwards; striking his head in falling against a large stone weight belonging to a steelyard. Hereupon Fonk said to Hamacher, *Lay hold of the fellow's throat, that he shall not sing out*; which he (Hamacher) did, and continued to do, until he had satisfied himself that it was no longer in Coenen's power to make any alarm. This done, Fonk drew the pocket-book out of Coenen's breast-pocket: Hamacher packed the dead body into a cask, enveloping the head in a sack, then filling up the cask with straw, and finally closing it up. After this they agreed with each other to have the cask carried out of the city by Adam Hamacher, the brother of Christian; and accordingly on the following day (Sunday) Adam had orders to attend on Monday with his cart at Fonk's house very early in the morning. Monday came; and by 4 o'clock in the morning Adam was with his cart at Mr Fonk's door. Mr Fonk was himself in attendance to see the cask regularly delivered, and everything done correctly. Mr Fonk opened the door, assisted to back the cart into his court-yard, and saw the cask carted; after which Adam set forward with his load to a place near Mühlheim* on the Rhine. Up to the time of his arrival at this place, Adam knew nothing at all of the contents of the cask; and, having unloaded it, was on the point of driving off: but, upon *that*, Christian called out to him in great agitation—'Adam, you must not leave me yet: there is a dead man packed up in the cask.' 'A dead man!' said Adam: 'had I known that, it should have been long before I would have carted a hogshead for Mr Fonk.' These were all the words that passed. Christian Hamacher, the cooper, took out his tools, and knocked the cask open; after which he and Adam took out the corpse between them; and Christian, attaching a heavy stone to it by a leathern thong, sank it in the Rhine; and in executing this part of his commission, in order to shove off the body into deep water, Christian waded in so far from the shore that his boots were filled with water. Meantime, what became of Coenen's pipe and hat? According to the confession of Hamacher, immediately after the murder Mr Fonk carried them both into the counting-house; then went to the door with them; and, after 10 minutes' absence, returned without them: so that Hamacher was not able to say what became of them. (Some reports stated that a pipe was found with Coenen's dead body on the 19th of December; but, as it was never produced judicially until the year 1822, it could not be identified, and therefore no stress is to be laid on that part of the case. As to the hat, a neighbour of Fonk's, one Engels, a baker by trade, sometime between Easter and Whitsuntide drew up from the common sewer *a* hat, but whether *the* hat or no—there is the question.) To Christian Hamacher, for his assistance and to purchase his silence, Mr Fonk promised a hundred dollars; and had in fact immediately paid him 30 upon account.

Such was Hamacher's confession; all which he repeated, for a second time, upon the 9th of May: but soon after he began to vacillate, and retracted first that part which related to his brother (who, together with Fonk's book-keeper Hahnenbein, and some others, had by this time been arrested); and finally he retracted the whole. He now alleged that the Procurator General, von Sandt, had seduced him into this false confession; had even composed it for him; and had taught it him by heart. Upon this recantation it is that the defenders of Fonk rely.

The judicial management of the affair now travelled a very lingering and unsteady course. Up to the 4th of October 1817 it remained in the hands of the authorities at Cologne: but upon that day it was transferred to the military tribunal at Triers,* from a jealousy of the undue influence exercized in the former city by the very respectable and extensive connexions of the family of Foveaux. In this new court however much more anxiety was discovered for censuring the proceedings of the former judges than for ascertaining the guilt of Fonk and his alleged accomplice. At length, on the 23rd of June 1818, a judgement was pronounced entertaining the charge against Christian Hamacher, but setting Fonk and Hahnenbein at liberty. Soon after, upon new grounds of suspicion, Fonk was again arrested: but, by a decree of the Senate of Cologne, was again discharged. Hamacher's trial meantime came on before the Assize court of Triers; and on the 31st of October 1820 he was convicted as an accomplice, but without premeditation, in the murder of Coenen, and was condemned to hard labor for 16 years.

On the 3rd of November 1820, Mr Fonk was again taken into custody: the preliminary investigation lasted until June 1821: on the 22nd of April 1822 the public and solemn trial of the case came on before the Assize-court of Triers; and on June 9th of the same year it closed,—the jury, by a majority of 7 against 5, finding Mr Fonk guilty of wilful and premeditated murder upon the body of William Coenen on the night between the 9th and 10th of November 1816; and thereupon the court proceeded to award sentence of death against Mr Peter Fonk. The trial lasted 7 weeks; and no less than 247 witnesses were examined in the course of it.

Upon this unpleasant turn in the affair Mr Fonk appealed against the sentence to the court of revision at Berlin: arguments were heard, and the case underwent another sifting before this court: however the issue of the matter was that the court rejected his appeal, and affirmed the judgement of the court below. This judgement however, before it can be carried into effect, must receive the Royal ratification; and, as that had not by the last accounts, as yet reached Cologne, the matter may be considered as still in suspense.

Great and earnest as were the pains taken with this case before the court, yet it may be truly affirmed that the extrajudicial examination of it, both during the trial and after it, was pursued with still more heat, passionateness, and <distraction> of opinion. The public mind in that part of Germany is yet agitated with the question of Mr Fonk's guilt. And certainly the grounds for suspension of judgement are unusually strong. Except a confession afterwards retracted, and the internal presumptions against him (slight or strong) from the circumstances of the case which brought him under a liability to two motives for committing the alleged murder—viz. revenge and pecuniary interest,—these excepted, there is positively no shadow of evidence against Mr Fonk. No article of Coenen's apparel or other property, no traces of blood, were discovered upon searching Fonk's house. As to the hat, which was found so near to it, *that* certainly would wear a very suspicious appearance, had it been identified as Coenen's hat: but this was not done. It is true undoubtedly that the murder is not only a most mysterious but absolutely an unaccountable one, if we suppose Mr Fonk *not* to have been the murderer: that Coenen was murdered in the brothel, is a hypothesis quite untenable: and that he could not have been murdered for the sake of plunder, is clear as well as on other considerations as particularly because his gold watch was not taken. Yet surely it would be a most precipitate line of argument to load Mr Fonk with the dreadful charge of murder merely because no other person could be produced who had any apparent interest in that act. On the other hand it cannot be denied that Fonk's behaviour, upon the first disappearance of Coenen, was liable to a most sinister construction: and again it is certain that one circumstance which has weighed much in his favor with the public, has been entirely misapprehended. A jury of merchants, on examining Fonk's books, declared that particular book, which Hahnenbein had pointed out as the fraudulent one, to be perfectly correct. But by '*correct*' they meant only *self-consistent*: all the parts were made to tally with one another: but this by no means proved that it was consistent with other books known to Coenen and Hahnenbein: entries might have been transferred to this book, that separately taken were not open to any suspicion, but which may have been evidently fraudulent in the eyes of Hahnenbein who had inspected all the books—and would have been so in the eyes of Coenen, had he also been allowed to go through them.

The whole stress of the evidence therefore, after all, lies in the confession of Hamacher. Yet here again there is a great perplexity besetting us. If we suppose Hamacher's recantation to have been sincere, we are then obliged to load the memory of the Procurator von Sandt (a man in the rest of his life of irreproachable character) with the odium of a crime more atrocious even than the murder itself. Yet again, if we decide for the truth of the confession, difficulties arise that are hard to get over. Some writers indeed have insisted that this confession is in some of it's circumstances absolutely contradictory. *That* is saying too much: yet undoubtedly the improbabilities are considerable. Mr Fonk appealed to the evidence of his servants on the question of time; and this evidence certainly goes near to invalidate the accuracy of Hamacher's statement. It is proved that he supped with his family after 9 o'clock. The nurse-maid and two other servants swear to the fact of his retiring to rest about 10, or (as one of them thinks) a little before 10. At half past eleven another servant carries the key of the house-door to his bed-side, and sees him in bed. This statement therefore leaves a bare possibility, and no more, on considerations of time that Hamacher's story might be true. That the maid-servants again should not have heard either the ringing at the door bell or the inevitable hurly burly* of that dreadful tragedy performed in the packing-room, (that is— immediately below their own sleeping room) is certainly within the verge of possibility, but must be allowed to be improbable. Laying all this together, most unquestionably no reflecting person would venture upon any evidence yet laid before the public, to pronounce the condemnation of Fonk; and even the Jury were so little satisfied with it, that their sentence of *guilty* was carried by the smallest majority of which the number 12 is capable—viz. 7 against 5. One man's voice turned the scale: will any person pretend that it was anything more than an accident which carried this man over to the 6 who were for condemning him rather than to the 5 who acquitted him? But not to insist upon the grievous defects which beset the jury system of trial,—even upon the German system the difficulties in the present case were unusually great[1] because, from the long interval between the disappearance of Coenen and the finding of his body, too much time was inevitably left to the accused persons for clearing away all traces of their crime. Two points however there were, and capital points, which a skilful administrator of the German system would have sifted far more elaborately: and these were

1. the particular degree of interest which Fonk had in Coenen's death. Had he so powerful an interest staked upon that event, was the alternative for instance bankruptcy, exposure as a swindler, &c., as that in this interest alone it is possible to find a sufficient inducement to commit murder? For certainly to a man in Fonk's situation, a husband, a father, a citizen, the mere prospect of evading the necessity for refunding a considerable sum of money was *not* a sufficient motive.

---

[1] The Germans are not much accustomed to value the probabilities of judicial evidence; and here is a proof of it. Surely an hour and a half were a sufficient allowance for murdering a man and packing him up. And that Christian Hamacher having no collusion with the servants should have fixed upon the only space of an hour and a half which afterwards the servants were unable to swear to as otherwise occupied, is certainly one presumption (be it little or much) in favor of his statement. The German critic represents this part of his confession as deducting something from his general credibility; whereas it adds a positive value to it.

2. the very perplexing mystery connected with the alleged visit of Coenen to Fonk on the fatal evening of Saturday Nov. 9:—what was the object of that visit? This is a question upon which greater skill and perseverance would undoubtedly have elicited more light. A passage in one of the last letters of Coenen to his friends, which was brought forward on Hamacher's trial, but afterwards suppressed on Fonk's, gave some ground to suspect that Coenen had not been proof against temptation, but had at last closed with Fonk's proposals for corrupting his integrity. He there expresses himself mysteriously about some great pecuniary advantages that he was speedily to reap. Ill-judged zeal for the honor of the unhappy deceased led his friends to suppress this document; and yet, supposing that the alleged fatal visit did in fact take place, some such guilty understanding between the parties is absolutely necessary to explain it in such a way as to account for Fonk's being aware of it beforehand. This was the view which Hahnenbein took of that matter on his death-bed. 'Coenen,' said he to his brother with his dying breath, 'went doubtless to Fonk's with the expectation of meeting a bribe or security for one, and instead of that God willed that he should meet his murderer.' Coenen and Fonk, it will be remembered, had a private interview on the Saturday morning previously to the conference with Schröder: and, if we suppose the first overtures towards such a collusion to have been made on that occasion, it became necessary that Coenen should endeavour to see Fonk once again without Schröder's privity. Yet for this he had no time left but the evening of the same day; for on the following morning the final conclusion of the negociation and the departure of Schröder from Cologne were settled to take place, after which Coenen would lose all power to compel Fonk into the fulfilment of his promises. Some pretence however was necessary to color his going out so late from his inn, which might else have roused suspicions in Schröder; and with that view he affected to walk home with Hahnenbein. It is much to be regretted that, in the final investigations of this extraordinary case, no allusion should have been made to the letter of Coenen: although indeed, as both Hahnenbein and Schröder were then dead, it was perhaps too late to turn it to much account.

Many other reflexions are suggested by this memorable affair, which upon the whole seems to justify the wish that with the German system of fundamental and deliberate investigation there might, if possible, be combined the publicity of the English system.[2] But after all it is probable that

---

[2] The German critic intermingles with the latter part of his remarks a comparison between the German and English modes of criminal process very much to the disadvantage of the latter, and written apparently with a good deal of party warmth. How far he is entitled to an opinion on the English forms of judicature, may be judged from this— that he says the English allow of no plea of *guilty*; manifestly confounding with this the

no system whatsoever would have sufficed to illuminate the guilty darkness of this transaction; and that it is one of those cases which are reserved for the perfect light of a heavenly tribunal—and for that day when the murderer and his victim shall meet once more and the grave shall give up it's secrets!

English rule of law which allows the accused person to refuse answering any question tending to criminate himself, and instructing the magistrate to put him on his guard against such questions.

B. To the Editor of Blackwood's Magazine

[This manuscript fragment is in the National Library of Scotland, MS 4789, fos. 33–6. The date of the manuscript is 1828. De Quincey observes that he is writing 'at a distance of 12 years' from the slaying of William Coenen, which took place in 1816. The 1828 date of composition is confirmed by De Quincey's letter of 24 April 1828 to William Blackwood asking for money 'for the half-sheet of Fonk accepted some time back', and assuring him that 'with an Introduction ready this evening it will make half a sheet' (Barry Symonds, 'De Quincey and his Publishers', Ph.D. thesis, University of Edinburgh, 1994, 329). The present transcription does not record De Quincey's deletions. Superscript letters are given in regular type ('M"' appears as 'Mr', for example). Underlined words are italicized. For full details of the manuscript, and a complete transcription, see *The Works of Thomas De Quincey: Volume Six*, ed. David Groves and Grevel Lindop (London, 2000), 294–301. The manuscript was intended by De Quincey as the introduction to his discussion of Peter Anthony Fonk (see above, pp. 143–54). William Blackwood seems provisionally to have accepted some combination of the two papers, but he must have changed his mind, for no such article appeared in *Blackwood's Magazine*. Groves and Lindop point out that in the present manuscript De Quincey has 'confused the finer points of his own fiction'. In the published 'On Murder' article of 1827, 'his persona "X.Y.Z." had professed to be shocked by the lecture he transmitted. Now the lecturer signs *himself* "X.Y.Z." and attacks the correspondent who transmitted his lecture to the magazine' (*The Works of Thomas De Quincey: Volume Six*, 294). De Quincey reworked parts of the dialogue with the servant (see below, p. 157) for his second paper 'On Murder' (see above, p. 84).]

SIR,
SEVERAL months ago, whilst travelling in Germany, I met with a number of your far-famed journal, in which I was surprized to find published a lecture of my own, delivered sometime back to a Society of Gentlemen Amateurs, on *Murder considered as one of the Fine Arts*. The person, who communicated that article, did so from no good will to me,—as he discovers pretty clearly by his very hypocritical preface. He would denounce me, forsooth, to Bow Street! and quotes Lactantius* against me. But I despise him, and defy his innuendoes and his threats. And it gratifies me to find that Christopher North* despises him no less. The few words he bestows upon your correspondent are just what I should have anticipated

from his known good sense and philosophy: and the whole club are as much pleased as myself; and I have it in command from them to make our united acknowledgements.

In saying this I discharge one part of my business in now addressing you; and I am further specially instructed to request the honor of your company upon any occasion when you may visit London. Two such celebrated public characters as Christopher North or Mr Blackwood, we should feel proud to welcome with a splendid banquet and the honors of an extraordinary sitting. Pray do not be alarmed by any superannuated old assassins whom you may see lounging about our ante-chambers: for they are all as good as muzzled, if not absolutely toothless. I dare say it has often happened to you, in calling upon a country gentleman, to make your way to his presence through a whole kennel of dogs littering the lawn or the vestibule—hounds, pointers, grey-hounds, and perhaps a wolf-dog or two, whose 'feud' you have to stand until they are called off by the master's voice. Few situations of petty danger require more nerve; nay, without exaggeration I might say, of extreme danger. For myself, I have during my life been four times in peril of instant death: yet on any one of those occasions I have had less need of steeling myself to firmness by an extraordinary effort than at the moment of standing that *burst* of sudden fury and hostile demonstration which follows the first discovery of a stranger's person by these canine loungers about rural dwellings: especially in cases where one is not quite assured that any controlling voice is immediately at hand. Yet, much as people suffer in nerves from these rencontres, it is seldom that one hears of their suffering anything worse. And so you will find it with us: for, as I have said, besides amateurs, we have a few old professional murderers at our board: and they will be apt to snarl a little as you pass them. But you need only hold up your stick at any one of them, and say—*Down, Sir, down*, when in all probability he will slink off growling to his seat. One of them undoubtedly is rather savage, and in the dark might be dangerous. Not but he is an excellent and solid character in the main, though rather given to stab his dearest friends when he can get behind their backs. But we all have our little faults. And now that you know the worst about us, I may say— 'Forewarned, fore-armed.'*

So much on the part of the club generally. And, now for myself in particular, I have something more pressing to trouble you upon; and *that* is—to clear myself of two calumnies with which malicious people have aspersed me. One is—that, in my character of a man of taste and *virtu*,* I have gone so far as to offer premiums—and bounties to my own servant for murders of a superior quality. I do assure you, Mr North, that this is not the fact: and what it may have grown out of I presume to be this.

Saturday is my day for regaling with the best murders that can be had in the public journals of the Empire. After the fatigues of the week it is delightful to the mind of sensibility to relax in this way, and to sacrifice to the muses and the fine arts. My servant therefore has it amongst his duties to cater for me on this occasion: his orders are always to have a murder ready for my inspection, and if possible a series of murders; fresh, if such are to be had,—if not, stale. Now my enemies would insinuate that, in default of any satisfactory murders turning up in the papers,—(as there are dull periods in this business no less than in others), he is incited to embark on a home manufacture of his own: and I do not deny that a faithful servant, who is zealous for his master's service, may be likely to entertain such a thought. But it is well known to all my friends that I uniformly set my face against anything of the sort. I tell my servant that, when the newspapers fail him, he is at liberty to supply my table out of the *Newgate Calendar, God's Revenge Against Murder,** or other books of that class. Indeed to me it seems to something like presumption in a mere illiterate serving-man to think that he can execute anything that is fit to meet the approbation of connoisseurs. Over and above which reason, it is well known to candid people that I am most decidedly for goodness and morality. Therefore, on both considerations, as soon as ever I hear of any fellow of mine throwing out hints that look that way,—I make up my mind to nip the thing in the bud;* and I have him up to the drawing-room without delay; and then I reason with him. Let *me* alone for reasoning with him. 'John,' I say to him, (or 'Thomas,' as the case may be), 'From having read Aristotle,* and the Scholiasts,* and Thomas a Kempis,* and what not, I am enabled to see to the bottom of this matter: and now suffer me to reason with you as a man and as a footman.' And so then I reason with him; and I show him clearly what comes of taking to professional practices. 'From Murder,' I say to him, 'you will soon come to highway robbery; and from highway robbery it is but a short step to petty larceny. And when once you are got to *that*, there comes in sad progression sabbath-breaking, drunkenness, and late hours; until the awful climax terminates in neglect of dress, non-punctuality, and general waspishness. Many a man has begun with dabbling a little in murder, and thought he would stop there, until from one thing to another he has been led so far that in a few years he has become generally disrespectable.' In this way I reason with them; and by these and similar pictures of the shocking tendencies of a taste for murder when immoderately indulged, I have sometimes brought a great stout cartilaginous fellow to tremble like an aspen tree and to sob like a child. Oh! Sir, it's awful to hear the scale of horrors that I set before them!—But if it happens that all I can say is thrown away, that one might as well talk to the wind, and that a man is clearly bent upon doing a little in the murderous line,—I then change my tone, and after expressing a hope that as soon as he has sown his wild oats in that seductive path, he will see his error, and cultivate less agitating studies than murder, which (as I tell them candidly) never fails in the long run to make a man an object of dislike and obloquy,—I then wind up by throwing in a few suggestions on the principles of good taste. For, because a man's morals are bad, that is no reason why his taste should not be improved:

Est aliquid prodire tenus, si non datur ultrà:*

and, if murders are to be committed, it can do no party any good that they should offend in point of elegance. It is from this latter part of my lecture, as I suppose, that the calumny I have mentioned takes it's rise.

But another calumny, which wounds my feelings no less, is—that, in my critical judgements upon murders, it is pretended I shew myself biassed by an unworthy nationality. This notion must have grown out of that particular lecture published by you, in which it is true that I draw my illustrations chiefly from English murders. But that is all an accident. I never had a thought of insinuating that most meritorious murders have not been committed in other parts of Great Britain and also in various regions of the continent. In particular, with respect to the Germans—who are loud in complaining that the only murder, I have condescended to notice as coming from their country (viz. the Mannheim baker's*) was due to an Englishman—I protest that this circumstance had no weight in my selection. I was undoubtedly influenced by the consideration that the author of that murder was a member of our club—a man of refined taste—and a particular friend of my own. But otherwise, as to mere national distinctions, I am above them: *Tros, Tyriusque mihi** &c. And, to shew that I am sincere, I send you herewith the most eminent German murder that has been produced for the last 50 years,* which kept all the states of the Rhine and the Danube in agitation for 7 years, and even yet, at a distance of 12 years, is the subject of conversation and profound interest.——As to French murders, I acknowledge that not one out of a hundred is entirely satisfactory to my mind: circumstances of outrage and unnatural horror disfigure most of them: and very rarely it is that you will find a French murder in a chaste and pure style. Yet the following murder of more than a century back, communicated to me by a Frenchman who writes in a very angry tone, is certainly unobjectionable. It belongs to that very valuable class of murders—the mysterious; for to this hour no light has been thrown upon it. The Frenchman insists upon it that the great Williams, in his last performance (viz. at the Williamsons'*) was indebted for some of his best ideas to this Parisian murder: indeed, he calls Williams a 'filthy plagiarist': but that is what nobody will admit but a jealous

Frenchman: though it must be owned that some of the circumstances in the Parisian case of 1720 and the London of 1811 are in remarkable coincidence.

In the year 1720 the murder of M. de Savary* made a prodigious sensation throughout France. He lived in Paris; was an unmarried man of dissipated life; and his house was the resort of many wits and courtiers. His establishment was a very small one, consisting only of a valet and a woman cook. One day a person unknown, of polished manners and elegant appearance, paid him a visit. This person was courteously received, and asked to dinner; an invitation which he readily accepted. A little before dinner the valet was sent down into the cellar for a few bottles of Champaigne; and, upon some pretence or other, the stranger followed him. In the cellar the valet, wholly off his guard and stooping down into a wine-binn, was easily and without noise despatched by a blow from a wooden mallet on the back of the head. A dog, confined in the same cellar, was despatched in the same way. This done, the murderer crept silently into the kitchen—where the cook was fricasseeing some chickens: her attention was called off by the noise of frying and stewing; and one blow from the mallet effectually stunned her, after which the murder was completed. Without any noise or disturbance the extermination was now complete below stairs. Reascending therefore to M. Savary, whom he had reserved for his *bonne bouche*,* the murderer found little difficulty with *him*; for he was disabled at this time from offering any resistance by an attack of gout which confined him to his easy chair. These circumstances came to be known in the most singular way possible: the murderer actually sate down and deliberately recorded them in the blank leaves of a book which he left open upon the table: after which he walked out, and shut the door. The first discovery was made pretty much in the same way as in the case of the Marrs: a person called in the evening, and knocked long and loud for above a quarter of an hour,* until the attention of the neighbours was roused; violent suspicions arose; the door was forced; and the corpses were found lying prostrate just as they had fallen, but without much bloodshed—the heads having in every case been thoroughly crushed by the mallet. The next mystery was as to the motive of the assassin. That it was not robbery, appeared clearly from the state of the dining table which was laid out for dinner and not one piece of plate missing. It was concluded therefore to have been revenge: to confirm which, on a small time-piece bearing a skull cut in ivory, with the following inscription—'Look on this, that you may regulate your life'—there was found written in pencil by the murderer—'Look at his life, and you will not be surprized at his death.' Another discovery was soon made which seemed to point to some dishonored husband as the author of this revenge. Amongst M. de

Savary's papers, when examined by the Police, was found one in a lady's hand-writing containing these words: 'We are lost! My husband has just learned all! think of some means to avert his anger. *Parapel* is the only one who can restore him to reason. Let him speak to my husband: for, unless he does, we have no hope of safety.' This billet had neither signature nor date. *Parapel* was arrested, and acknowledged himself an acquaintance of M. de Savary's: but, after many examinations and long confinement, persisting in his first declaration that he knew nothing of the circumstances to which the note referred, he was set at liberty. Many others were arrested on suspicion: and it was then ascertained that a prince of the blood and numerous persons of the highest rank frequented the house; and either because the suspicions took a dangerous direction, or because no clue really could be gained,—the affair was gradually hushed up: all the parties arrested were liberated; and the whole investigation was dismissed by the police: though the matter was not forgotten, and even to the time of the revolution* it remained a mystery of profound interest.

My judgement upon this transaction, which I solemnly pronounce of the first water,* is—that, whether the murderer were a dishonored husband or not, he was clearly an amateur of the finest genius; so fine, that I must be allowed to doubt of his being a Frenchman: a point which I must remind my angry French correspondent is not quite established.

I now pass to my German murder: requesting however that your printer will not disfigure me so much as he did in the case of my lecture. If he does, I must inform him what he has to look for: my friend the Mannheim amateur, who did the baker, is come home; and, in case of necessity, he may be as well contented to operate on a couple of compositors as one baker. Thurtell, speaking of some person whom Weare* had cheated, said in a most sentimental tone—'He is my friend'; insinuating that tender apology for murdering the man who had injured him. Now I can assure your printer as a very suspicious circumstance that, upon my pointing out to the Mannheim amateur such horrid outrages upon my text as 'Deipno-sophi*lae*'* (what Pagans be they?), 'reddere *ex*cutum',* and many others, he took me by the hand, his eyes filled with tears, and he said movingly— 'You are my friend: I shall go to Edinburgh.' For that time I diverted his purpose; but I cannot answer for another case, if another should occur of equal atrocity.

Yours ever,

X.Y.Z.

C. A New Paper on Murder as a Fine Art

[The following transcription is made up of two different manuscript fragments. The narrative begins with a manuscript in the Dove Cottage Library, 1988:193. The manuscript is dated 1844, and runs from 'A new paper on Murder as a Fine Art' to 'ready to grant than Fielding to ask'. The manuscript contains a number of different and sometimes unrelated paragraphs. In the present transcription, only that material bearing directly on murder is reproduced. De Quincey's deletions are not recorded. His abbreviations are expanded (for example, his 'more ready to grant y^n F to ask' is rendered as 'more ready to grant than Fielding to ask'). Underlined words are italicized. The narrative is continued in *The Posthumous Works of Thomas De Quincey*, ed. Alexander Japp, 2 vols. (London, 1891–3), i. 77–84. Japp's transcription is apparently compiled from one or more manuscript sources, and runs from 'But this was, after all, a small matter' to 'giving them celebration and malediction in one breath'. For full details of the manuscripts, and a complete transcription, see *The Works of Thomas De Quincey, Volume Fifteen*, ed. Frederick Burwick (London, 2003), pp. 448, 456–61.]

A NEW paper on Murder as a Fine Art—might open thus—that on the model of those Gentlemen Radicals who had voted a monument to Palmer & Co.*—it was proposed to erect statues to such murderers as should by their next of kin or other person interested in their glory—make out a claim rather of superior atrocity—or in equal atrocity of superior neatness, concinnity of execution, perfect finish, or felicitous originality—(the facilitas aequalis*—smoothness—or curiosa felicitas* (elaborate felicity). The men who murdered the *Cat.* in Newgate Calendar* these were—good: but Williams better, who murdered the baby.*—And perhaps—(but the hellish felicity of the last act makes us demur). Fielding* was superior. For you never hear of a fire swallowing up a fire—or a river stopping a deluge—this would be = Kilkenny cats*—but what fire, deluge, or all Killkenny cannot do, Fielding proposed—viz., to murder the murderers—to become himself the Nemesis* of his own atrocity. [. . .]

Fielding the Murderer of Murderers (in a double sense rhetorical and literal)—This is the most terrific revelation yet known. If a gang of robbers draws 12 murderers together, it is not the men at random—der erste der letzte* are all ready for murder: those who come are the murderers by exception whom to form as a gang has found out. But here men hired as sailors—1–2–3–4–5–6—viz. Jones, Heselton, Johnstone, Anderson,

Carr, Gulloway, the 1st 6 asked (tho' so far not at random that some
observation had concurred) are all ready; more ready to grant than Fielding to ask. [. . .]

But that was, after all, a small matter compared with the fine art of the
man calling himself Outis,* on which for a moment we must dwell. Outis—
so at all events he was called, but doubtless he indulged in many aliases—
at Nottingham joined vehemently and sincerely, as it seemed, in pursuit of
a wretch taxed with having murdered, twelve years previously, a wife and
two children at Halifax,* which wretch (when all the depositions were
before the magistrate) turned out to be the aforesaid Mr Outis. That
suggests a wide field of speculation and reference.

Note the power of murderers as fine-art professors to make a new start,
to turn the corner, to retreat upon the road they have come, as though it
were new to them, and to make diversions that disarm suspicion. This
they owe to fortunate obscurity, which attests anew the wonderful com-
pensations of life; for celebrity and power combine to produce drawbacks.

A foreigner who lands in Calcutta at an hour which nobody can name,
and endeavours to effect a sneaking entrance at the postern-gate[1] of the
governor-general's palace, *may* be a decent man; but this we know, that he
has cut the towing-rope which bound his own boat to the great ark of his
country. It may be that, in leaving Paris or Naples, he was simply cutting
the connection with creditors who showed signs of *attachment* not good
for his health. But it may also be that he ran away by the blaze of a burning
inn, which he had fired in order to hide three throats which he had cut,
and nine purses which he had stolen. There is no guarantee for such a
man's character. Have we, then, no such *vauriens** at home? No, not in the
classes standing favourably for promotion. The privilege of safe criminality, not liable to exposure, is limited to classes crowded together like leaves
in Vallombrosa;* for *them* to run away into some mighty city, Manchester or
Glasgow, is to commence life anew. They turn over a new leaf with a
vengeance. Many are the carpenters, bricklayers, bakers' apprentices, etc.
who are now living decently in Bristol, Newcastle, Hull, Liverpool, after
marrying sixteen wives, and leaving families to the care of twelve separate
parishes. That scamp is at this moment circulating and gyrating in society,
like a respectable *te-totum,** though we know not his exact name, who, if he
were pleased to reveal himself in seventeen parts of this kingdom, where
(to use the police language) he has been 'wanted' for some years, would be
hanged seventeen times running, besides putting seventeen Government
rewards into the pockets of seventeen policemen. Oh, reader, you little
know the unutterable romances perpetrated for ever in our most populous

[1] 'Postern-gate.' See the legend of Sir Eustace the Crusader, and the good Sir
Hubert,* who 'sounded the horn which he alone could sound',* as told by Wordsworth.

empire, under cloud of night and distance and utter poverty. Mark *that*— of utter poverty. Wealth is power; but it is a jest in comparison of poverty. Splendour is power; but it is a joke to obscurity. To be poor, to be obscure, to be a baker's apprentice or a tailor's journeyman, throws a power about a man, clothes him with attributes of ubiquity, *really* with those privileges of concealment which in the ring of Gyges* were but fabulous. Is it a king, is it a sultan, that such a man rivals? Oh, friend, he rivals a spiritual power.

Two men are on record, perhaps many more *might* have been on that record, who wrote so many books, and perpetrated so many pamphlets, that at fifty they had forgotten much of their own literary villainies, and at sixty they commenced with murderous ferocity a series of answers to arguments which it was proved upon them afterwards that they themselves had emitted at thirty—thus coming round with volleys of small shot on their own heads, as the Whispering Gallery at St Paul's* begins to retaliate any secrets you have committed to its keeping in echoing thunders after a time, or as Sir John Mandeville under Arctic skies heard in May all those curses thawing, and exploding like minute-guns, which had been frozen up in November.* Even like those self-replying authors, even like those self-reverberators in St Paul's, even like those Arctic practitioners in cursing, who drew bills and *post-obits** in malediction, which were to be honoured after the death of winter, many men are living at this moment in merry England who have figured in so many characters, illustrated so many villages, run away from so many towns, and performed the central part in so many careers, that were the character, the village, the town, the career, brought back with all its circumstances to their memories, positively they would fail to recognise their own presence or incarnation in their own acts and bodies.

We have all read the story told by Addison of a sultan who was persuaded by a dervise to dip his head into a basin of enchanted water,* and thereupon found himself upon some other globe, a son in a poor man's family, married after certain years the woman of his heart, had a family of seven children whom he painfully brought up, went afterwards through many persecutions, walked pensively by the seashore meditating some escape from his miseries, bathed in the sea as a relief from the noonday heat, and on lifting up his head from the waves found himself lifting up his head from the basin into which that cursed dervise had persuaded him to dip. And when he would have cudgelled the holy man for that long life of misery which had, through *his* means, been inflicted upon himself, behold! the holy man proved by affidavit that, in this world, at any rate (where only he could be punishable), the life had lasted but thirty-three seconds. Even so do the dark careers of many amongst our obscure and migratory villains from years shrink up to momentary specks, or, by their very multitude, altogether evanesce. Burke and Hare,* it is well known, had lost all count of their several murders; they no more remembered, or could attempt to remember, their separate victims, than a respectable old banker of seventy-three can remember all the bills with their indorsements made payable for half-a-century at his bank; or than Foote's turnpike-keeper,* who had kept all the toll-bar tickets to Kensington for forty-eight years, pretended to recollect the features of all the men who had delivered them at his gate. For a time, perhaps, Burke (who was a man of fine sensibility) had a representative vision of spasms, and struggles, and convulsions, terminating in a ten-pound note indorsed by Dr ——.* Hare, on the other hand, was a man of principle, a man that you could depend upon—order a corpse for Friday, and on Friday you had it—but he had no feeling whatever. Yet see the unity of result for him and Burke. For both alike all troublesome recollections gathered into one blue haze of heavenly abstractions: orders executed with fidelity, cheques on the bankers to be crossed and passed and cashed, are no more remembered. That is the acme of perfection in our art.

———————

One great class of criminals I am aware of in past times as having specially tormented myself—the class who have left secrets, riddles, behind them. What business has any man to bequeath a conundrum to all posterity, unless he leaves in some separate channel the solution? This must have been done in malice, and for the purpose of annoying us, lest we should have too much proper enjoyment of life when he should have gone. For nobody knows whether the scoundrel could have solved it himself— too like in that respect to some charades which, in my boyish days (but then I had the excuse of youth, which they had not), I not unfrequently propounded to young ladies. Take this as a specimen: My first raises a little hope; my second very little indeed; and my whole is a vast roar of despair. No young lady could ever solve it, neither could I. We all had to give it up. A charade that only needs an answer, which, perhaps, some distance generation may supply, is but a half and half, tentative approach to this. Very much of this nature was the genius or Daimon (don't say *De*mon) of Socrates.* How many thousands of learned writers and printers have gone to sleep over too profound attempts to solve *that*, which Socrates ought to have been able to solve at sight. I am myself of opinion that it was a dram-bottle, which someone raised a ghost to explain. Then the Entelecheia of Aristotle;* did you ever read about that, excellent reader? Most people fancy it to have meant some unutterable crotchet in metaphysics, some horrible idea (lest the police should be after it) without a name; that is, until the Stagyrite repaired the injustice of his conduct by giving it a pretty long one. My opinion now, as you are anxious to know it, is, that it was a lady, a sweetheart of Aristotle's; for what was to hinder Aristotle having a sweetheart? I dare say Thomas Aquinas,* dry and arid as he was, raised his unprincipled eyes to some Neapolitan beauty, began a sonnet to some lady's eyebrow,* though he might forget to finish it. And my belief is that this lady, ambitious as Semele,* wished to be introduced as an eternal jewel into the great vault of her lover's immortal Philosophy, which was to travel much farther and agitate far longer than his royal pupil's conquests.* Upon that Aristotle, keeping her hand, said: 'My love, I'll think of it.' And then it occurred to him, that in the very heavens many lovely ladies, Andromeda, Cassiopeia, Ariadne,* etc., had been placed as constellations in that map which many chronologists suppose to have been prepared for the use of the ship *Argo*,* a whole generation before the Trojan war.* Berenice,* though he could not be aware of *that*, had interest even to procure a place in that map for her ringlets; and of course for herself she might have. Considering which, Aristotle said: 'Hang me! if I don't put her among the ten Categories!'* On after thoughts he put her higher, for an Entelecheia is as much above a Category as our Padishah Victoria* is above a Turkish sultan. 'But now, Stag', said the lady (privileged as a sweetheart she called him *Stag*, though everybody else was obliged to call him Stagyrite), 'how will they know it's meant for me, Stag?' Upon which I am sorry to say the philosopher fell to cursing and swearing, bestowing blessings on his own optics and on posterity's, meaning yours and mine, saying: 'Let them find it out.' Well, now, you see I *have* found it out. But that is more than I hope for my crypto-criminals, and therefore I take this my only way of giving them celebration and malediction in one breath.

EXPLANATORY NOTES

ABBREVIATIONS

Fairburn's Account   *Fairburn's Account of the Dreadful Murder of Mr Marr and Family* (London, 1812).

The Maul and the Pear Tree   T. A. Critchley and P. D. James, *The Maul and the Pear Tree: The Ratcliffe Highway Murders, 1811* (London, 1971).

Newgate Calendar   *The Complete Newgate Calendar*, ed. G. T. Crook, 5 vols. (London, 1926).

Works of Hobbes   *The English Works of Thomas Hobbes*, ed. William Molesworth, 11 vols. (London, 1839–45).

Unless otherwise noted, all references to classical sources are to the Loeb editions.

ON THE KNOCKING AT THE GATE IN MACBETH

First published in the *London Magazine*, 8 (October 1823), 353–6. This short essay, along with another unrelated essay on the English economist and demographer Thomas Robert Malthus, forms the fifth instalment of De Quincey's nine-part series of 'Notes from the Pocket-Book of a Late Opium-Eater'. It appeared in the October 1823 issue of the *London*, alongside Lamb's 'Letter of Elia to Robert Southey, Esquire', William Hazlitt's 'Pictures at Wilton, Stourhead, &c.', and Thomas Carlyle's 'Schiller's Life and Writings'.

  3 *Macbeth . . . murder of Duncan*: in William Shakespeare's tragedy *Macbeth* (*c.*1606), the knocking at the gate startles Macbeth and Lady Macbeth after their murder of Duncan: 'Whence is that knocking?', asks Macbeth. 'How is't with me, when every noise appalls me?' (II. ii. 54–5).

  4 *quoad*: 'to the extent of, as regards, with respect to' (*OED*).

    Mr Williams: John Williams (1784–1811), a seaman, is presumed responsible for a series of brutal murders in Ratcliffe Highway in the East End of London in December 1811 (not '1812', as De Quincey writes). De Quincey details these murders in his 'Postscript' to 'On Murder' (see above, pp. 95–141).

    The Marrs: on 7 December 1811 John Williams entered 29 Ratcliffe Highway and killed Timothy Marr, linen draper; Celia Marr, his wife; Timothy Marr, junior, their infant son; and James Gowen, Marr's apprentice. The servant girl, Margaret Jewell, returned from an errand and knocked on the door while Williams, surrounded by the four dead bodies, was still inside the house.

5 *'the poor beetle that we tread on'*: Shakespeare, *Measure for Measure*, III. i. 78–80: 'And the poor beetle that we tread upon | In corporal sufferance finds a pang as great | As when a giant dies'.

'with its petrific mace': John Milton (1608–74), *Paradise Lost*, X. 293: 'Death with his mace petrific'.

hell within him: cf. Milton, *Paradise Lost*, iv. 20–1: 'The hell within him, for within him hell | He brings'.

'the gracious Duncan': Shakespeare, *Macbeth*, III. i. 65.

'the deep damnation of his taking off': Shakespeare, *Macbeth*, I. vii. 20.

6 *the goings-on of human life*: cf. Coleridge, 'Frost at Midnight', 12: 'With all the numberless goings-on of life'.

'unsexed': Shakespeare, *Macbeth*, I. v. 40–1: Lady Macbeth prays, 'Come, you spirits | That tend on mortal thoughts, unsex me here.'

Macbeth . . . born of woman: Shakespeare, *Macbeth*, V. viii. 15–16. De Quincey, however, has confused the reference. It was Macduff, not Macbeth, who 'was from his mother's womb | Untimely ripp'd'.

7 *a critic in the LONDON MAGAZINE*: George Darley (1795–1846), poet and critic, published his seven 'Letters to the Dramatist of the Day' in the *London Magazine* (1823–4) under the pseudonym 'John Lacy'. In the September 1823 'Letter', Darley discusses *Macbeth*, II. ii, in terms that anticipate De Quincey's investigation of the knocking at the gate one month later: 'The breath seems to stop in one's throat whilst reading these lines; the vital principle is almost suspended, whilst the intellectual is in a state of preternatural excitement' (*London Magazine*, 8 (1823), 276).

X. Y.Z.: one of De Quincey's favourite signatures. He signed his manuscript 'Letter to the Editor of Blackwood's Magazine' in the same way (see above, p. 160).

ON MURDER CONSIDERED AS ONE OF THE FINE ARTS

First published in *Blackwood's Magazine*, 21 (February 1827), 199–213. 'The best article in the N° is De Quincey on Murder', wrote David Macbeth Moir to William Blackwood after reviewing the February 1827 issue. 'I can easily suppose that you must have had some qualms in publishing the article, but it is blameless, and will be generally read and relished.' Moir thought he detected the presence of De Quincey's closest friend and fellow *Blackwood's* contributor, John Wilson, for 'in some parts' he approaches Wilson 'so closely that I can scarcely persuade myself of there not being a little intermingling'. De Quincey published both the present essay and 'The Last Days of Kant' in the same February 1827 issue of *Blackwood's* (Eugene A. Nolte, 'The Letters of David Macbeth Moir to William Blackwood and his Sons', 2 vols. (Ph.D. thesis, Texas Technological College, 1955), i. 332).

8 *Editor of Blackwood's Magazine*: William Blackwood (1776–1834) edited *Blackwood's Magazine* from 1817 to 1834, but the magazine also had a fictive editor, 'Christopher North', who was most often personated by John Wilson (1785–1854), voluminous *Blackwood's* contributor and Professor of Moral Philosophy in the University of Edinburgh, 1820–51. De Quincey undoubtedly had both Blackwood and Wilson in mind when he addressed himself to the editor of *Blackwood's* (see Robert Morrison, 'John Wilson and the editorship of *Blackwood's Magazine*', *Notes and Queries*, 46/1 (1999), 48–50).

Society for the Promotion of Vice: De Quincey probably parodies the Society for Promoting Christian Knowledge, founded by Thomas Bray (1656–1730) in 1698 to encourage the distribution of Christian literature and counteract the growth of vice and immorality.

Hell-Fire Club: the first of several early eighteenth-century Hell-Fire Clubs is reputed to have been founded around 1720 by Philip, duke of Wharton (1698–1731). These informal aristocratic groups were allegedly devoted to drink, sacrilege, and sexual excess, and were bombastically condemned in the anonymous *Hell-Fire-Club: Kept by a Society of Blasphemers . . . With the King's Order in Council, for Suppressing Immorality and Prophaneness* (London, 1721). Sir Francis Dashwood (1708–81) founded a similar but better-known Club around 1750.

Society . . . for the Suppression of Virtue: De Quincey parodies the Society for the Suppression of Vice, founded in 1802 by William Wilberforce (1759–1833), abolitionist and politician.

ευφημισμὸς: 'euphemism'.

Bow-street: the chief magisterial business of London was for many years carried on in the Bow Street Police Court. Its officers were popularly known as the 'Bow-Street Runners', the first London police force. In 1829, two years after De Quincey published this article, the 'Runners' were officially replaced by the Metropolitan Police.

Lactantius: Lactantius (*c.* AD 240–*c.*320), North African Christian apologist and one of the most reprinted of the Latin Church Fathers. De Quincey quotes from Lactantius, 'Epitome 58' in *Epitome Divinarum Institutionum*, ed. Eberhared Heck and Antonie Wlosok (Stuttgart, 1994), 91. De Quincey distorts the quotation in a number of ways, including the omission of the opening question ('What is as horrid, as foul as the murder of a man?') and the translation of 'voluptas' ('pleasure' or 'delight') as 'demands of taste'.

9 *'proemia postulavit'*: 'he has demanded rewards'.

'interfectori favit': 'he has shown favour to the killer'.

X. Y. Z.: see above, p. 167.

Note of the Editor: the note is almost certainly the addition of either William Blackwood or John Wilson, and seems to have been inserted without De Quincey's consent.

Erasmus ... Praise of Folly: Desiderius Erasmus of Rotterdam (1469–1536), the greatest of the Renaissance humanists, satirized theologians and widely practised religious observances in his celebrated *Moriae encomium*, or *Praise of Folly* (1509).

Dean Swift ... eating children: Jonathan Swift (1667–1745), Anglo-Irish author and Dean of St Paul's, Dublin. In 'A Modest Proposal' (1729), Swift satirically suggested eating the children of the Irish poor.

Williams': for John Williams, see above, p. 166.

10 *pari passu*: 'at an equal pace'.

Aeschylus ... Michael Angelo: Aeschylus (525–456 BC), Greek tragedian. Michelangelo (1475–1564), Italian painter, sculptor, architect, and poet.

Wordsworth. ... 'created the taste by which he is to be enjoyed': William Wordsworth (1770–1850) declared in his 'Essay, Supplementary to the Preface' (1815) that 'every author, as far as he is great and at the same time *original*, has had the task of *creating* the taste by which he is to be enjoyed' (*The Prose Works of William Wordsworth*, ed. W. J. B. Owen and Jane Smyser, 3 vols. (Oxford, 1974), iii. 80; Wordsworth's italics).

Majesty's Judges of Assize: High Court judges who presided in county criminal and civil cases.

Everything ... two handles: De Quincey borrows from Laurence Sterne, *The Life and Opinions of Tristram Shandy, Gentleman*, ed. Ian Campbell Ross (Oxford, 1998), 83: 'Every thing in this world, continued my father, (filling a fresh pipe)—every thing in this earthly world, my dear brother *Toby*, has two handles.'

Old Bailey: the Central Criminal Court in London.

Kant ... unconditional veracity ... his reasons: in 1797 the Franco-Swiss novelist and political writer Benjamin Constant (1767–1830) accused the German philosopher Immanuel Kant (1724–1804) of going 'so far as to maintain that it would be a crime to lie to a murderer who asked us whether a friend of ours whom he is pursuing had taken refuge in our house'. Kant admitted that 'I actually said this somewhere or other, though I cannot now recall where', and then reaffirmed his view in *On the Supposed Right to Lie from Philanthropy* (1797), in which he states that 'if you have *by a lie* prevented someone just now bent on murder from committing the deed, then you are legally accountable for all the consequences that might arise from it. But if you have kept strictly to the truth, then public justice can hold nothing against you, whatever the unforeseen consequences might be' (see Kant, *Practical Philosophy*, ed. Mary J. Gregor (Cambridge, 1996), 611–12). Kant, however, did not argue that one should 'point out [the] victim's hiding-place' (as De Quincey's lecturer claims).

11 *Howship*: John Howship (1781–1841), English surgeon and author.

Berners' Street ... men of genius: Samuel Taylor Coleridge (1772–1834) lived with his friends John and Mary Morgan at 71 Berners Street,

London, from 1812 to 1813. Other 'men of genius' who lived in Berners Street include the architect Sir William Chambers (1726–96) and the painters John Opie (1761–1807) and Henry Fuseli (1741–1825).

11 *Plotinus from the attic lips*: Plotinus (AD 205–70), Platonist philosopher. 'Attic' is 'of or pertaining to Attica, or to its capital Athens'; thus, 'marked by simple and refined elegance, pure, classical' (*OED*).

ὁι περί τον Πλάτωνα: 'those around Plato'.

'Fire — fire!' . . . *spectacle*: De Quincey invokes John Wilson, 'Noctes Ambrosianae (XIV)' in *Blackwood's Magazine*, 15 (April 1824), 382: 'I call this a very passable fire. . . . I fear the blockheads will be throwing water upon the fire, and destroying the effect. Mr Ambrose, step over the way, and report progress.' Revealingly, Wilson then proceeds to a discussion of John Thurtell. Cf. William Hazlitt, 'Mr Kean's Iago' in *The Complete Works of William Hazlitt*, ed. P. P. Howe, 21 vols. (London, 1930–4), v. 213: Shakespeare 'knew that the love of power . . . was natural to man. . . . Why do we always read the accounts in the newspapers, of dreadful fires and shocking murders, but for the same reason?'

additional keys: the first five and a half octave piano appeared in the late eighteenth century, and by the early nineteenth century piano keyboards reached six and a half octaves.

morality . . . on the insurance office: fire brigades were employed by the insurance companies, and responded only to fires at premises insured by their own companies. The government was not involved in fire-fighting until 1865.

Stagyrite . . . a perfect thief: Aristotle (384–322 BC) was born in Stagira and known as the 'Stagirite'. In his *Metaphysics*, v. xvi, he defines 'excellence' as that which 'cannot be surpassed relative to its genus . . . transferring it to the case of bad things, we speak of a complete scandalmonger and a complete thief – as indeed we even call them good: a good thief and a good scandalmonger'.

'a beautiful ulcer': De Quincey almost certainly has in mind Howship, *Practical Remarks upon Indigestion* (London, 1825), 155: 'External to the cavity . . . was now seen, quite distinct from the fine injected membrane, the section of a small white soft tumor. . . . The contrast was beautiful, the natural structure well injected, that of the tumor not injected at all'.

12 *Nicomachéan Ethics . . . Magna Moralia, or Big Ethics*: Aristotle's *Nicomachean Ethics* was dedicated to or edited by his son, Nichomachus. The authorship of the *Magna Moralia* is uncertain: it may have been written by Aristotle, or it may have been compiled from his lectures by one of his students after his death.

Spartam nactus es, hanc exorna: adapted from Cicero, *Letters to Atticus*, IV. vi. 2, which itself quotes Euripides, *Fragments*, 723: 'Sparta is your portion: embellish it!'

Autolycus or Mr Barrington: Autolycus is the thief and rogue in

Shakespeare's *The Winter's Tale*. George Barrington (1755–1804) was an Irish adventurer and notorious pickpocket.

phagedaenic ulcer: 'spreading ulcer' (*OED*).

'bright consummate flower': Milton, *Paradise Lost*, v. 481.

inkstand . . . Coleridge . . . Blackwood: Coleridge, 'Selection from Mr Coleridge's Literary Correspondence with Friends, and Men of Letters', *Blackwood's Magazine*, 10 (1821), 256: 'What qualities and properties would you wish to have combined in an ink-stand? . . . The union of these *desiderata* will be *your ideal* of an ink-stand.'

paulo-post-futurum: a grammatical term referring to the verb form used for an event that is about to happen.

Τετέλεσαι . . . είργασαι: respectively, 'it is completed' and 'it is done'. A molossus is 'a metrical foot consisting of three long syllables' (*OED*). De Quincey's reference seems to be to *Medea*, a Greek tragedy by Euripides (*c.* 485–406 BC). But the word είργασαι does not appear in the play. De Quincey probably has in mind Euripides, *Hecuba*, 1122.

'abiit, evasit': Cicero, *In Catilinam*, ii. 1: 'Abiit, excessit, evasit, erupit' ('He has gone, left us, got away, broken out').

13 *Vertu*: variant of 'Virtu', 'a knowledge of, or interest in, the fine arts' (*OED*).

Cain to Mr Thurtell: Cain was the first-born son of Adam and Eve, and murdered his brother Abel (Genesis 4: 1–16). John Thurtell (1794–1824) believed his fellow gambler William Weare had cheated him of £300 and, after enticing Weare into the country, he murdered him. Thurtell's trial and execution attracted enormous attention, including William Maginn, 'The Lament for Thurtell' in *Blackwood's Magazine*, 15 (January 1824), 101: 'What if, after swallowing brains and blood, he ate pork chops like turtle, | Sure, don't *we* swallow anything? Alas! for Whig Jack Thurtell'.

father of the art: De Quincey parodies Pierce Egan (1772–1849), sporting writer, whose *Boxiana* (1812) opens with a lively survey of 'the origin, rise, and progress of pugilism in England', and ponders 'whether our first parent, ADAM, had any pretensions to this art' (Egan, *Boxiana*, ed. Scott Noble (Toronto, 1997), 1).

Tubal Cain: Eve 'also bare Tubal-Cain, an instructor of every artificer in brass and iron' (Genesis 4: 22).

Sheffield: Sheffield, in south Yorkshire, was in the nineteenth century the world centre of high-grade steel manufacture.

Whereat . . . Par. Lost, B. XI: Milton, *Paradise Lost*, xi. 444–7.

14 *'It has . . . a large wound'*: Jonathan Richardson (1667–1745), portrait painter, *Explanatory Notes and Remarks on Paradise Lost* (1734), 497.

Polypheme: in Homer's *Odysseus*, Polyphemus is the most famous of a race of savage, one-eyed giants known as Cyclopes. In Book IX Odysseus narrowly escapes being killed and eaten by Polyphemus.

14 *Duke of Gloucester, in Henry VI.*: Shakespeare, *2 Henry VI*, III. ii.

Duncan's, Banquo's: Shakespeare, *Macbeth*, II. ii and *Macbeth*, III. iii.

age of Pericles: Pericles (*c.*495–429 BC), Athenian statesman, led Greece during an age of great political and cultural achievement.

Interfectus est, interemptus est: 'He was killed, he was destroyed'.

Murdratus est: De Quincey playfully Latinizes German stems: 'He was murdered'.

Jewish school . . . Hugh of Lincoln . . . Lady Abbess: in Geoffrey Chaucer's *Canterbury Tales*, the Prioress (not 'Abbess') relates the story of a choir-boy in Asia who was murdered by Jews. At the end of the tale she likens him to Hugh of Lincoln (1245–55), a legendary English child martyr whose alleged murder by Jews became a focal point of medieval anti-Semitism.

Catiline, Clodius . . . Cicero: Cicero (106–43 BC), statesman, lawyer, scholar, and writer, was also the greatest Roman orator. Catiline (*c.*108–62 BC), aristocrat and demagogue, plotted to overthrow the Roman republic and murder its leading citizens, including Cicero. He was denounced by Cicero in the Senate and died in battle shortly thereafter. Clodius (*c.*93–52 BC), politician and thug, was a bitter enemy of Cicero.

15 *Cethegus*: Cethegus was the most dangerous of Catiline's associates and undertook to murder Cicero. He was executed by order of the Senate.

utile . . . cloaca . . . honestum: De Quincey means the useful ('utile') as opposed to the honourable ('honestum') thing. A 'cloaca' is a 'sewer'.

'assassin': the 'Assassins', whose name derives from the Arabic 'Hash-shash' ('hashish smoker'), were an Islamic sect dating from the eleventh century, and infamous for their alleged practice of taking hashish to induce ecstatic visions and then murdering their religious enemies. Rashid ad-Din (d. 1192), leader of the Syrian branch of the Assassins, was known in the West as the Old Man of the Mountain.

settled a pension on him for three lives: the anecdote has not been traced, and is probably De Quincey's own apocryphal addition.

William I. of Orange, of Henry IV. of France: William I, Prince of Orange (1533–84), leader of the Protestant Netherlands in their revolt against Spanish rule, was shot dead by a fanatical Roman Catholic, Franc-Comtois Balthasar Gérard. Henri IV (1553–1610), first Bourbon King of France, was stabbed to death by a deranged Roman Catholic, François Ravaillac (1578–1610).

Duke of Buckingham . . . Mr Ellis: George Villiers, 1st Duke of Buckingham (1592–1628), statesman and royal favourite, was murdered in Portsmouth by a disaffected naval lieutenant, John Felton (*c.*1595–1628). Sir Henry Ellis (1777–1869), principal librarian of the British Museum, published a letter 'announcing the Assassination of the Duke of Buckingham' in *Original letters, illustrative of English History*, 3 vols. (London, 1824),

iii. 254–60: 'the Duke of Buckingham . . . was by one Felton . . . slaine at one blow, with a dagger-knife. In his staggering he turn'd about, uttering onely this word, "Villaine!" '

Gustavus Adolphus . . . Wallenstein: Gustavus Adolphus (1594–1632), king of Sweden and champion of the Protestant cause in the Thirty Years War, was not murdered, but died in battle at Lützen. Albrecht Wenzel Eusebius von Wallenstein (1583–1634), Bohemian soldier and commander of the armies of the Holy Roman Empire in the Thirty Years War, was stabbed to death by an English mercenary, Walter Devereux.

Harte amongst others: De Quincey refers to Walter Harte (1709–74), miscellaneous writer, *The History of the Life of Gustavus Adolphus, King of Sweden* (1759). Harte's account does not tally with De Quincey's: as Gustavus's followers 'were preparing to retreat, an Imperial cavalier advanced, unobserved . . . and having cried out, *Long have I fought thee*, transpierced his majesty with a pistol-ball through the body' (Harte, *The History of Gustavus Adolphus*, 2 vols. (London, 1807), ii. 377).

exemplaria: 'models' or 'examples'.

Nocturnâ versatâ manu, versate diurne: Horace, *Ars Poetica*, 269: 'handle [them] by night, handle them by day'.

16 *Locke's*: John Locke (1632–1704), philosopher and author of *An Essay Concerning Human Understanding* (1690), the seminal work of British empiricist philosophy.

Galileo . . . Des Cartes: Galileo (1564–1642), Italian mathematician, astronomer, and physicist. René Descartes (1596–1650), French mathematician, scientist, and philosopher.

Baillet . . . tom. I. p. 102–3: Adrien Baillet (1649–1706), *La Vie de Monsieur Des-Cartes*, 2 vols. (Paris: Horthemels, 1691), i. 102–3. The incident appears almost exactly as Baillet recounts it.

Gluckstadt . . . Hamburg: Gluckstadt lies north-west of Hamburg on the River Elbe estuary in northern Germany.

East Friezland . . . West Friezland: 'Friesland', or 'Frisia', is a historic region of Germany and the Netherlands fronting the North Sea.

'des scélérats': 'villains'.

17 *quand il viendroit à manquer*: 'should he happen to go missing'.

'funk,' (as the men of Eton call it,): Eton College was founded by Henry VI in 1440, and is located in Berkshire, southern England. 'Funk' is 'cowering fear' (*OED*, which notes that 'funk' is 'first mentioned as Oxford slang').

'game': 'showing "fight"; plucky, spirited' (*OED*).

respectable trunk-maker to declare: the paper from unsold books was proverbially used for lining trunks.

18 *Zuyder Zee*: 'Zuiderzee', or 'Southern Sea', is a former inlet of the North

Sea that penetrated into the central Netherlands. In 1927–32 it was dammed and most of the area reclaimed as farm land.

18 *Flying Dutchman*: in European maritime legend, the Flying Dutchman is a spectre ship doomed to sail for ever. Its appearance is believed to signal imminent disaster.

'Caesarem vehis et fortunas ejus': Plutarch, *Parallel Lives*, Caesar, xxxviii: 'You carry Caesar and his fortunes'. The phrase was used by Caesar to identify himself to a boat captain who was anxious to turn back to port because of a storm.

German emperor: not identified.

Spinosa: Benedict de Spinoza (1632–77), Dutch-Jewish philosopher.

died in his bed: it is generally accepted that Spinoza died of tuberculosis.

La Via . . . Jean Colerus: Johannes Colerus (1647–1707), Lutheran minister in The Hague, *The Life of Benedict de Spinosa* (1705). De Quincey's summary of Colerus is lively but accurate.

'que sa mort . . . naturelle': 'that his death was not entirely natural'.

Rev. Mr Henry Teonge: Henry Teonge (1621–90), naval chaplain, kept a spirited diary of his sea travels from 1675 to 1679. De Quincey's good friend Charles Knight (1791–1873) first edited and published the diary in 1825. De Quincey's reference is to page four of Knight's edition.

Fryer's Travels to the East Indies, 1672: John Fryer (d. 1733), surgeon in the East India Company, *A New Account of East India and Persia in Eight Letters: being nine years travels, begun in 1672 and finished in 1681* (1698).

Diapente . . . Diatessaron . . . Evangelical: literally, 'harmony of five' and 'harmony of four'. 'Evangelical', De Quincey wittily suggests, because 'diatessaron' is also 'a harmony of the four Gospels' (*OED*).

19 *'extrêmement sobre en son boire et en son manger'*: 'a very abstemious eater and drinker'.

mandragora . . . and opium: 'His Bill amounted to sixteen Florins and two pence. . . . there is no Opium nor *Mandrake* mentioned therein' (John Colerus, 'The Life of Benedict de Spinoza', in Frederick Pollock, *Spinoza: His Life and Philosophy* (London, 1899), 416).

these two letters, L. M.: Colerus writes simply of the 'Medicus L. M. Van Amsterdam' ('the physician L. M. from Amsterdam'; 'The Life of Benedict de Spinosa', p. 414).

ducatoon: 'a silver coin formerly current in Italian and some other European states' (*OED*).

Lindley Murray: Lindley Murray (1745–1826) was born in Pennsylvania but settled near York in England. He is best known for his *Grammar of the English Language* (1795).

Hebrew grammar: In 1670 Spinoza began to compose a Hebrew grammar, *Compendium Grammatices Linguae Hebraeae*, but did not finish it.

Hobbes: Thomas Hobbes (1588–1679), English political philosopher.

20 *irresistible power ... highest species of right*: in *Leviathan* (1651), Hobbes systemically set out an ingenious model for authoritarian government, and argued that the supremacy and unity of the sovereign power was the essential condition of a stable society, and to this even moral law must be subordinated.

1640 ... little MS. ... king's behalf: Hobbes's *De Corpore Politico* circulated in 1640 in manuscript form, and argued in favour of undivided sovereignty.

'had not his Majesty ... (in May) ... danger of his life': in April 1640 Charles I summoned parliament for the first time in eleven years. His requests for funds were blocked and he brought proceedings to an abrupt close in early May. De Quincey quotes from Hobbes's 'Considerations upon the Reputation, Loyalty, Manners, and Religion of Thomas Hobbes', in *Works of Hobbes*, iv. 414.

Long Parliament: the Long Parliament was summoned by Charles I in November 1640 and not officially dissolved until 1660, following the English Civil Wars and the Protectorate. Hobbes feared he would be called to account for *De Corpore Politico* and fled to France.

John Dennis ... Louis XIV ... Queen Anne: John Dennis (1657–1734), critic and dramatist whose only successful play, *Liberty Asserted* (1704), contained bitter attacks on the French. His egotism approached mania. He is said to have believed that the French would not agree to the Peace of Utrecht that ended the War of the Spanish Succession unless he was handed over to them. The anecdote is recounted in Theophilus Cibber, *The Lives of the Poets of Great Britain and Ireland*, 5 vols. (London, 1753), iv. 221–2.

Cromwell ... Leviathan: Oliver Cromwell (1599–1658), leading general on the parliamentary side in the English Civil War, was lord protector from 1653 to 1658. In 1651 Hobbes published *Leviathan* and returned to England.

ambassadors at the Hague and Madrid: Isaac Dorislaus (1595–1649), diplomat and lawyer, was appointed the Commonwealth's ambassador to the Dutch Republic, but was assassinated at The Hague by Royalists. Anthony Ascham (1618–50), parliamentarian, went to Madrid as an ambassador of the Commonwealth, and was murdered by Royalist henchmen.

Tum venit ... terror ubique aderat: Hobbes, 'Vita Carmine Expressa', in *Works of Hobbes*, vol. i. p. xciii: 'Then Dorislaus and Ascham came to mind for me | Just as the terror was present everywhere for the one proscribed (ordained for death)'.

'terror ubique aderat!': Hobbes has written what purports to be an elegiac couplet, but the second half of the second line is clumsily composed from a metrical point of view, especially in the elision of the syllables 'que' and 'a'.

20 *bounce*: 'a loud or audacious boast' (*OED*).

Wallis the mathematician: Hobbes addressed his 'Considerations upon the Reputation, Loyalty, Manners, and Religion of Thomas Hobbes' to John Wallis (1616–1703), mathematician and Savilian professor of geometry at Oxford. On the title-page he described Wallis as 'a learned person' (*Works of Hobbes*, iv. 409).

'because he would not trust . . . the French clergy': *Works of Hobbes*, iv. 415.

Tom's being brought to the stake for religion: *Leviathan* was widely condemned as cynical and irreligious.

21 *Mr Coleridge . . . as good as manuscript*: De Quincey is almost certainly paraphrasing Coleridge's wry observation on his newspaper *The Friend*, in *Biographia Literaria*, ed. James Engell and W. Jackson Bate, 2 vols. (Princeton, 1983), i. 175: 'To establish this distinction was one main object of THE FRIEND; if even in a biography of my own literary life I can with propriety refer to a work, which was printed rather than published, or so published that it had been well for the unfortunate author, if it had remained in manuscript!'

Tennison . . . Tillotson: Thomas Tenison (1636–1715) published *The Creed of Mr Hobbes Examined* in 1670. He succeeded John Tillotson (1630–94) as archbishop of Canterbury upon the latter's death.

introductory anecdote is as follows: De Quincey quotes from Tenison, 'The Introduction' in *The Creed of Mr Hobbes Examined* (London, 1670), 2–5.

Peak in Derbyshire . . . Hobbes's description of it: Hobbes extolled the splendour of the Peak District in a Latin poem, *De Mirabililus Pecci* (1636).

Chattsworth: Hobbes was for many years tutor to the young Earls of Devonshire. The family's country seat is Chatsworth House in Derbyshire.

same water with Leviathan: Hobbes took the title *Leviathan* from the description of the sea monster in Job 41. The title suggests the kind of power he believed was necessary to create a civil society.

Deipnosophilae: the printer has spelled the title incorrectly. It should be *Deipnosophitae* (*The Gastronomers*), an aristocratic symposium on food and other subjects by Athenaeus (*fl. c.* AD 200). De Quincey himself noted the spelling error in his 'Letter to the Editor of Blackwood's Magazine' (see above, p. 160).

22 *Sextus Roscius . . . murthered . . . Balneae Palatinae*: Cicero, *Pro Roscio Amerino*, vii: 'the father, while returning one evening from supper, was killed near the baths of Pallacina'.

Epicurus the Atheist . . . Death and the Gods: Cicero, *De Natura Deorum*, I. xxxi.

'frightened from his propriety': adapted from Shakespeare, *Othello*, II. iii. 175–6: 'it frights the isle | From her propriety'.

Malebranche: Nicolas Malebranche (1638–1715), French Roman Catholic priest and philosopher.

Bishop Berkeley: George Berkeley (1685–1753), Anglo-Irish Anglican bishop, scientist, and philosopher. He is reported to have visited Malebranche in Paris in 1713. De Quincey draws this anecdote from Joseph Stock (1740–1813), Bishop of Waterford and Lismore, *An Account of the Life of George Berkeley* (London, 1776), 9: Berkeley found Malebranche 'in his cell, cooking in a small pipkin a medicine for a disorder with which he was then troubled. . . . The conversation naturally turned on our author's system, of which the other had received some knowledge from a translation just published. But the issue of this debate proved tragical to poor Malebranche. — In the heat of disputation he raised his voice so high, and gave way so freely to the natural impetuosity of a man of parts and a Frenchman, that he brought on himself a violent increase of his disorder, which carried him off a few days after.'

genus irritabile: Horace, *Epistles*, II. ii. 102: 'Much do I endure, to soothe the fretful tribe of bards'.

So the whole ear of Denmark is abused: Shakespeare, *Hamlet*, I. v. 36–8: 'so the whole ear of Denmark | Is by a forged process of my death | Rankly abus'd'.

'every virtue under heaven': Alexander Pope (1688–1744), 'Epilogue to the Satires: Dialogue II', l. 73.

turn-up: 'a boxing contest' (*OED*).

Occasional Causes: 'Occasionalism' asserts that the relations between human minds and physical things, which we intuitively suppose to be causal, are in fact a consequence of God's will. Malebranche played a central role in developing the theory.

Leibnitz: Gottfried Wilhelm Leibniz (1646–1716), German mathematician and philosopher.

a fortiori: with greater reason or more convincing force.

23 *gold . . . Vienna . . . his throat*: De Quincey blends fact and fiction. Leibniz was accused of miserliness and he left a substantial sum for his heirs, but he died peacefully in his bed in Hanover after a week of confinement with gout and colic.

Dr Parr: Samuel Parr (1747–1825), clergyman, schoolmaster, Whig commentator, and disputatious scholar. Parr was born at Harrow-on-the-Hill near London, but in 1783 he became the perpetual curate at Hatton in Warwickshire. The village lay on the road from Warwick to Birmingham. De Quincey met Parr in the summer of 1812, and produced a four-part assessment of his career in *Blackwood's* for 1831.

salus reipublicae: 'the safety of the republic'.

2¼ Spital sermons: Parr delivered his Spital sermon on 15 April 1800, and published it later that same year. De Quincey had a low opinion of Parr's Whiggery.

23 *anonymous life of this very great man*: untraced.

Königsberg: Kant was born, spent his entire life, and died in Königsberg in East Prussia (now Kaliningrad, Russia).

little child . . . Kant escaped: De Quincey seems to draw this incident at least in part from an account of an 1819 English murder that he published when he was editor of the *Westmorland Gazette*. See Robert H. Super, 'De Quincey and a Murderer's Conscience', *Times Literary Supplement* (5 December 1936), 1016: the murderer Robert Dean 'first thought of murdering Miss Longman, but considering that she might have some sins to answer for he determined upon killing the innocent child; and he accordingly took the poor infant out, and cut her throat'.

24 *Edmondbury Godfrey*: Sir Edmund Berry Godfrey (1621–78), English magistrate, was murdered, allegedly by Roman Catholics. The incident set off a wave of anti-Catholic hysteria, and shook the government of Charles II. A Catholic silversmith confessed that he had witnessed the event, but later admitted that he had lied. The murder has never been satisfactorily explained. James Joyce noted that 'the murder of Sir Edmund Godfrey' was 'so artistically secret that it evoked the admiration of De Quincey' (*James Joyce: Occasional, Critical, and Political Writings*, ed. Kevin Barry (Oxford, 2000), 84).

Sint Maecenates, non deerunt, Flacce, Marones: Martial (*c.* AD 41–*c.*103), *Epigrams*, VIII. lvi. 5: 'Let there be many a Maecenas, many a Maro, Flaccus, will not fail, and even your fields will give you a Virgil'. Gaius Maecenas (*c.*74–8 BC), statesman and trusted adviser to Augustus, was the munificent patron of several Roman literary figures, including Virgil (70–19 BC), eminent poet.

Consulting Grant's . . . about 4 three-tenths per annum: John Graunt (1620–74), statistician and generally accepted as the founder of the science of demography, *Natural and Political Observations . . . made upon the Bills of Mortality*, ed. Walter Willcox (Baltimore, 1939), 35: 'That but few are *Murthered*, viz., not above 86' of the 229,250 who have 'died of other diseases, and casualties'.

Mrs Ruscombe: Frances Ruscombe and her maid Mary Sweet were murdered on 27 September 1764. The assassin carried away £90 in gold coin and was never brought to justice, though several suspects were arrested. For details see John Casberd, *A Vindication of Peaceable Robert Matthews, from the Charge of Mrs Ruscombe's Murder* (Bristol, 1781); and John Latimer, *The Annals of Bristol in the Eighteenth Century* (Bristol, 1893), 362–3.

George III: George III (1738–1820), king of Great Britain and Ireland, 1760–1820.

College Green: the area immediately in front of Bristol Cathedral.

25 *surgeon . . . assisted at his dissection*: Charles White (1728–1813), Manchester surgeon and family physician to the Quincey family during De

Quincey's childhood, had a private museum in which he housed the skeleton of an executed highwayman. White and others had helped to dissect the body shortly after the execution. De Quincey believed the highwayman was also very probably responsible for the Bristol murders. White gave De Quincey a tour of his museum on at least two occasions.

Cruickshank: William Cumberland Cruickshank (1745–1800), anatomist.

coup de grace: death blow.

26 *Bland*: De Quincey means Mary Blandy (1720–52), who murdered her father with poison. Cf. 'Mary Blandy' in *Newgate Calendar*, iii. 219–20: 'Miss Blandy conveyed some of the powder and gave it to her father; and repeating this draught on the following day, he was tormented with the most violent pains in his bowels'. For more details, see the *Trial of Mary Blandy*, ed. William Roughead (London, 1914).

Donnellan . . . Boughton: John Donnellan (d. 1781) was executed at Warwick after being convicted of using poison to murder his brother-in-law Sir Theodosius Edward Allesley Boughton (1760–80). Cf. 'John Donnellan' in *Newgate Calendar*, iv. 151: 'Dr Rattray, of Coventry . . . was of opinion, from the symptoms that followed the taking of the draught, that it was poison, and the certain cause of . . . death'.

Italy?: Italy was thought of as a place where the use of poisons was particularly prevalent, in part because of the notorious Borgia family, powerful in political and ecclesiastical circles in the fifteenth and six-teenth centuries, and rumoured to be highly adept at using poison to dispatch enemies.

Volpato: Giovanni Volpato (1733–1803), Italian sculptor and engraver.

Candid: here meaning 'free from malice; not desirous to find faults' (*OED*).

Taylor . . . leaps . . . influence of fear: Jeremy Taylor (1613–67), Anglican writer and clergyman, was much admired by De Quincey, who almost certainly has in mind 'Of Fear and Violence, and how these can make an Action Involuntary' in *The Rule of Conscience*, book IV, chapter 1, section iii, rule 7 (*The Whole Works of Jeremy Taylor*, ed. Reginald Heber, 15 vols. (London, 1822), xiv. 389–98).

M'Keands: in May 1826 Alexander and Michael McKean (or McKeand) cut the throat of Elizabeth Bate, a servant at the Jolly Carter Inn at Winton, Eccles, near Manchester. They also drugged the landlord, Joseph Blears, and wounded his wife, Martha Blears. A servant boy, William Higgins, witnessed the crime and was pursued by the killers. At the trial he testified that in order to escape he 'jumped over the bannister of the staircase on to the landing' (R. Bulfield, *The Trial of Alexander & Michael McKean* (Manchester, 1826), 42). De Quincey himself tells the story of the McKeans in his 1854 'Postscript' to 'On Murder' (see above, pp. 137–41).

27 *Mannheim*: Mannheim is in south-western Germany, on the right bank of

the River Rhine. De Quincey's story is fictitious but it may have been inspired by the notorious April 1824 murder of a Mannheim baker (see Frederick Burwick, 'De Quincey and the Aesthetics of Violence', *Words-worth Circle*, 27 (1996), 77–80).

27 *"fancied"*: 'the fancy' was a term applied to those who were fond of a particular amusement or closely attached to some subject. It was generally used of the boxing fraternity.

Master of the Rolls: Jack Martin, a celebrated boxer, was a baker by profession and nicknamed 'the master of the rolls'. He was an associate of John Thurtell (see above, p. 171). William Hazlitt mentions Martin in his famous essay 'The Fight' (1822).

28 *Round the 14th*: De Quincey's blow-by-blow account of various rounds parodies Pierce Egan's account of several fights in *Boxiana* (see above, p. 171).

geometrical exploits: fancy slang: lying horizontal (i.e., being knocked down).

mug: fancy slang: face.

pins: fancy slang: legs.

conk: fancy slang: nose.

29 *'Certainly . . . affliction than a strangury'*: Taylor, 'Of the practise of the Grace of Repentance in the time of Sicknesse', in *Holy Dying*, ed. P. G. Stanwood (Oxford, 1989), 140.

Aurelius . . . Collers' Translation: Marcus Aurelius (AD 121–80), Roman emperor, *Meditations*, III. i. De Quincey cites from the famous 1701 translation by Jeremy Collier (1650–1726), English bishop and critic.

entire lecture . . . expound their merits: De Quincey devotes most of his 'Postscript' to a detailed account of the Williams murders (see above, pp. 97–136).

30 *John Petersen*: the mallet 'belonged to a German sailor from Hamburg named John Peterson' (*The Maul and the Pear Tree*, 97).

murder of the Williamsons: on 19 December 1811 John Williams concealed himself in the King's Arms pub in New Gravel Lane and then murdered John Williamson, the owner; his wife, Elizabeth Williamson; and their servant, Bridget Anna Harrington.

L. S——: the initials have not been explained. A personal reference seems possible, but no likely candidate has been identified in the *Black-wood's* or De Quincey circles.

laudator temporis acti: Horace, *Ars Poetica*, 173: 'a praiser of time past'.

Durer . . . Fuseli: Albrecht Dürer (1471–1528), German Renaissance painter and printmaker. Henry Fuseli, Swiss-born painter (see above, p. 170).

31 *falsetto*: 'a forced voice of a range or register above the natural' (*OED*).

opinionum commenta . . . judicia confirmat: Cicero, *De Natura Deorum*, II. ii. 5: 'The years obliterate the inventions of the imagination, but confirm the judgements of nature'.

Thurtell's . . . dumb-bells: dumbbells were used by boxers for training and were thus a natural weapon for Thurtell, an accomplished amateur boxer.

Aeneid . . . Iliad: Virgil's *Aeneid* was modelled on Homer's *Iliad*.

place where . . . time when: De Quincey parodies Shakespeare, *Love's Labour's Lost*, I. i. 230–48.

ought to be a good man: De Quincey parodies Aristotle, *Poetics*, xv. 1–2: 'Concerning "character" there are four points to aim at. The first and most important is that the character should be good.'

'diamond-cut-diamond': a contest between equally matched rivals. Cf. Aristotle, *Poetics*, xiv. 7–9: 'Now if an enemy does it to an enemy, there is nothing pitiable either in the deed or the intention'.

32 *'to cleanse the heart . . . of pity and terror'*: Aristotle, *Poetics*, vi. 2–4: 'Tragedy . . . through pity and fear . . . effects relief to these and similar emotions'.

Abraham Newland: Abraham Newland (1730–1807) was Chief Cashier of the Bank of England from 1778 to 1807. For legal reasons, his signature appeared in the promissory clause on the Bank's notes, with the result that these notes became known popularly as 'Abraham Newlands'. His semi-legendary status was enhanced by the fact that, during his thirty years as Chief Cashier, he never slept away from the Bank.

Prester John: Prester John was a legendary Christian ruler of the East. In the thirteenth and fourteenth centuries, various missionaries and lay travellers sought unsuccessfully to find his kingdom.

an affair of honour: a duel, especially one fought over a woman.

'with every delicacy of the season': the standard cliché for reporting society dinners in newspaper gossip columns.

Cockney: a slighting reference to Londoners, and part of *Blackwood's* ongoing campaign against the *London Magazine* and its support of 'Cockney School' writers such as John Keats, William Hazlitt, and Leigh Hunt.

tailors . . . to murder eighteen: proverbial, 'Nine tailors make a man'. Cf. Thomas Carlyle seven years later in *Fraser's Magazine*: 'Does it not stand on record that the English Queen Elizabeth, receiving a deputation of Eighteen Tailors, addressed them with a: Good morning, gentlemen both!' (Carlyle, *Sartor Resartus*, ed. Rodger Tarr (Berkeley, Calif.: 2000), 212).

33 *Ingenuas didicisse . . . sinit esse feros*: Ovid, *Ex Ponto*, II. ix. 47–8: 'a faithful study of the liberal arts humanizes character and permits it not to be cruel'.

Annals of Edinburgh . . . undiscovered: De Quincey has his facts straight except for the date. In November 1806 William Begbie, Porter to the British Linen Company's Bank, was stabbed to the heart with a bread knife and robbed of more than £4,000. A sizeable reward was offered, but Begbie's assassin was never found (for details, see Mary Cosh, *Edinburgh: The Golden Age* (Edinburgh, 2003), 587–9).

33 *Sed fugit interea . . . circumvectamur amore*: Virgil, *Georgics*, iii. 284–5: 'But time meanwhile is flying, flying beyond recall, while we, charmed with love of our theme, linger around each detail'.

   '*Semper . . . nunquamne reponam?*': Juvenal, *Satires*, i. 1–2: 'What? Am I to be a listener only all my days? Am I never to get my word in . . . ?'

   '*animus*': 'animating spirit or temper, usually of a hostile character' (*OED*).

34 *Brutus*: Marcus Junius Brutus (85–42 BC) was leader of the conspirators who assassinated Julius Caesar in 44 BC. Brutus died two years later by his own hand.

   called aloud . . . his country hail!: Mark Akenside (1721–70), poet and physician, *The Pleasures of the Imagination*, i. 496–8: 'call'd aloud | On Tully's name, and shook his crimson steel, | And bade the father of his country, hail!'

   '*small deer*': Shakespeare, *King Lear*, III. iv. 138: 'But mice and rats, and such small deer'.

   fungar vice . . . exsors ipsa secandi: Horace (65–8 BC), Latin lyric poet, *Ars Poetica*, 304: 'So I'll play a whetstone part, which makes steel sharp, but of itself cannot cut'.

THE AVENGER

First published in *Blackwood's Magazine*, 44 (August 1838), 208–33. On 25 May 1838 De Quincey told John Wilson that he was writing 'a German Tale (*scene laid in Germ.*, I mean, but entirely my own invention), turning upon secret murder'. Two weeks later De Quincey had almost finished the tale. 'I am sure of your liking the final part,' he told Robert Blackwood. 'Never was [the] secret of a catastrophe better kept.' When Blackwood and his advisers read the tale, however, they felt it needed to be cut. De Quincey, cash-strapped and anxious to make a sale, agreed, and told Blackwood's friends that they 'need feel under no restraint or reserve or scruple in canceling or correcting upon the widest scale'. It is not known what cuts were made, or who made them (*The Works of Thomas De Quincey: Volume Nine*, ed. Grevel Lindop, Robert Morrison, and Barry Symonds (London, 2001), 264).

35 *Why callest thou me murderer . . . with blood?*: the first part of the epigram recalls Jesus's 'Why callest thou me good?' (Matthew 19: 16; Mark 10: 18; Luke 18: 19). No other source has been traced.

36 *the shadowy – the uncertain . . . palpable – and human*: De Quincey draws on the aesthetics outlined by Edmund Burke in his 1757 *Philosophical*

Enquiry into the Origin of our Ideas of the Sublime and Beautiful, ed. Adam Phillips (Oxford, 1990), 54: 'To make any thing very terrible, obscurity seems in general to be necessary. When we know the full extent of any danger . . . a great deal of the apprehension vanishes'.

37 *one deep calling to another*: cf. Psalm 42: 7: 'Deep calleth unto deep'.

battle of Waterloo: on 18 June 1815 Napoleon Bonaparte (1769–1821), Emperor of the French, was finally defeated at the Battle of Waterloo, ending twenty-three years of almost continual warfare between France and other powers in Europe. The French were beaten by an allied army of British, Prussian, Dutch, Belgian, and German forces.

38 *French anabasis to Moscow*: an 'anabasis' is 'a military advance' (*OED*). Napoleon's invasion of Russia began in June 1812, and ended in disastrous retreat five months later.

en prince: in a princely manner.

39 *haute noblesse*: the old aristocracy.

Pharsalia: Pharsalia, in Thessaly, was the scene of the decisive battle of the Roman civil war (48 BC) in which Julius Caesar defeated Pompey.

Antinous: Antinoüs (*c.* AD 110–30) was a Bithynian youth of great beauty and a favourite of the emperor Hadrian.

modern Pygmalion: in Ovid, *Metamorphoses*, x. 243–97, Pygmalion, a sculptor, makes an ivory statue representing his ideal of womanhood and then falls in love with his own creation. The goddess Venus brings the statue to life in answer to his prayer.

40 *Blending . . . summer skies*: Wordsworth, 'A Jewish Family', ll. 19–20.

Jewish prophet . . . inspirations of wo: De Quincey links Maximilian to the legendary figure of the Wandering Jew, hinting broadly at his background and at his doomed status as exile and sinner. Cf. John Barrell, *The Infection of Thomas De Quincey* (New Haven, 1991), 29: 'Throughout De Quincey's autobiographical writings, he takes to himself the identity of the Wandering Jew'.

41 *Margaret Liebenheim*: De Quincey has chosen the name carefully. His wife's name was Margaret, and he was deeply affected by her death in 1837, just one year before he published this tale. In German, 'lieben' is 'to love', and 'heim' is 'home'.

43 *'Lead us not into temptation!'*: Luke 11: 4.

44 *stricken deer*: Shakespeare, *Hamlet*, III. ii. 271: 'Why, let the strooken deer go weep'.

'recoiled into the wilderness': Wordsworth, 'In the Pleasure-Ground on the Banks of the Bran, Near Dunkeld', l. 128.

doing or suffering: Milton, *Paradise Lost*, i. 157–8: 'to be weak is miserable | Doing or suffering'.

47 *bijouterie*: jewellery or ornate objets d'art.

48 *tessellae*: small squares or cubes, especially those forming part of a mosaic.

50 *Amurath or Mahomet*: De Quincey intends these names as representative of Islamic sultans such as Murad IV (1612–40) or Mahmud II (1785–1839).

52 *acharnement*: relentless ferocity.

53 *wanderjahre*: 'journeyman years', and famous as the title of the second volume of Johann Wolfgang von Goethe's novel *Wilhelm Meister* (1821–9).

Silesian: Silesia is a historic region in what is now south-western Poland.

58 *acmé*: highest point.

65 *he heard me not – he saw me not*: cf. Percy Shelley, *The Revolt of Islam*, xi. 1: 'She saw me not – she heard me not'. De Quincey quotes directly from Shelley's *Revolt* in the 'Postscript' to 'On Murder' (see above, p. 131).

66 *'dust to dust – ashes to ashes!'*: from the funeral service in the Book of Common Prayer.

68 *My trial is finished*: cf. John 19: 30: 'Jesus . . . said, It is finished, and bowed his head, and gave up the ghost.'

"warfare is accomplished": Isaiah 40: 2: 'Speak ye comfortably to Jerusalem, and cry unto her, that her warfare is accomplished, that her iniquity is pardoned'.

70 *the funds*: the 'Funds' were 'the stock of the National Debt, considered as a mode of investment' (*OED*).

transpired: figuratively, 'to escape from secrecy to notice; to become known, especially by obscure channels' (*OED*).

Morganatic marriage: a marriage which does not raise the status of the bride or confer rights of succession upon her children.

Maccabees: the Maccabees were a priestly Jewish family who organized a successful rebellion against the Syrian rulers of Palestine and reconsecrated the defiled Temple of Jerusalem in 164 BC.

71 *Friedland and Eylau*: Napoleon invaded East Prussia in 1807. At Eylau, on 7–8 February, he suffered his first major deadlock in a battle fought against the Russians and Prussians. At Friedland, on 14 June, he compensated for the setback at Eylau with a decisive victory over the Russians.

trepanned: 'trepan' is 'to entrap, ensnare, beguile' (*OED*).

73 *scandalum magnatum*: 'offence to the authorities'.

74 *daughter of Jerusalem!*: cf. Song of Solomon 1: 5: 'I *am* black, but comely (O ye daughters of Jerusalem)'. The phrase 'daughters of Jerusalem' is repeated six more times in the Song of Solomon.

75 *"chamber of desolation"*: De Quincey describes a tradition that seems never to have existed, although he may be distorting the actual Jewish custom of leaving part of the wall opposite the front door of a house bare (unplastered or unpainted) in memory of the destruction of the ancient Temple of Jerusalem.

77 *great assembly of Jews at Paris*: in 1807 Napoleon convened a so-called Sanhedrin of Jewish leaders with the objective of promoting integration and assimilation. He agreed to important reforms that promoted Jewish emancipation, but also extracted numerous concessions, including a declaration that France alone had claim on the political allegiances of the Jews.

80 *Forty thousand lives*: De Quincey alludes to Shakespeare, *Hamlet*, v. i. 269–71: 'Forty thousand brothers | Could not with all their quantity of love | Make up my sum'.

SECOND PAPER ON MURDER CONSIDERED AS ONE OF THE FINE ARTS

First published in *Blackwood's Magazine*, 46 (November 1839), 661–8. De Quincey sent the 'Second Paper' to Robert Blackwood on 24 September 1839 'in continuation of one published many years ago by your Father on *Murder considered as one of the Fine Arts*' (National Library of Scotland, MS 4048, fos. 234, 235). De Quincey also compiled a series of fragmented notes relating to the 'Second Paper on Murder' (see *The Works of Thomas De Quincey: Volume Eleven*, ed. Julian North (London, 2003), 596–7).

81 *DOCTOR NORTH*: 'Christopher North' was the pen name of John Wilson, the fictive editor of *Blackwood's Magazine* and De Quincey's oldest and closest friend (see above, p. 168).

crutch: Christopher North, an athletic octogenarian, was closely identified with his crutch. Cf. Charles Dickens in 1841: 'that old man of might, with his lion heart and sceptred crutch, Christopher North' (*The Speeches of Charles Dickens*, ed. Kenneth Fielding (Oxford, 1960), 11).

A good many years ago ... dilettante in murder: De Quincey reminds *Blackwood's* readers of his first paper 'On Murder', published twelve years earlier in 1827 (see above, pp. 8–34).

82 *civilation*: as De Quincey explains in his 1852 essay on Sir William Hamilton, 'civilation' is 'civilization' as pronounced by 'a gentleman taking his ease of an evening ... after 10 P.M.' (*The Works of Thomas De Quincey: Volume Seventeen*, ed. Edmund Baxter (London, 2001), 158).

Stagyrite ... two extremes: Aristotle was known as 'The Stagyrite' (see above, p. 170). He detailed his doctrine of the ethical mean in *Nicomachean Ethics*, II. vi. 15–17.

born to be hanged: Shakespeare, *The Tempest*, I. i. 32–3: 'If he be not born to be hang'd, our case is miserable'. Cf. Henry Fielding, *Tom Jones*, book III, chapter ii: 'It was the universal opinion of all Mr Allworthy's family that [Tom Jones] was certainly born to be hanged'.

83 *shambles ... attelier*: respectively, a slaughter-house and a studio.

coup d'oeil: the scene that the beholder of a picture takes in.

83 *Cyclops*: in Greek mythology, Cyclopes were man-eating, one-eyed giants (see above, p. 171).

quid valeant humeri, quid ferre recusent?: De Quincey adapts Horace, *Ars Poetica*, 39–40: 'Ponder long what your shoulders refuse, and what they are able to bear.'

84 *liberavi animam meam*: St Bernard of Clairvaux (1090–1153), Cistercian monk and mystic, *The Letters*, trans. Bruno Scott James (Guildford, Surrey, 1998), 474: 'I have delivered my soul'.

in toto: entirely.

Principiis obsta: Ovid, *Remedia Amoris*, 91: 'Stand firm against the onset (of a disease)'.

laudator temporis acti: Horace, *Ars Poetica*, 173: 'a praiser of time past'. De Quincey quotes this same line in his first essay 'On Murder' (see above, p. 30).

85 *God's Revenge upon Murder, by Reynolds*: John Reynolds (*fl.* 1620–40), *The Triumph of God's Revenge* (1621–35), a series of ostensibly fictional tales of revenge and murder in which a wrathful God tracks down and punishes sinners. Cf. William Godwin in his 1832 account of the composition of his terror novel *Caleb Williams* (1794): 'I turned over the pages of a tremendous compilation, entitled "God's Revenge Against Murder", where the beam of the eye of Omniscience was represented as perpetually pursuing the guilty, and laying open his most hidden retreats to the light of day' (Godwin, *Caleb Williams*, ed. David McCracken (Oxford, 1970), 340).

Scott in his Fortunes of Nigel: Sir Walter Scott (1771–1832), novelist and poet; chapter 24 in *The Fortunes of Nigel*, ed. Frank Jordan (Edinburgh, 2004), 267: 'The book was entitled, "God's Revenge against Murther"; not . . . the work which Reynolds published . . . but one of a much earlier date'. The work which Scott has in mind, however, has not been traced. Jordan writes that it is 'probably imaginary' (p. 619).

Newgate Calendar: *The Newgate Calendar* was the generic title of various eighteenth- and nineteenth-century collections recounting the careers of infamous criminals.

listless . . . filth that muddled by: De Quincey adapts Thomas Gray, 'Elegy Written in a Country Churchyard', ll. 103–4: 'His listless length at noontide would he stretch, | And pore upon the brook that babbles by'.

One morning in 1812: as in his essay 'On the Knocking at the Gate in Macbeth', De Quincey is out by a year. The date should be '1811' (see above, p. 166).

brushing . . . the postman by the conduit side: De Quincey adapts Thomas Gray, 'Elegy Written in a Country Churchyard', ll. 99–100: 'Brushing with hasty steps the dews away | To meet the sun upon the upland lawn'.

86 *chef-d'oeuvre*: masterpiece.

Williams . . . Marr's . . . Williamson's: De Quincey details these murders in his 'Postscript' to 'On Murder' (see above, pp. 97–136).

'reclaimed': 'To cry out, or protest, against (a thing or person)' (*OED*).

gout de comparaison, as La Bruyère calls it: the French phrase is 'taste for making comparisons'. De Quincey's reference is to Jean de La Bruyère (1645–96), French satirist, *Les Caractères de Théophraste traduits du grec avec les caractères ou les mœurs de ce siècle* (1688; *The Characters, or Manners of the Age, with the Characters of Theophrastus*).

Iliad . . . Odyssey: the two Greek epic poems traditionally attributed to Homer.

ne plus ultra: the highest point capable of being attained.

87   *Leo the Tenth*: Giovanni de' Medici (1475–1521), elected Pope Leo X in 1513, made Rome the cultural centre of the Western world.

en attendant: literally, 'as we wait'.

Thugs and Thuggism: the Thugs were a confederacy of robbers and murderers who travelled in gangs throughout India for several hundred years.

persimmon: a persimmon is a plum-like fruit. In the nineteenth century the word had a wide range of humorous slang senses, apparently emanating from America. Here it seems to mean 'my greatest efforts'.

'non est inventus': the phrase is taken from Psalm 37: 36: 'I sought him, but he could not be found'. In the present legal context, it means the return of a sheriff on a writ, when the defendant is not found in his county.

88   *Et interrogatum . . . Non est inventus*: 'And it was asked by Toad-in-the hole — Where is that reporter? And it was replied with laughter — He has not been found. Then it was repeated by everyone with waves of laughter — He has not been found.'

Burke-and-Hare: William Burke (1792–1829) and William Hare (*c.*1790–*c.*1860), Irish-born murderers, smothered sixteen people in Edinburgh in 1828 and then delivered the corpses to the back door of the celebrated anatomist Robert Knox, where they received payment. At their trial in 1829, Hare turned King's evidence, and Burke was hanged (and dissected). Copycat 'burkings' occurred throughout the early 1830s; cf. the 1831 tale of terror 'The Victim' in *The Vampyre and Other Tales of the Macabre*, ed. Robert Morrison and Chris Baldick (Oxford, 1997), 87–98.

The Old Man of the Mountains: De Quincey discussed 'The Old Man of the Mountains' in his first essay 'On Murder' (see above, p. 15).

Mr Von Hammer: Joseph von Hammer-Purgstall (1774–1856), Austrian orientalist, *The History of the Assassins* (1835).

malleus haereticorum: 'hammer of heretics'. Johann Faber (1478–1541), bishop of Vienna, was given the title after publishing his celebrated attack on Martin Luther, *Malleus in haeresim Lutheranam* (1524).

tickle your catastrophes: Shakespeare, *2 Henry IV*, II. i. 60: 'I'll tickle your catastrophe'.

89 *Williams . . . ship carpenter's mallet*: as De Quincey discusses in his first essay 'On Murder', Williams used a mallet to assassinate the Marr family (see above, p. 30).

Charles the Hammer . . . the Martel: Charles Martel (*c.*688–741), Frankish ruler, was known as 'the hammer'.

Charlemagne: Charlemagne (742–814), King of the Franks, was the grandson of Charles Martel.

Abdera: Abdera was a Greek city on the coast of Thrace, and proverbial for the stupidity of its inhabitants.

Jewish Sicarii: the Sicarii were a first-century Jewish terrorist sect. They kidnapped or murdered persons friendly to Rome.

Nero: Nero (AD 37–68), fifth Roman emperor, was infamous for his extravagance and debauchery.

90 *Josephus*: Flavius Josephus (AD 37/38–*c.*100), Jewish priest, scholar, and historian, is celebrated for *The History of the Jewish War* and *Jewish Antiquities*.

Pontifex Maximus?: at Rome, the Pontifex Maximus was head of the college of pontiffs.

'*Et interrogatum . . . est inventus*': 'And it was asked by Toad-in-the hole—Where is the assassin? And it was replied by all—He has not been found'.

Book XX . . . his Antiquities: Josephus, *Jewish Antiquities*, xx. 160–6.

Book I . . . his Wars: De Quincey intends Josephus, *The Jewish War*, ii. 254–7.

"*They tooled . . . Roman sickles or sicae*": Josephus, *Jewish Antiquities*, xx. 186.

justus exercitus: a righteous army.

Festus: Porcius Festus, Procurator of Judaea (*c.*60–62), acted with rigour against the Sicarii, pursuing them with cavalry and infantry (see Josephus, *Jewish Antiquities*, xx. 187–8).

'*Et interrogatum . . . est inventus*': 'And it was asked by Toad-in-the hole—Where is that army? And it was replied by all—It has not been found'.

91 *Mersenne . . . Commentary on Genesis*: Marin Mersenne (1588–1648), French mathematician, philosopher, and theologian, *Quaestiones Celeberrimae in Genesim* (1623). De Quincey's page reference to *Quaestiones* is correct. 'Operose' is 'laborious; tedious; elaborate' (*OED*).

Abelem fuisse morsibus dilaceratum à Cain: 'Abel was torn apart by Cain's bites'. These words do not appear in Mersenne.

St Chrysostom: St John Chrysostom (*c.* AD 347–407), eloquent orator and archbishop of Constantinople, produced a large number of scriptural homilies and other sermons.

Irenaeus: St Irenaeus (*c.* AD 120/130–*c.* 200), bishop of Lyons, wrote *Adversus haereses* (*Against Heresies*) to refute Gnosticism.

Prudentius: Aurelius Clemens Prudentius (AD 348–after 405), Christian Latin poet, is best known for *Psychomachia* (*The Contest of the Soul*).

Frater . . . sarculo: i.e. his . . . hedging-bill: Prudentius, 'Preface' to *Hamartigenia*, 15–16.

92 *Madeira . . . Cape*: Madeira is fortified wine from the Portuguese island of Madeira. Cape is wine from the Cape of Good Hope in South Africa.

Pancirollus . . . de rebus deperditis: Guido Panciroli (1523–99), professor of law, *Rerum memorabilium jam olim deperditarum, & contrà recens atque ingeniose inventarum libri duo* (1599). 'De rebus deperditis' is 'concerning things utterly lost'.

Planudes: Maximus Planudes (1260–*c.*1310), Greek Orthodox scholar, theologian, and anthologist, revised (and bowderlized) *The Greek Anthology*, a celebrated and anonymous collection of Greek poetry and prose comprising authors from about 700 BC to AD 1000.

epigram itself . . . at this moment: De Quincey has in mind *The Greek Anthology*, xi. 125: 'The physician Crateas and the sexton Damon made a joint conspiracy. Damon sent the wrappings he stole from the grave-clothes to his dear Crateas to use as bandages and Crateas in return sent him all his patients to bury.'

Salmasius: Claudius Salmasius (1588–1653), French classical scholar, discovered the Palatine manuscript of *The Greek Anthology* and published a famous edition of the *Scriptores Historiae Augustae* (1603).

Vopiscus: Flavius Vopiscus, reputed author of several biographies in the *Scriptores Historiae Augustae*.

"Est et elegans . . . commissos occideret": De Quincey quotes (and slightly modifies) Salmasius's note in Vopiscus, 'Life of Divus Aurelianus' in *Scriptores Historiae Augustae*, 2 vols. (Leiden, 1671), ii. 422: 'There is indeed an elegant epigram of Lucilius where a physician and an undertaker have agreed that the physician should kill any patient entrusted to his care'. Lucilius (*fl.* first century AD) is a Greek epigrammatist. The Loeb edition of *The Greek Anthology* lists this epigram as anonymous.

"Et ut pollinctori amico suo traderet pollingendos": 'And should hand the body over to his friend the undertaker to be prepared for burial'.

93 *"Et ut pollinctor . . . quos curabat"*: 'And that the undertaker should in turn pass on to the physician as gifts the linen bandages which he would filch from the corpses being prepared for burial so that the doctor could use them to bind the wounds of those under his care.'

re infectâ: the business being unfinished.

Pylades . . . Orestes: in Greek mythology, Pylades was the constant companion of Orestes, son of Agamemnon and his wife, Clytemnestra. Pylades helped Orestes murder Clytemnestra.

93 ἐπιμύθιον . . . *Aesop*: the Greek word is 'moral of the story'. Aesop is the reputed author of a collection of Greek fables, and almost certainly a legendary figure. De Quincey draws from 'Fable 307' in *Corpus Fabularum Aesopicarum*, ed. Herbert Hunger (Leipzig, 1959), 116.

94 *uno pede*: 'with one foot'. De Quincey plays on 'una voce', 'with one voice'.

POSTSCRIPT [TO ON MURDER CONSIDERED AS ONE OF THE FINE ARTS]

First published in volume 4 of *Selections Grave and Gay* (Edinburgh, 1854), 60–111. The volume also contained revised versions of the 1827 and 1839 essays 'On Murder'.

95 *bagatelle*: 'a trifle, a thing of no value or importance' (*OED*).

cooking and eating them: as in the first essay 'On Murder', De Quincey's reference is to Jonathan Swift's satire 'A Modest Proposal' (see above, p. 169).

jeu d'esprit: 'a witty or humorous trifle' (*OED*).

Lilliput . . . Laputa . . . Yahoos: in Jonathan Swift's *Gulliver's Travels* (1726), book I, Gulliver is shipwrecked on the island of Lilliput, where the inhabitants are only six inches tall. In book III, he travels to the flying island of Laputa, where the absent-minded inhabitants quite literally have their heads in the clouds. In book IV, he describes the country of the Houyhnhnms, rational and virtuous horses who share their island with the vicious and filthy Yahoos.

Telamonian shield: in Homer's *Iliad*, Ajax, son of Telamon, is of great stature and dogged courage. His characteristic attribute is a strong and all-enveloping body-shield. De Quincey draws from Pope in his translation of *The Iliad*, viii. 321–2: 'Secure behind the *Telamonian* Shield | The skilful Archer wide survey'd the Field'.

96 *spectacle of a great fire*: De Quincey used a similar example in his first essay 'On Murder' (see above, p. 11).

Drury Lane: De Quincey was in London on 25 February 1809 when the Drury Lane Theatre burned to the ground. In *De Quincey to Wordsworth*, ed. John Jordan (Berkeley, 1963), 102–3, he describes the 'sublime' spectacle of the fire, and the 'great multitude of people . . . gathered on all sides of the Theatre'.

Apollo: Apollo was the most widely revered and influential of all the Greek gods. Cf. De Quincey's account in *De Quincey to Wordsworth*, 103: 'a person in the room described the fine spectacle of the roof falling in at Drury Lane: – he saw the Apollo fall fm. his pedestal; and could have counted the strings on his harp by the light'.

Goree: the Goree warehouses, named after the island just south of Cape Verde Peninsula, Senegal, were destroyed by fire in 1802.

97 *arrowy sleet*: De Quincey draws from Milton, *Paradise Regained*, iii. 323–5: 'flying behind them shot | Sharp sleet of arrowy showers against the face | Of their pursuers'.

Williams' murders of 1812: as in previous essays, De Quincey is out by a year in dating the atrocities attributed to John Williams (see above, pp. 166, 186).

98 *Never, throughout the annals . . . Cain*: cf. the opening sentence from 'John Williams' in *Newgate Calendar*, v. 119: 'The metropolis – indeed the whole nation – was never so completely horror-struck at any private calamity as at the daring and inhuman murders perpetrated, in the very heart of the City of London, at the close of the year 1811.'

three hundred miles from London: when the Williams murders took place, De Quincey was living in Wordsworth's former home of Dove Cottage in Grasmere.

Attila, or 'scourge of God': Attila (d. 453), king of the Huns, 434–53. His Latin byname was 'Flagellum Dei' ('Scourge of God').

castra stativa: 'a stationary camp'.

99 χλῆμα ἐς αει: 'a possession for ever'. De Quincey draws from Thucydides, *The Peloponnesian War*, I. xxii. 4. Cf. Horace, *Odes*, III. xxx. 1: 'I have finished a monument more lasting than bronze'.

Coleridge . . . London . . . panic: *The Maul and the Pear Tree*, 50: in the week following the murder of the Marrs, 'the *London Chronicle* had offered its news in adjacent, incongruous columns. While one headline shrieked, "Murder of Mrs Marr and Family", the next announced, "Mr Coleridge's Lectures" '.

Southey: Robert Southey (1774–1843), historian, biographer, essayist, and poet laureate, was for many years De Quincey's neighbour in the Lake District.

'Edinburgh Annual Register' . . . the whole: Southey edited the *Edinburgh Annual Register* from 1809 to 1813. A summary of the events surrounding Williams's two attacks appeared in the *Edinburgh Annual Register for 1811* (Edinburgh, 1813), 206–11, 219–31.

100 *Bow Street*: De Quincey also mentions the Bow Street police in his first essay 'On Murder' (see above, p. 168).

Lascars, Chinese, Moors, Negroes: cf. the coroner in his charge to the jury in the *Edinburgh Annual Register for 1811*, 223: 'in the eastern part of the metropolis . . . the number of strangers and seamen discharged from time to time at the East and West India and London docks, and the influx of foreign sailors from all parts of the globe, imperiously call for the solemn attention of those . . . intrusted with the administration of government'.

middle stature . . . superfluous flesh: reports of Williams differed widely. In the *Edinburgh Annual Register for 1811*, 220, John Turner, the key witness in the Williamson murders, reported that the man he saw rifling through

Mrs Williamson's pockets was 'about six feet in height, dressed in a genteel style, with a long dark loose coat on'. *The Times*, 8481, 24 December 1811, described Williams as 'a short man' with 'a lame leg'. But the *Morning Chronicle*, 13302, 26 December 1811, declared that 'Williams ... had large red whiskers ... he is about five feet nine inches in height, of an insinuating manner and pleasing countenance, and is not lame, as stated in some of the papers'.

100 *upon the Indus*: the River Indus rises in Tibet and empties into the Arabian Sea.

Scinde and Lahore: more commonly, 'Sindh', is a province in what is now south-eastern Pakistan. Lahore is the capital of Punjab province in eastern Pakistan.

101 *young women ... favourable reception*: not all women gave Williams a favourable reception. Cf. *The Times*, 8485, 28 December 1811: the father of a Miss Laurence owned a public house and 'Williams used to come ... and sit in the bar with the utmost familiarity. She never approved of his conduct. She gave him notice last Saturday week not to shew his face any more'.

'Now, Miss R ... be tranquil': De Quincey seems to conflate the testimony of at least two different witnesses. 'Miss R.' is probably '*Margaret Reilly*, a girl of the town', whose testimony appeared in the *Morning Chronicle*, 13304, 28 December 1811: 'She saw two men run out of Gravel-lane, one of them ... with large whiskers, the other lame'. De Quincey's anecdote concerning the 'gentle-mannered girl ... Williams had undoubtedly designed to murder', however, is much closer to the story told by a Mrs Hoare that appeared in the *Edinburgh Annual Register for 1811*, 230: on the Saturday night a week before the Marr family was killed, she heard 'a knocking at the wall' and asked, ' "Who is there?" "It is I, – I am coming to rob your house", answered Williams. She immediately knew his voice. ... "Robber or no robber, I'll let you in, and I am glad you are come" '.

coup d'essai: trial effort.

'all that mighty heart': Wordsworth, 'Composed Upon Westminster Bridge, September 3, 1802', 14.

102 *surtout*: 'a man's great-coat or overcoat' (*OED*).

Titian ... Rubens ... Vandyke ... full dress: Titian (*c.*1488–1576), Peter Paul Rubens (1577–1640), and Sir Anthony Van Dyck (1599–1641), all eminent painters.

going out as Grand Compounder: at Oxford, those 'who paid higher fees for their degrees in consideration of being possessed of an independent income' (*OED*). The practice was abolished in 1853.

long blue frock ... silk: *Edinburgh Annual Register for 1811*, 230: According to William Hassel, 'clerk to the prison', Williams was 'dressed in a brown great-coat lined with silk, a blue under-coat with yellow buttons, blue and white waistcoat, stripped blue pantaloons, brown worsted stockings, and shoes'.

103 *Marr*: De Quincey first mentions Timothy Marr in 'On the Knocking at the Gate in Macbeth' (see above, p. 166).

Mrs Marr . . . enmity towards each other: cf. *Morning Chronicle*, 13304, 28 December 1811: 'It appears that Williams was a shipmate of Mr Marr's, and came home with him about a year and a half ago, in the Dover Castle East Indiaman. . . . Williams . . . had often mentioned being in company with Marr.'

causa teterrima: foulest cause.

104 *Jewish superstition . . . limits of Sunday*: the Jewish calendar is a lunar–solar one determined by complex calculations. There are differences of religious and legal opinion concerning the definition of sunset (the latest beginning point for the Sabbath) and the appearance of the stars (the earliest end point). De Quincey is probably thinking in particular of Jewish merchants, some of whom were allowed to open on Sunday, which would technically have begun at sundown on Saturday.

young man of twenty-seven: De Quincey's recollection of the ages of the victims is inaccurate. Timothy Marr was 24 years old, as was his wife. Their son Timothy Marr, junior, was 3 months old (see Margo Ann Sullivan, *Murder and Art: Thomas De Quincey and the Ratcliffe Highway Murders* (New York, 1987), 23).

108 *hell-kite*: cf. Shakespeare, *Macbeth*, IV. iii. 216–17: 'All my pretty ones? | Did you say all? O hell-kite! All?'

fifty minutes: most reports indicate that the servant girl Margaret (De Quincey calls her 'Mary') Jewell was gone a much shorter period of time. Cf. *Fairburn's Account*, 4, 6: 'She returned in about half an hour. . . . it is conjectured . . . [she] alarmed the wretches, who therefore had not an opportunity to rob the premises'.

Help there is none: cf. Psalm 22: 11: 'for trouble *is* near; for *there is* none to help'.

oyster shop . . . remoter district: cf. 'John Williams' in *Newgate Calendar*, v. 119: 'The girl left the shop door ajar, expecting to return in a very few minutes; but, unfortunately, the nearest place of sale for oysters had disposed of the whole, and she therefore went farther on her errand.'

Mr Winsor: Frederick Winsor (1763–1830), inventor and entrepreneur, formed the first coal-gas lighting company in 1806. A year later he erected gas streetlights in Pall Mall, London.

109 *past one o'clock*: cf. Margaret Jewell's testimony in *Fairburn's Account*, 14: 'I thought I would wait till the watchman came, which he shortly did, and called the hour of one.'

very gently knocked: cf. Margaret Jewell's testimony in *Fairburn's Account*, 14: 'I certainly heard some one coming down stairs, which I thought was my master coming to let me in. . . . I rang again, and knocked at the door with my foot repeatedly.'

109 *reflections this way or that*: cf. Wordsworth, *The Borderers*, 1539–41: 'a step, a blow, | The motion of a muscle – this way or that – | 'Tis done'.

112 *pawnbroker*: cf. *Fairburn's Account*, 15: John Murray was 'a pawnbroker, residing at No. 30, Ratcliffe-highway, next to the house of the deceased Mr Marr'.

116 *octave*: De Quincey adapts the ecclesiastical meaning of the term: 'The eighth day after a festival (both days being counted, and so always falling on the same day of the week as the festival itself)' (*OED*).

117 *The earthquake is not satisfied at once*: Wordsworth, *The Prelude* (1805), x. 74.

118 *second atrocity took place*: Williams carried out the Williamson murders on 19 December 1811 (see above, p. 180).

   Mr Williamson: De Quincey discusses John Williamson in his first essay on murder (see above, p. 30).

   following five persons: John Williamson was 56; his wife Elizabeth was 60; their housemaid Anna Bridget Harrington was in her fifties; and their granddaughter Kitty Stillwell was 14. The lodger was John Turner, a journeyman.

119 *Banquo . . . regal banquet*: Shakespeare, *Macbeth*, III. iv. 9–31.

121 *'Lord Jesus . . . murdered!'*: De Quincey in his account habitually expands the passage of time, in this instance between when the door banged and when the housemaid cried out. Cf. Turner in the *Edinburgh Annual Register for 1811*, 221: 'I heard the front door bang to very hard. Immediately afterwards I heard the servant exclaim, – "We are all murdered" '.

   Medusa's head: in Greek mythology, Medusa was a winged female creature whose head of hair consisted of snakes.

122 *scrutoire*: more commonly 'escritoire', a 'writing desk constructed to contain stationery and documents' (*OED*).

125 *bed-tester*: the canopy over the bed.

126 *first thought . . . share his chances*: De Quincey appears to have invented John Turner's concern for the sleeping Kitty Stillwell. Cf. Turner's own account in the *Morning Chronicle*, 13298, 21 December 1811: 'I went down stairs, and saw one of the villains. . . . I immediately ran up stairs; took off the sheets from my bed, fastened them together, and lashed them to the bed-posts; I called to the watchman to give the alarm.'

   half-carious: 'carious' is 'decayed; rotten with dry rot' (*OED*).

   Sovereigns as yet were not: the sovereign was introduced in 1816, five years after the Williams murders.

   strophe and antistrophe: these terms describe metrically corresponding groups of lines in Greek choral and lyric poetry.

Pull baker, pull devil!: E. Cobham Brewer, *The Dictionary of Phrase and Fable* (London, 1963), 732: 'Pull Devil, Pull Baker' is to 'let each one do the best for himself in his own line of business, but let not one man interfere in that of another'.

127 *creaking shoes*: cf. *Morning Chronicle*, 13301, 25 December 1811: 'JOHN TURNER . . . described to the Magistrates' how he was 'sure he heard a man slowly walking in the sitting room, and that his shoes cracked, and that he was confident the man could not have nails in his shoes'.

128 *odour of sanctity*: the odour of sanctity is a beautiful scent that is said to exude from a number of holy persons and certain European saints.

130 *Three or four people ran up*: cf. Turner's own account in *Morning Chronicle*, 13298, 21 December 1811: 'I was hanging out of the front window by the sheets; the watchman received me in his arms . . . a great mob had then assembled opposite the door.'

131 *seven bishops at Westminster in 1688*: William Sancroft (1617–93), archbishop of Canterbury, was the leader of a group of seven bishops who were imprisoned for opposing the policies of the Roman Catholic king James II. The acquittal of the group in June 1688 was greeted with widespread popular rejoicing.

'Revolt of Islam,' canto xii: Shelley, *The Revolt of Islam*, XII. i. 1–9. De Quincey's transcription is accurate, except that in line 3 Shelley writes 'winds', not 'wings'.

132 *sword . . . shirt into the street*: De Quincey seems to modify and heighten the experience of George Fox, whose deposition appeared in the *Edinburgh Annual Register for 1811*, 222: 'I reside . . . opposite the house of the deceased. . . . While they were breaking open the door, I ran across to my own house for a hanger.' A 'hanger' is 'a kind of short sword, originally hung from the belt' (*OED*). Cf. *Newgate Calendar*, v. 122: Fox 'obtained an entrance . . . with a cutlass in his hand'.

133 *only one man had been concerned in the affair*: cf. *Morning Chronicle*, 13302, 26 December 1811: 'As far as can officially be learned, there were only two men concerned in both of the atrocious murders.' The same opinion was iterated in the *Morning Chronicle*, 13304, 28 December 1811: 'The witness felt certain that more than one man had been concerned in the murders.'

134 *'J. P.'*: as De Quincey discusses in the first essay 'On Murder', the mallet used to kill the Marr family belonged to John Petersen (see above, p. 30).

135 *men of various nations, at a public-house*: Williams lodged at the Pear Tree, Pear Tree Alley, Wapping. The members of the household were Robert Vermilloe, the publican; his wife Sarah Vermilloe; their washerwoman (and sister-in-law to Sarah Vermilloe), Mary Rice; and Mary Rice's son William Rice. There were five lodgers: John (or Michael) Cuthperson, John Harrison, John Petersen, John Fredrick Richter, and

John Williams. Petersen was from Hamburg (see above, p. 180). In *The Times*, 8484, 27 December 1811, Richter was described as 'a young foreign seaman'.

135 *Courvoisier (the murderer of Lord William Russell)*: in May 1840, François Benjamin Courvoisier, a valet, murdered his master Lord William Russell (1767–1840).

136 *One iron bar ... by his braces*: cf. *The Times*, 8485, 28 December 1811: The turnkey found Williams 'suspended by the neck, from an iron bar ... on which the prisoners hang their clothes. He was quite cold and lifeless.'

137 *wild natural justice:* De Quincey alludes to the famous first sentence of Lord Bacon, 'Of Revenge': 'Revenge is a kind of wild justice, which the more man's nature runs to, the more ought law to weed it out.'

138 *Manchester Infirmary ... statuesque interest*: cf. R. Bulfield, *The Trial of Alexander & Michael McKean* (Manchester, 1826), 64: 'After they had hung about an hour their bodies were taken down. – The body of Alexander was left for dissection at Lancaster, and that of Michael was sent to the Manchester Infirmary for the same purpose.'

hocussing ... drugging ... with laudanum: cf. Dickens, *The Pickwick Papers*, ed. James Kingsley (Oxford, 1986), 151: ' "What do you mean by 'hocussing' brandy-and-water?" inquired Mr Pickwick ... "Puttin' laud'num in it", replied Sam.'

141 *cabarets*: drinking houses.

law as it then stood ... quadrivium: cf. Leon Radzinowicz, *A History of English Criminal Law*, 5 vols. (London, 1948–86), i. 198: 'The Magistrate had an interview with the Secretary for the Home Department in order to consider whether the usual practice of burying the body at the cross-roads might be departed from in this instance. . . . It was decided that the body should be exhibited to public view in the same neighbourhood in which Williams had committed his crimes. . . . The procession stopped twice, each time for a quarter of an hour, at the two houses formerly inhabited by Williams's victims. . . . Finally the body was taken from the platform, lowered into the grave, a stake was driven through it and the pit was then covered.'

driven through his heart: cf. the *Morning Chronicle*, 13306, 31 December 1811: Williams's body 'will be conveyed to Ratcliffe Highway, and thrown into a hole six feet deep; after which a stake will be driven through it'. See also G. M. H. Playfair, 'De Quincey: The Murderer Williams', *Notes and Queries*, 11th series, 5 (January 1912), 6: in 1886, during excavation of a trench for a gas company, workmen 'discovered the skeleton of a man with a stake driven through it. . . . It is believed that the skeleton is that of a man who murdered a Mr and Mrs Marr, their infant child, and a young apprentice.'

APPENDIX A. Peter Anthony Fonk

143 *Cologne*: Cologne is located below Bonn on the west bank of the River Rhine in western Germany.

Enfeld: 'Enfeld' is properly Ehrenfeld, a small town near Cologne.

145 *Neuss*: Neuss is in western Germany, on the west bank of the River Rhine.

147 *cooper's knife*: a cooper is 'a craftsman who makes and repairs wooden vessels formed of staves and hoops, as casks, buckets, tubs' (*OED*).

149 *Mühlheim*: Mühlheim is south-east of Cologne, near Frankfurt, in western Germany.

150 *Triers*: properly, 'Trier', a city in south-western Germany, on the right bank of the River Mosel.

152 *hurly burly*: cf. Shakespeare, *Macbeth*, I. i. 3–4: 'When the hurly-burly's done, | When the battle's lost and won'.

APPENDIX B. To the Editor of Blackwood's Magazine

155 *Lactantius*: see above, p. 168.

Christopher North: see above, pp. 168, 185.

156 *'Forewarned, fore-armed'*: Miguel de Cervantes, *Don Quixote*, trans. Tobias Smollett, ed. Martin Battestin and O. M. Brack (Athens, Ga., 2003), 450: 'Sir, forewarned and forearmed is half the day'.

virtu: see above, p. 171.

157 *Newgate Calendar, God's Revenge Against Murder*: see above, p. 186.

nip the thing in the bud: cf. Ovid, *Remedia Amoris*, l. 91: 'Principiis obsta' (see above, p. 186).

Aristotle: see above, pp. 170, 185.

the Scholiasts: a scholiast is 'one who writes explanatory notes upon an author' (*OED*). De Quincey's ignorant author probably intends the 'Scholastics', the medieval university teachers of theology and logic.

Thomas a Kempis: Thomas à Kempis (1379/80–1471), Christian theologian and the probable author of *Imitation of Christ*. De Quincey's ignorant author, however, may be confusing à Kempis with Thomas Aquinas (1224/5–74), the greatest of medieval philosopher-theologians.

158 *Est aliquid prodire tenus, si non datur ultrà*: Horace, *Epistles*, I. i. 32: 'It is worth while to take some steps forward, though we may not go still further'.

Mannheim baker's: see above, pp. 27–9.

Tros, Tyriusque mihi: Virgil, *Aeneid*, i. 574: 'Tros Tyriusque mihi nullo discrimine agetur' ('Trojan and Tyrian I shall treat with no distinction').

send you . . . German murder . . . last 50 years: De Quincey is referring to his essay on Peter Anthony Fonk, which he completed around 1825. The present essay was intended as an introduction to the Fonk essay (see above, pp. 143–54).

158 *Williamsons'*: De Quincey details the murder of the Williamsons in his 'Postscript' to 'On Murder' (see above, pp. 118–36).

159 *M. de Savary*: De Quincey errs by twenty-one years in his dating of the event, but he clearly has in mind the May 1699 murder of Jean Baptiste Savary, brother of Mathurin Savary, bishop of Sées. De Quincey may have drawn his account in part from the Marquis de Dangeau, *Memoirs of the Court of France from the year 1684 to the year 1720, now first translated*, 2 vols. (London, 1825), i. 379: 'The King was informed, that M. Savari had been assassinated at his house, in Paris. There were a valet and a female servant also killed, and the crime has apparently been committed in the day time. . . . It seems, by some writings, which have been found, to have been an act of revenge; nothing has been stolen in the house. M. Savari . . . was a virtuoso, and a man of pleasure, and had many friends.' Cf. the Duke of Saint-Simon, *Memoirs of Louis XIV and the Regency*, 3 vols. (London, 1901), i. 157: 'A strange adventure, which happened at this time, terrified everybody, and gave rise to many surmises. Savary was found assassinated in his house at Paris. . . . Few doubted but that the deed had been done by a very ugly little man, but of a blood so highly respected, that all forms were dispensed with, in the fear lest it should be brought home to him; and, after the first excitement, everybody ceased to speak of this tragic history.'

bonne bouche: the mouthful that one saves for the last, in order to savour it and have the flavour linger on the tongue.

Marrs . . . knocked . . . quarter of an hour: De Quincey details the murder of the Marr household in his 'Postscript' to 'On Murder' (see above, pp. 97–118).

160 *time of the revolution*: De Quincey means the first French Revolution of 1789.

first water: 'of the highest excellence or purity' (*OED*).

Thurtell . . . Weare: John Thurtell and William Weare feature in De Quincey's first essay 'On Murder' (see above, p. 171).

'Deipnosophilae': properly, '*Deipnosophitae*'. The word was misspelled by the printer in the first paper 'On Murder' (see above, p. 21).

'reddere excutum': the reference is confusing because the phrase 'reddere excutum' does not appear in the first paper 'On Murder'. De Quincey probably has in mind either a misremembrance or an uncorrected proof of the paper's closing quotation from Horace, which contains the phrase 'acutum | Reddere' (see above, p. 34).

APPENDIX C. A New Paper on Murder as a Fine Art

161 *Palmer & Co.*: in 1844, the year De Quincey wrote this manuscript, Joseph Hume (1777–1855), radical Scottish MP, organized the building of a monument in Edinburgh to commemorate Thomas Fyshe Palmer (1747–1802) and four other 'Scottish Martrys' who in 1793 were con-

victed of writing pamphlets in support of parliamentary reform and sent to Australia.

facilitas aequalis: just facility.

curiosa felicitas: Petronius, *Satyricon*, cxviii, 4: 'Homerus testis et lyrici Romanusque Vergilius et Horatii curiosa felicitas' ('Homer proves this, and the lyric poets, and Roman Virgil, and the studied felicity of Horace').

Cat. in Newgate Calendar: De Quincey is thinking of the case of 'John Bodkin, Dominick Bodkin and Others' in *Newgate Calendar*, iii. 122: 'The assassins had even been so wanton in their cruelties as to kill all the dogs and cats in the house.'

Williams . . . murdered the baby: De Quincey describes John Williams's murder of the infant Timothy Marr in his 'Postscript' to 'On Murder' (see above, pp. 115–16).

Fielding: not identified.

Kilkenny cats: a pair of proverbial cats from Kilkenny, Ireland, who fought until only their tails were left.

Nemesis: in Greek myth, 'Nemesis' is the personification of retribution or righteous anger.

der erste der letzte: the first, the last.

162 *Outis*: Greek for 'nobody', 'no man', and the name famously adopted by Odysseus to dupe Polyphemus in Homer, *Odyssey*, ix.

wife . . . two children . . . Halifax: not identified.

vauriens: a 'vaurien' is 'a worthless, good-for-nothing fellow; a scamp' (*OED*).

like leaves in Vallombrosa: cf. Milton, *Paradise Lost*, i. 302–3: 'Thick as autumnal leaves that strew the brooks | In Vallombrosa'.

te-totum: 'any light top . . . spun with the fingers, used as a toy' (*OED*).

Sir Eustace . . . Sir Hubert: a legend concerning Sir Eustace de Lucey and his younger brother Hubert. Whilst on the Crusades in Palestine, Hubert arranged to have Eustace killed, and then returned home to England to a life of revelry. But Eustace escaped death, and returned to Egremont Castle to sound the horn as its rightful owner. De Quincey has confused the two brothers: Hubert is the treacherous one.

'sounded the horn which he alone could sound': Wordsworth, 'The Horn of Egremont Castle', l. 112.

163 *ring of Gyges*: Gyges (*c.*685–*c.*657 BC), king of Lydia, was a shepherd who found a ring that made him invisible. He used it to seduce the queen and murder the king. The story is recounted in Plato, *Republic*, book II.

Whispering Gallery at St Paul's: the Whispering Gallery is directly beneath the dome of St Paul's Cathedral, London. De Quincey's account is inaccurate. A whisper uttered at any point is carried round the outer wall at almost its original volume, but is not amplified.

163 *Mandeville . . . curses . . . November*: Sir John Mandeville (*fl.* 14th century), reputed author of a collection of travellers' tales from around the world, *The Voyage and Travels of Sir John Mandeville, Knight*. De Quincey, however, almost certainly draws this reference from Joseph Addison (1672–1719), essayist, poet, and dramatist, 'No. 254' in *The Tatler*, ed. Donald F. Bond, 3 vols. (Oxford, 1987), iii, 289–90: Addison prints 'an Extract of Sir *John's* journal' in which words freeze in the air until a thaw brings 'a Volley of Oaths and Curses'.

post-obits: an abbreviation for 'post-obit bond', 'a bond given by a borrower, securing to the lender a sum of money to be paid on the death of a specified person from whom the borrower has expectations' (*OED*).

Addison . . . dervise . . . enchanted water: Addison, 'No. 94' in *The Spectator*, ed. Donald F. Bond, 5 vols. (Oxford, 1965), i. 398–9. A 'Dervise' or 'Dervish' is a 'Mohammedan friar, who has taken vows of poverty and austere life' (*OED*).

164 *Burke and Hare*: De Quincey toasts William Burke and William Hare in his second essay 'On Murder' (see above, pp. 92–3).

Foote's turnpike-keeper: De Quincey's reference seems to be to Samuel Foote (1720–77), actor, wit, mimic, and playwright. But no Kensington turnpike-keeper with a superb memory has been traced in any of Foote's plays.

Dr ——: Dr Robert Knox (1791–1862), anatomist and conservator at the Museum of the Royal College of Surgeons at Edinburgh, paid Burke and Hare £7 10s. for the first corpse they delivered, but soon increased the payment to £10 per body.

Daimon . . . of Socrates: Socrates claimed a personal demon. Plato, *Apology for Socrates*, 31: 'I have had this from my childhood; it is a sort of voice that comes to me, and when it comes it always holds me back from what I am thinking of doing, but never urges me forward.'

Entelecheia of Aristotle: for Aristotle, see above, p. 170. 'Entelechy' is a term for the complete actualization or full expression of a potentiality.

165 *Thomas Aquinas*: St Thomas Aquinas (see above, p. 197, note to p. 157) wrote the *Summa theologiae* and the *Summa contra gentiles*.

some lady's eyebrow: De Quincey alludes to *As You Like It*, II. vii. 147–9: 'And then the lover,/sighing like furnace, with a woeful ballard/Made to his mistress's eyebrow'.

Semele: in Greek mythology, Semele is a daughter of Cadmus and Harmonia. She was ambitious because she wanted to be Zeus's wife.

royal pupil's conquests: Alexander the Great (356–323 BC), king of Macedonia and conqueror of what was then most of the civilized world, was one of Aristotle's pupils.

Andromeda, Cassiopeia, Ariadne: Greek heroines commemorated in the stars.

Argo: in Greek mythology, Jason and his crew (the 'Argonauts') went in the ship *Argo* to retrieve the Golden Fleece.

Trojan war: the legend of the Trojan War is the most notable theme from ancient Greek literature and forms the basis of Homer's *Iliad*. The conflict was between the early Greeks and the people of Troy in Asia Minor, and is traditionally dated to the twelfth or thirteenth century BC.

Berenice: Berenice II (*c.*269–221 BC), wife of Ptolemy Euergetes, king of Egypt. When he set forth to avenge the murder of his sister, Berenice dedicated a lock of her hair to his safe return. It was later transferred to heaven, where it formed a new constellation.

ten Categories!': in *Categories*, Aristotle proposes ten fundamental types of predicates.

Padishah Victoria: 'Padishah' is 'a Persian title'. In India, it was applied 'by natives to the sovereign of Great Britain as the Emperor of India' (*OED*). Victoria (1819–1901), queen of Great Britain and Ireland, 1837–1901.